EQUALITY:
A NEW FRAMEWORK

EQUALITY: A NEW FRAMEWORK

Report of the Independent Review of the Enforcement of UK Anti-Discrimination Legislation

BOB HEPPLE QC

MARY COUSSEY

TUFYAL CHOUDHURY

HART PUBLISHING
OXFORD – PORTLAND OREGON
2000

Hart Publishing
Oxford and Portland, Oregon

Published in North America (US and Canada) by
Hart Publishing
c/o International Specialized Book Services
5804 NE Hassalo Street
Portland, Oregon
97213-3644
USA

Distributed in Netherlands, Belgium and Luxembourg by
Intersentia, Churchillaan 108
B2900 Schoten
Antwerpen
Belgium

Hart Publishing is a specialist legal publisher based in Oxford, England.
To order further copies of this book or to request a list of other
publications please write to:

Hart Publishing
Salters Boatyard, Folly Bridge, Abingdon Rd, Oxford, OX1 4LB
Telephone: +44 (0)1865 245533 Fax: +44 (0) 1865 794882
email: mail@hartpub.co.uk
WEBSITE: http//:www.hartpub.co.uk

British Library Cataloguing in Publication Data
Data Available

ISBN 1 84113-159-8 (paperback)

Typeset by John Saunders and Printed in Great Britain

CONTENTS

PREFACE

We are rightly proud of having been the first European country to introduce anti-discrimination legislation administered by independent commissions and enforced by courts and tribunals. But this legislation is now outdated, and there is a really pressing need for reform to make the law comprehensive, consistent, effective, and user-friendly. During the quarter-century since its enactment, the limits and defects of the legislation have become more and more apparent, and the passing of each new measure has added to the incoherence and opaqueness of the UK's equality codes.

The legislation has been enacted in a characteristically British piecemeal and pragmatic way, responding with detailed specificity to the political needs of the times, but without the benefit of a constitutional framework guaranteeing the equal protection of the law and equal access to justice.

The Commission for Racial Equality, the Equal Opportunities Commission and many others have repeatedly called for the reform of this tangled web of legislation, drawing attention to the unnecessary fetters on the commissions' powers to promote equality of opportunity and secure compliance with the law. Like the courts, they have complained of the tortuous and unworkable procedures for achieving equal pay for men and women, three decades after the enactment of the Equal Pay Act. And they have called for the legislation to give direct effect to the rights and obligations guaranteed by European law. But successive Governments have failed to heed their recommendations, preferring instead to make limited and piecemeal changes. The defective state of the law helps no-one except lawyers.

This report of the independent review of the enforcement of UK anti-discrimination legislation is the most profound study of what is wrong with the existing laws, and of what can and should be done to develop an accessible legislative framework, together with other measures to promote equal opportunities policies. It provides Government and other decision-makers with a uniquely well-researched practical guide, based on the experience of those directly affected by the legislation. It explains the options for reform, drawing upon lessons from other countries. It does not treat legislation as a panacea. It recommends an inclusive, pro-active, non-adversarial approach, which avoids unnecessary bureaucratic requirements, while ensuring that the law is effectively enforced.

The authors of this brilliant report are to be congratulated for producing a major study which diagnoses the main problems and recommends wise and workable ways of tackling them. It is to be hoped that the necessary political commitment will now be found to translate their proposals into legislation as a high priority.

ANTHONY LESTER
Chair, Advisory Committee

ACKNOWLEDGMENTS

This project was the brainchild of Anthony (Lord) Lester. Without his enthusiasm, guidance and unfailing support the review could not have been undertaken. The members of our advisory committee and panel of experts (Appendix 6) put the project on solid and realistic lines, and contributed ideas and contacts. Their confidence in our purposes has been crucial, as has the support of Jack Beatson QC, Director of the Centre for Public Law. Those who wrote working papers (Appendix 7) made a major contribution to our thinking.

We wish to thank the Joseph Rowntree Charitable Trust and the Nuffield Foundation for funding the project, and Stephen Pittam and Sharon Witherspoon for their understanding and encouragement. We are also grateful to Organisational Resources Counselors Inc. for providing financial support for travel to the USA, and for arranging and hosting meetings with employers in New York. Bruce McLanahan was unstinting in his advice and in arranging meetings with groups of lawyers in the USA.

The project rests on the experiences of a large number of people: those who gave us interviews and those who participated in our case studies; those who responded to our initial consultation paper and our Options for Reform paper; those who attended our regional consultation meetings, and allowed us to participate in other meetings relevant to our work (Appendix 4). For help in organising meetings, we thank especially Noreen Burrows, Evelyn Ellis, Claire Kilpatrick, Elspeth Reid, Paul Brown, Richard Steele and Ann Holton, and for organising our consultation conference Phillip Greenwood and staff in the Faculty of Law at Cambridge. John Prophet, Doris Littlejohn, Alice Leonard and Barbara Cohen were most helpful in arranging access to the tribunals and commissions.

Sections of the draft report were read by Sandra Fredman, Tess Gill, Alice Leonard, Doris Littlejohn, Christopher McCrudden, Aileen McColgan, Onora O'Neill, and John Prophet. None of them, nor any of the others whom we have consulted, is responsible for the contents of the report or for the blemishes that remain.

We acknowledge the use of data from the workplace employee relations survey made available by the ESRC Data Archive at the University of Essex (para.1.39), data supplied by the EOC and CRE (tables 4.1 and 4.2), *Equal Opportunities Review* (tables 4.3 to 4.7), and the Employment Tribunals Service (para. 4.33).

ABBREVIATIONS

ACAS	Advisory, Conciliation and Arbitration Service
CAB	Citizen's Advice Bureau
CAC	Central Arbitration Committee
CCT	Compulsory competitive tendering
CLS	Community Legal Service
CLSF	Community Legal Service Fund
CRE	Commission for Racial Equality
DDA	Disability Discrimination Act 1995
DfEE	Department for Education and Employment
DRC	Disability Rights Commission
DRCA	Disability Rights Commission Act 1999
EAT	Employment Appeal Tribunal
ECHR	European Convention on Human Rights and Fundamental Freedoms
ECJ	European Court of Justice
ECNI	Equality Commission for Northern Ireland
EEOC	Equal Employment Opportunity Commission
EOC	Equal Opportunities Commission
EqPA	Equal Pay Act 1970
ERA 1996	Employment Rights Act 1996
ERA 1999	Employment Relations Act 1999
ET	Employment tribunal
ETD	Equal Treatment Directive 76/207
FEA	Fair Employment Act 1989
FEC	Fair Employment Commission
FET	Fair Employment Tribunal
FETO	Fair Employment and Treatment (Northern Ireland) Order 1998
GPA	WTO Agreement on Government Procurement
GOQ	Genuine Occupational Qualification
HREOC	Human Rights and Equal Opportunities Commission
HMIC	Her Majesty's Inspectorate of Constabulary
HMIP	Her Majesty's Inspectorate of Prisons
HRA	Human Rights Act 1998
IHA	Interlocutory Hearing Applications
IPPR	Institute of Public Policy Research
LGA 1988	Local Government Act 1988
LGA 1999	Local Government Act 1999
LRA	Labour Relations Agency
NIA	Northern Ireland Act 1998
OFCCP	Office of Federal Contract Compliance Programs
OFSTED	Office for Standards in Education
ONS	Office of National Statistics
ORC	Organisation Resource Counselors Inc.
PHA	Pre-Hearing Assessments
PHR	Pre-Hearing Reviews
RADAR	The Royal Association for Disability and Rehabilitation
RRA	Race Relations Act 1976
RR(NI)O	Race Relations (Northern Ireland) Order
RNIB	Royal National Institute for the Blind
SACHR	Standing Advisory Commission on Human Rights
SDA	Sex Discrimination Act 1975
SD(NI)O	Sex Discrimination (Northern Ireland) Order
TULRCA	Trade Unions and Labour Relations (Consolidation) Act 1992
TUPE	Transfer of Undertakings (Protection of Employment) Regulations 1981
WERS	Workplace Employee Relations Survey
WTO	World Trade Organisation

EXECUTIVE SUMMARY

Introduction: aims and methodology

This report presents the findings of the independent review of the enforcement of UK anti-discrimination legislation which was conducted under the auspices of the Centre for Public Law and the Judge Institute of Management Studies in the University of Cambridge. The project was funded by the Joseph Rowntree Charitable Trust and the Nuffield Foundation.

The general aim of the project was to review and evaluate proposals for the reform of UK anti-discrimination legislation, based on an assessment of the experience of those affected by the legislation. The specific objectives were to develop an accessible legislative framework, to propose other measures that will promote equal opportunity policies and to spur compliance with those polices, and to ensure that the UK is in full compliance with its obligations under EU law and international human rights law.

The principal methods used were targeted case studies and interviews, an initial consultation paper, regional and other consultation meetings, a consultation paper *Options for Reform* published with seven working papers in December 1999, and a consultative conference.

Chapter one: Why a new framework is needed

There are numerous reasons why the prevailing framework of anti-discrimination legislation in Britain needs to be reviewed:

- dissatisfaction with outdated legislation and the fragmentation and inconsistencies between four separate anti-discrimination regimes in the UK and three separate commissions in Britain
- demands for the legislation to be made more user-friendly and accessible
- pressures to extend the grounds of unlawful discrimination beyond race, sex and disability
- the commitment of the government to impose positive duties on public authorities to have due regard to equal opportunities
- the relative success of fair employment legislation in Northern Ireland in reducing inequality and segregation
- the need to keep in line with EU law
- the possibility that devolution will lead to a fragmentation of equality policies
- the new political and legal culture based on the Human Rights Act
- while anti-discrimination legislation has broken down many barriers for individuals in their search for jobs, housing and services, and there are fewer overt expressions of discrimination, women still face occupational segregation, concentration in low-paid, part-time work, unequal pay, pregnancy discrimination and harassment; and members of ethnic minorities, disabled persons and older people still suffer from stereotypes about their abilities
- discrimination and exclusion are more complex and covert than they were three decades ago when the present framework was conceived; there are attitudes, policies and practices within organisations of the kind identified as "institutional racism" by the Stephen Lawrence inquiry; eliminating institutional barriers requires greater emphasis on changing organisational culture
- although in the past five years most organisations have adopted equal opportunities policies, the main initiatives tend to be reactive and separate from each other

The present framework places too much emphasis on state regulation and too little on the responsibility of organisations and individuals to generate change. This framework adopts an inconsistent and incoherent approach to different manifestations of inequality. It was designed largely to deal with a model of organisations with hierarchical, vertically integrated and centralised bureaucracies. This is not appropriate for modern flatter organisational structures in which equality depends not simply on avoiding negative discrimination but on the active participation of all stakeholders, on training and improving skills, developing wider social networks and encouraging adaptability.

Chapter two: harmonising legislation and institutions

Several defects in the present framework can be identified:

- there is too much law and it is inaccessible to those whose actions it is intended to influence; this is a major cause of the protraction of legal proceedings, and makes it difficult and costly for employers to bring about changes in the attitudes and practices of managers
- people have come to think that eliminating discrimination and promoting equality is a matter of detailed rules imposed by external agencies, rather than on the responsibility of organisations and individuals to change themselves
- the legislation is inconsistent and inherently unsatisfactory

The report proposes that there should be a single Equality Act in Britain, supplemented by regulations and codes of practice, written in plain language. There should be a Human Rights Commission with responsibility to promote human rights including equality and a single Equality Commission with responsibility for the enforcement of equality legislation. Merger with the Disability Rights Commission should be deferred for at least five years.

The framework should be based on the following five principles:

- the goal of legislation and other measures is to eliminate unlawful discrimination and to promote equality regardless of sex, race, colour, ethnic or national origin, religion or belief, disability, age, sexual orientation, or other status
- there must be clear, consistent and easily intelligible standards
- the regulatory framework must be effective, efficient and equitable, aimed at encouraging individual responsibility and self-generated efforts to promote equality
- there must be opportunities for those directly affected by change to participate, through information, consultation and engagement in the process of change
- individuals should be free to seek redress for the harm they have suffered as a result of unlawful discrimination, through procedures which are fair, inexpensive and expeditious, and the remedies should be effective

Detailed recommendations are made for clarifying the concepts of direct and indirect discrimination, justification, and victimisation. An inclusive approach to the definition of grounds of unlawful discrimination is favoured, and there is a discussion of the exceptions which may be necessary if this is done. It is proposed that there should be a separate statutory tort of harassment and bullying at work. The legislation should be interpreted according to the underlying purpose of protecting the dignity, autonomy and worth of every individual, and the promotion of good relations between different groups.

Anti-discrimination measures should be augmented by positive duties to promote equality which do not depend upon proof of fault by an individual complainant. These positive duties should aim at securing fair participation of under-represented groups in the workforce, fair access to education, training, goods, facilities and services and a fair distribution of benefits.

Chapter three: changing organisational policy and behaviour

The debate about regulation has fallen into the trap of posing one form of regulation (e.g. voluntarism) as preferable to another (e.g. enforced self-regulation). A voluntary approach may influence the behaviour of some organisations, but it will not work in others that for economic or social reasons are resistant to change. The report draws on modern regulatory theory and on the findings of our targeted case studies, to offer a design of an enforcement pyramid which starts from a base of persuasion, information and voluntary action plans, and if these fail, moves upwards to commission investigation, compliance notice, judicial enforcement, sanctions and withdrawal of contracts or subsidies. This builds on three interlocking mechanisms: internal scrutiny by the organisation to ensure effective self-regulation, the participation of interest groups in the process of change, and the commission which provides a back-up role of assistance and ultimately enforcement where voluntary methods fail.

This design informs the proposals which are made for a new framework that seeks to encourage an inclusive, pro-active, non-adversarial approach to achieve fair participation and fair access:

- a duty on public authorities to promote equality
- employment equity plans
- pay equity plans
- contract and subsidy compliance

In drawing up these proposals regard has been had to experience elsewhere, particularly in the USA, Canada, and in Northern Ireland. One lesson from those countries is that there will not be significant improvements without positive action. Another lesson is the need to avoid unnecessary bureaucratic requirements. With this in mind, the report does not propose prior approval of equality schemes or equity plans, nor does it recommend compulsory monitoring and reporting requirements. Instead, it is proposed that employers with more than 10 full-time employees should be required to conduct a periodical review (once every three years). If significant under-representation of women, ethnic minorities or disabled persons is found, an employment equity plan must be drawn up in consultation with interest groups, in particular employees or their representatives. The plan should include provision for reasonable adjustments to achieve fair participation.

In the case of pay equity, the report favours periodic pay audits and pay equity plans in negotiation with recognised unions or, where there are none, in consultation with employees or their representatives. In order to encourage employers to do this, it should be possible to contract-out of the individual's right to equal pay by collective agreement or workforce agreement in respect of a defined and reasonable period so far as is appropriate and necessary to allow the employer time to absorb the costs of implementation of an agreed pay equity plan. The Central Arbitration Committee should be able to arbitrate in respect of disputes, and to strike down or amend any agreement that is directly or indirectly discriminatory. Proposals are made for widening the basis of comparison between men's and women's pay.

Chapter four: making procedures and remedies more effective

The underlying principle is that individuals should be free to seek redress for the harm they have suffered as a result of unlawful discrimination through procedures which are fair, inexpensive and expeditious, and that the remedies should be effective. With this in mind, the report makes a number of recommendations, including

- regular basic discrimination training for chairmen and members of employment tribunals, and additional training for selected chairmen and members
- an equality scheme for employment tribunals setting targets of 50% women and a percentage that reflects the proportion of ethnic minority communities in each region by 2006
- all discrimination cases should be commenced in employment tribunals, but there should be a power to transfer a matter to the county court or sheriff court where certain criteria are met

- the commission should have power to institute proceedings in its own name or jointly with individuals where there is a common question of fact or law affecting a number of persons, whether identified or not
- there should be more active case management of equal pay cases
- the Lord Chancellor should direct the Community Legal Service Fund to give priority to all kinds of discrimination case in respect of both legal help and representation
- there should be a statutory reversal of the burden of proof, as required by EC law
- the time limit for making a complaint of unlawful discrimination should be six months
- exemplary or punitive damages should be available for unlawful discrimination, as recommended by the Law Commission
- tribunals should have power to make an order of engagement, reinstatement or re-engagement
- conciliation in non-employment cases should be attempted in respect of all grounds of unlawful discrimination
- a pilot project for mediation in sexual harassment and other cases should be supported
- employers' grievance and harassment procedures should include provision for mediation

Appendix 1 sets out the findings of the case studies. These show that the main impact of the law on employers in Northern Ireland and the USA has been in having to reduce under-representation. This can be achieved by using a range of marketing techniques already familiar to business. Managers with experience of affirmative action or employment equity plans are wholly in favour of them. Employers are almost all recognise the need for regulation, but are opposed to increased reporting requirements. They generally favour a single equality commission.

Appendix 2 has a table of UK and EC legislation, and *Appendix 3* compares the provisions of the main enactments.

SUMMARY OF RECOMMENDATIONS

Recommendation 1 (2.1–2.12)
- There should be a single Equality Act in Britain
- This Act should be supplemented by regulations and by regularly up-dated codes of practice on specific subjects
- The Act and other documents should be written in plain language so as to facilitate comprehension, and should be available in forms which take into account the needs of disabled people

Recommendation 2 (2.13–2.20)
The framework should be based on the following five principles:
- the goal of legislation and other measures is to eliminate unlawful discrimination and to promote equality regardless of sex, race, colour, ethnic or national origin, religion or belief, disability, age, sexual orientation, or other status
- there must be clear consistent and easily intelligible standards
- the regulatory framework must be effective, efficient and equitable, aimed at encouraging personal responsibility and self-generating efforts to promote equality
- there must be opportunities for those directly affected to participate, through information, consultation and engagement in the process of change
- individuals should be free to seek redress for the harm they have suffered as a result of unlawful discrimination, through procedures which are fair, inexpensive and expeditious, and the remedies should be effective

Recommendation 3 (2.21–2.23)
- The concept of direct discrimination should be interpreted in accordance with the overall purposes of the legislation, as set out in Recommendation 8 below
- Adverse treatment of a woman for a reason related to pregnancy or childbirth should be a substantive wrong, without any requirement for comparison with the treatment of another person

Recommendation 4 (2.24–2.25)
- Victimisation should be defined as any adverse treatment of a person (including an ex-employee) by reason that such person has brought proceedings, given or collected evidence or information, made an allegation, supported another person, or done any other act under or by reference to the equality legislation; it should not be necessary to show that the person victimised has been less favourably treated than in those circumstances other persons are or would be treated

Recommendation 5 (2.26–2.27)
- The definition of discrimination should make it clear that intention or conscious motivation is not a necessary ingredient
- For the avoidance of doubt, the legislation should declare that specific knowledge of the disability as such or as to whether its material features fall within schedule 1 of the DDA, is not a necessary ingredient in establishing discrimination on that ground

Recommendation 6 (2.28–2.33)
- Indirect discrimination should be defined as the application of an apparently neutral provision, criterion or practice which disadvantages a substantially higher proportion of the members of a "designated group" in comparison with other groups unless that provision, criterion or practice is appropriate and necessary and can be justified by objective factors unrelated to any of the grounds of unlawful discrimination
- The concept of indirect discrimination should be applied to all prohibited grounds of discrimination, including disability
- A provision, criterion or practice should not be regarded as appropriate and necessary in the case of indirect discrimination which disadvantages disabled persons or persons of a religious group, unless the needs of that group cannot be reasonably accommodated without causing undue hardship on the person responsible for

accommodating those needs, having regard to factors such as financial and other costs and health and safety requirements
- The "designated groups" should be those covered by the legislation (see below, Recommendation 14)

Recommendation 7 (2.34–2.40)
- Anti-discrimination measures should be augmented by positive duties to promote equality which do not depend upon proof by individual complainants that a respondent is "at fault"
- Positive duties should be aimed at securing fair participation of under-represented groups in the workforce, fair access to education, training, goods, facilities and services, and a fair distribution of benefits

Recommendation 8 (2.41–2.42)
The purposes of the legislation should be explicitly stated in the legislation and should be defined as-
- the protection of the dignity, autonomy, and worth of every individual
- the promotion of equality and the elimination of discrimination so that no person should be denied opportunities or benefits for reasons related to one of the prohibited grounds
- the application of the principle of equality in a way which does not require a reduction in the level of protection already afforded to any person
- the identification and removal of barriers against persons in designated groups
- the encouragement of positive policies and practices and such reasonable adjustments as will ensure that persons in the designated groups achieve fair participation in employment, fair access to education, training, goods, facilities and services and a fair distribution of benefits
- the promotion of good relations between persons of different racial or religious group or belief, age, marital status or sexual orientation, between men and women generally, and between persons with a disability and persons without

Recommendation 9 (2.45)
- The general defence of justification of discrimination in employment in the DDA should be amended so as to permit discrimination only on specified rational grounds such as that the individual would not be able to perform the essential functions of the job, with or without reasonable adjustment, or to protect the health and safety of any person, including the disabled person

Recommendation 10 (2.46)
- The specific lists of genuine occupational requirements in the SDA and RRA should be replaced by a general defence that the essential functions of the job required it to be done by a person of a particular ethnic or national origin, religious or other belief, sex, or age
- This should be amplified by examples given in a code of practice

Recommendation 11 (2.47)
- The proposals by the Disability Rights Task Force in relation to the statutory duty to make reasonable adjustments should be implemented

Recommendation 12 (2.48–2.49)
- There should be a general exception for positive action intended to provide specific advantages for persons from designated under-represented groups to pursue a vocational activity or to prevent or compensate for disadvantages in professional careers
- Codes of practice should give examples of such positive action taking into account current models of training
- For this purpose the "designated groups" should be racial or ethnic groups, women, and disabled persons

Recommendation 13 (2.50–2.56)
- There should be a statutory tort of harassment and bullying at work
- The elements of this tort should be that: (1) the act or other conduct is unwelcome and offensive to the recipient; (2) it could reasonably be regarded as creating an intimidating, hostile, offensive or humiliating work environment; and (3) the recipient has suffered or is likely to suffer some harm whether physical, psychological or emotional (including anxiety and injury to feelings)

Recommendation 14 (2.57–2.63)
- The prohibited grounds of discrimination should be race, colour, ethnic or national origin, sex, gender reassignment, marital status, family status, sexual orientation, religion or belief, disability, age, or other status

Recommendation 15 (2.64–2.67)
- Legislation against age discrimination should apply to all persons aged 18 or over
- There should be research and consultation on the question of prohibiting compulsory retirement ages
- The guiding principle for specific exceptions should be that they are objectively justified by a legitimate aim and are appropriate and necessary to the achievement of that aim

Recommendation 16 (2.68)
- Legislation should be framed so as to prohibit discrimination on the specified grounds, without the need to show that the victim belongs to the protected group.

Recommendation 17 (2.69)
- The recommendations of the Disability Rights Task Force on the definition of disability and disabled person should be implemented

Recommendation 18 (2.70–2.71)
- The legislation should declare for the avoidance of doubt that discrimination on the grounds of membership of Roma, gypsy or Irish traveller communities constitutes discrimination on grounds of race or ethnic origin

Recommendation 19 (2.72–2.75)
- The recommendations of the Human Genetics Advisory Commission on genetic discrimination should be reviewed no later than 2004

Recommendation 20 (2.76)
- The legislation should specifically prohibit discrimination on grounds of marital status and family status

Recommendation 21 (2.77–2.82)
- The legislation should prohibit direct and indirect discrimination on grounds of religion or belief
- There is no need for a statutory definition of "religion or belief" bearing in mind that practices which are contrary to human rights, as guaranteed by the HRA, will not be lawful
- Employers, schools and other institutions should be under a duty to make reasonable adjustments to accommodate a person's religious observance or practice provided that this can be done without undue hardship on the employer's business or the conduct of the school or other institution
- There should be specific exception for employment for the purposes of an organised religion (1) as a cleric or minister of that religion, or (2) in any other occupation where the essential functions of the job require it to be done by a person holding or not holding a particular religion or belief, or (3) where employment is limited to one sex or to persons of a particular sexual orientation, or who are not undergoing or have not undergone gender reassignment, if the limitation is imposed to avoid offending the religious susceptibilities of a significant number of its followers
- A similar exception should apply to an authorisation or qualification for purposes of an organised religion

Recommendation 22 (2.83–2.84)
- Legislation should prohibit direct and indirect discrimination on grounds of sexual orientation
- There should be specific exceptions for (1) employment for purposes of a private household; (2) employment where the holder of the job provides persons with services promoting their welfare, and those services can most effectively be provided by a person of a particular sexual orientation; (3) accommodation in small premises provided by a resident owner or occupier; and (4) membership of small private associations
- Distinctions between same-sex partners and unmarried different-sex partners should be treated as direct discrimination on grounds of sexual orientation, but distinctions between same-sex partners and married different-sex partners should not be treated as either direct or indirect discrimination on grounds of sexual orientation

Recommendation 23 (2.85–2.94)
- There should be a human rights commission for Britain the functions of which will include the review of legislation, scrutiny of draft legislation, giving advice and assistance to individuals, conducting investigations and inquiries, giving guidance to public authorities, and generally promoting human rights including equality
- There should be a separate single equality commission for Britain covering all grounds of unlawful discrimination

- The internal structure of the equality commission should be the subject of discussion and consultation after the decision has been taken to merge the existing commissions
- The DRC should not be included initially in a merged commission, but this should be reviewed after five years

Recommendation 24 (3.8–3.13)

There should be a duty on specified public authorities in the exercise of their functions to eliminate unlawful discrimination and to have due regard to the need to promote equality
- between persons of different racial groups, religious belief, age, marital status or sexual orientation
- between men and women generally
- between persons with a disability and without
- between persons with dependants and persons without

Recommendation 25 (3.14–3.16)

Every specified public authority should be required to collect and publish such information as is appropriate and necessary to facilitate the performance of its duty to promote equality, and to publish an equality scheme, setting out its arrangements-
- for assessing its compliance with the duty and for consulting on matters to which the duty is likely to be relevant
- for assessing and consulting on the likely impact of policies adopted or proposed to be adopted on the promotion of equality
- for monitoring any adverse impact of policies adopted by the authority on the promotion of equality, and in doing so to have regard to the aims of the policy, measures capable of mitigating any adverse impact, and alternative policies which might better achieve the promotion of equality

Recommendation 26 (3.17–3.19)

The duty should apply -
- in respect of all their functions, including procurement and employment, to government departments, the Scottish Administration, the National Assembly for Wales and its subsidiaries, police authorities, health authorities and boards, NHS trusts and primary care trusts and local education authorities
- in respect of specified functions to such other public authorities as the Secretary of State may designate, after consultation

Recommendation 27 (3.20–3.22)

- Performance of the duty should be measured through performance management frameworks which use a basket of indicators on equality showing progress towards fair participation and fair access over a period of time
- Inspection and audit should be carried out, wherever possible, by those bodies which have general inspection and audit functions in the public sector
- The commission should have residual power to issue a compliance notice, after allowing the authority an opportunity to make representations, requiring evidence of compliance to be produced within a specified time
- The public authority should be able to appeal against the notice to a tribunal
- In the event of non-compliance, the commission should be able to apply to a tribunal for an order requiring the authority to comply

Recommendation 28 (3.23–3.40)

- Every employer (including an associated employer) with more than 10 employees should be required to conduct a periodical review (once every three years) of its employment practices (affecting recruitment, training, promotion or redundancy) for the purpose of determining whether members of ethnic minorities, women and disabled persons, are enjoying, and are likely to continue to enjoy, fair participation in employment in the undertaking
- If the employer finds, following such a review, that there is significant under-representation of any group, it should be under a duty draw up and implement an employment equity plan to identify and remove barriers to the recruitment, training and promotion of members of ethnic minorities, women and disabled persons, whether as full-time or part-time employees
- The plan should include provision for such reasonable adjustments as may be necessary to ensure that people from the designated groups achieve a degree of representation in each occupational group and in the employer's workforce that reflects their representation in the national workforce or in those segments of the workforce from which the employer may reasonably be expected to recruit employees
- The employer should not be obliged to take any action which would involve undue hardship to the employer's undertaking, nor to recruit or promote a person who would not be qualified for the job

- This review should be conducted in consultation with interest groups, in particular employees or their representatives, with a view to reaching agreement on the action plan
- The employer should be obliged to disclose information as to the results of the review and of any employment equity plan in the company report, and to employees or their representatives
- The failure of an employer to conduct a periodic review, or, where appropriate, to draw up an employment equity plan, or to disclose information about the review or plan, should be admissible in evidence in any proceedings for unlawful discrimination, and the tribunal should be entitled to draw an adverse inference from this fact, having regard to the size and administrative resources of the employer
- The commission should have power, after due notice, to publish the fact that an employer has failed to conduct a review or to consult or to draw up and implement an employment equity plan
- The commission should publish a code of practice giving guidance to employers on periodic reviews and employment equity plans
- The commission should have power to require information on the review and action plan, and to make recommendations as to the action to be taken
- Where the commission is of the opinion that the employer is not carrying out a satisfactory review, it should use its best endeavours to secure satisfactory written undertakings
- If such undertakings are not given, the commission should be able to serve a notice giving directions to the employer; similarly if an undertaking, although given, is not complied with the commission should be able either to serve a directions notice or to apply to a tribunal for enforcement of the undertaking
- The commission should also have power to serve a notice about goals and timetables, against which to measure progress, on an employer who has given an undertaking, or been directed to take action, or has been subject to a tribunal order to take any action
- The commission should be able to apply to an employment tribunal to enforce an undertaking or directions, or goals and timetables notice, and the tribunal should have power to make an order specifying the steps to be taken
- In the event of failure to comply with a tribunal order, the tribunal should be able either to certify the failure to the High Court for contempt proceedings, or itself to award a monetary penalty

Recommendation 29 (3.41–3.50)

- Employers with more than 10 full-time employees should be obliged to conduct a periodic pay audit (once every three years),covering both full- and part-time employees, and to publish this in the company's report, and to inform employees or their representatives and, on request, the commission
- The failure of an employer to conduct an audit or to disclose, should be admissible in evidence in any proceedings for unlawful discrimination, and the tribunal should be entitled to draw an adverse inference from this fact, having regard to the size and administrative resources of the employer
- The commission should have power, after due notice, to publish the fact that an employer has failed to conduct a pay audit or to disclose
- If, following an audit, the employer finds a significant disparity between predominantly female and predominantly male job classes, it should be obliged to draw up a pay equity plan in negotiation with recognised trade unions with a view to reaching a collective agreement, or where no union is recognised in respect of pay, after consultation with a view to reaching a workforce agreement with employees or their representatives
- When bargaining on pay, the employer and recognised union should have due regard to the need to promote equal pay for work of equal value for men and women
- The minimum (default) contractual right of an employee to equal pay for work of equal value should apply where there is no collective agreement or workforce agreement on the subject
- There should be the possibility of CAC arbitration in the event of a dispute, and the CAC should have power to award a pay equity plan, which should operate in the same way as a collective agreement or workforce agreement
- Individual employees should be able to bring proceedings in an employment tribunal for breach of a collective agreement or workforce agreement or CAC award relating to equal pay
- The CAC should have power to strike out or amend provisions in collective or workforce agreements or employer's pay structures which are directly or indirectly discriminatory

Recommendation 30 (3.51–3.52)

- It should be possible to contract-out of the individual's right to equal pay by collective agreement or workforce agreement in respect of a defined and reasonable period so far as is appropriate and necessary to allow the employer time to absorb the costs of implementation of an agreed pay equity plan
- A CAC pay equity award should operate in the same way as a collective agreement or workforce agreement

Recommendation 31 (3.53–3.54)
- The principle of proportionality in relation to the defence of objective justification for a difference in pay between men and women should be codified, by providing that a difference in pay for work of equal value is justified only to the extent that the difference is attributable to factors which are not related to sex

Recommendation 32 (3.55)
- The definition of "same employment" should be clarified so as to conform to EC law, by including any employment by the same employer or by an associated employer or by any other employer who forms part of the same public service

Recommendation 33 (3.56)
- An employer should be obliged to achieve pay equity at the level of the entire undertaking, rather than within a particular establishment or establishments as at present, subject to the general defence of objective justification

Recommendation 34 (3.57–3.59)
- The EOC code of practice on equal pay should be revised, simplified, and expanded in the light of recent experience
- There should be encouragement to review existing job evaluation schemes against the EC code, the EOC guidelines on good equal opportunities practice in analytical job evaluation and other sources
- Chairmen and members of employment tribunals (and, if our proposals in Recommendation 29 are accepted members of the CAC), who hear equal value claims, should receive training in the nature of job evaluation schemes

Recommendation 35 (3.60)
- Section 2A(2) of the Equal Pay Act should be repealed. An existing scheme should be admissible and relevant evidence in determining whether the work is of equal value, but it should not be conclusive

Recommendation 36 (3.61–3.77)
- The positive duty on specified public authorities to promote equality and eliminate unlawful discrimination should apply to their procurement, grant and subsidy, licensing and franchising functions
- Equality standards should be included among the core performance indicators for the purposes of compliance with the duty to secure best value
- The normal system of best value reviews, audit and inspection should include measures for fair participation and fair access, and in addition, the commission should be able to make inquiries and request information, and, where an authority has failed to take appropriate steps to comply, the commission should be able to apply to a tribunal for an appropriate order
- The "approved questions arrangement", with suitable amendments, should be applied to all grounds of unlawful discrimination
- Contractors should be excluded from approved lists, not invited to tender, not selected against competing bids and be liable to have their contracts terminated, if they have been found by an employment tribunal, after a fair hearing, to have committed gross misconduct, including persistent discrimination or any other serious breach of equality legislation
- The UK Government should press the European Commission for a less restrictive approach to contractual obligations to achieve equal opportunities, and for a clarification and simplification of the EC rules in this respect

Recommendation 37 (4.2–4.7)
- Regular discrimination training should continue to be received on a national basis by all chairmen, but additional refresher courses should be provided for experienced chairmen
- Discrimination cases should be assigned only to chairmen with the requisite experience or specialist training

Recommendation 38 (4.8–4.9)
- The current programme of discrimination training for lay members should be continued and additional resources should be provided for specialist training to a selected number of lay members
- The practice should continue that lay members are not called to sit on discrimination cases unless they have the requisite experience or training
- The specialist race panel should be discontinued
- Chairmen should give clear guidance to lay members to avoid prejudice and stereotyped attitudes, and members who are unable or unwilling to do so, should not be called for discrimination cases

Recommendation 39 (4.10)

- An equality scheme for the employment tribunals should set targets for achieving a lay membership of not less than 40% women by 2003, and 50% by 2006, and a percentage that reflects the proportion of ethnic minority communities in each region by 2006
- Barriers on the service of disabled persons as members of tribunals should be removed, unless they can be justified as appropriate and necessary

Recommendation 40 (4.11)

- The title of chairman of employment tribunals should be changed to employment judge

Recommendation 41 (4.12–4.17)

- All discrimination cases should be commenced in the employment tribunals
- Where the matter does not relate to employment, the tribunal should be designated as an "equality tribunal"
- The lay members should be called to hear cases having regard to their knowledge and experience of the relevant field. If necessary, additional members should be appointed with relevant knowledge in respect of education and consumer affairs
- The President of tribunals or a regional chairman should have the power to transfer a matter to the county court, either on application by a party, or on his or her own motion
- Equivalent provisions should be made for the transfer of cases to the sheriff court in Scotland
- The criteria for transfer should include: (1) whether it would be more convenient or fair for the hearing to be held in that court, having regard to the facts, legal issues, remedies and procedure; (2) the availability of a judge specialising in this type of claim; (3) the facilities available at the tribunal and at the court where the claim is to be dealt with and whether they may be inadequate because of the disabilities of a party or a potential witness; and (4) the financial value of the claim and the importance of the claim to the public in general

Recommendation 42 (4.20–4.21)

- Tribunals should continue to use IHAs where they are satisfied that unrepresented parties will not be at a disadvantage
- The parties should be sent in advance pro forma questions which are to be raised at the IHA

Recommendation 43 (4.22–4.23)

- A simplified single questionnaire should be used for all types of discrimination claim
- The form should be made available to applicants by the Employment Tribunals Service together with the originating application IT1
- The form should state clearly the consequences of failure to reply or an evasive or equivocal reply
- Respondents should be required to reply within eight weeks of service of the questionnaire, failing which the tribunal should have power, on application or of its own motion, to strike out all or part of the notice of appearance or to debar the respondent from defending altogether, but this should not be done without giving the respondent an opportunity to show cause why such an order should not be made

Recommendation 44 (4.24–4.26)

- The commission should have power to institute proceedings in its own name or jointly with individuals in respect of unlawful discrimination where there is a common question of fact or law affecting a number of persons, whether identified or not
- The commission should be able to claim injunctive and declaratory relief and also an order requiring compensation to be paid to a defined group of individuals
- Individuals who fall within the defined group should be able to register within a specified time, and, if they do so, to enforce any order for compensation to the extent of their own loss or injury
- If our recommendation in respect of exemplary damages is accepted, then in any proceedings brought by the commission the amount of such damages should be paid to the commission

Recommendation 45 (4.27–4.32)

- There should be more active case management by chairmen of tribunals in equal pay cases, speedier appointment of the expert, an early meeting between the expert and the parties (under the chairman's management) to establish a strict timetable, with any departure from this being subject to a directions hearing

Recommendation 46 (4.34–4.36)
- The Lord Chancellor should direct the CLSF to give priority to all types of discrimination case in respect of both legal help and representation

Recommendation 47 (4.37–4.39)
- There should be a statutory reversal of the burden of proof in respect of all unlawful discrimination along the lines set out in Article 4 of the Burden of Proof Directive 97/80/EC

Recommendation 48 (4.40–4.41)
- The time limit for making a complaint of unlawful discrimination should be six months from the date of the alleged act of discrimination, unless in all the circumstances of the case the court or tribunal considers it just and equitable to hear the complaint out of time

Recommendation 49 (4.42–4.44)
- There should be an up-to-date digest of current awards for injury to feelings
- Damages should be available as a remedy for unintentional indirect discrimination in respect of all grounds of unlawful discrimination and in all fields to which the law applies

Recommendation 50 (4.45–4.48)
- Tribunals in England, Wales and Northern Ireland should make greater use of their power to award aggravated damages
- Punitive damages should be available for unlawful discrimination as recommended by the Law Commission in respect of England and Wales
- Consideration should be given to the award of aggravated and punitive damages for unlawful discrimination in Scotland

Recommendation 51 (4.49–4.50)
- An employment tribunal should have power to order engagement, re-engagement or reinstatement, unless the employer shows that it would not be practicable to comply with such an order
- If an order is made but not observed, the tribunal should be able to award additional compensation, including aggravated and punitive damages

Recommendation 52 (4.51–4.53)
- An employment tribunal should have power to recommend that the applicant be engaged in or promoted to a particular job
- The power to make a recommendation that action be taken to obviate or reduce the adverse effect of the discrimination on the applicant should be extended to non-employment cases
- In the event of a recommendation not being complied with in the period specified the tribunal or court should have power to award additional compensation, including aggravated and punitive damages

Recommendation 53 (4.59–4.65)
- The power of the commission to make arrangements for conciliation in non-employment cases should be extended to all grounds of unlawful discrimination
- A pilot project for mediation in sexual harassment cases, and subsequently in other discrimination cases, should be supported
- Employers' grievance and harassment procedures should include provision for mediation
- The ERA 1996, s.3 should be amended so as to require an employer to specify in the note about grievance procedures a person or body to whom the employee can apply for mediation of any grievance relating to alleged discrimination or harassment, if other procedures fail

INTRODUCTION

AIMS AND METHODOLOGY

Aims

This report presents the findings of the independent review of the enforcement of UK anti-discrimination legislation which was conducted under the auspices of the Centre for Public Law and the Judge Institute of Management Studies in the University of Cambridge between 1 April 1999 and 31 May 2000. The project was funded by the Joseph Rowntree Charitable Trust and the Nuffield Foundation. The research team had the benefit of an Advisory Committee, chaired by Lord Lester of Herne Hill QC, and also a panel of experts (see Appendix 6). Those advisers and experts are not, however, responsible for our conclusions. A paper entitled *Options for Reform* together with a series of working papers was published in December 1999 (see Appendix 7).

The general aim of the project was to review and evaluate proposals for the reform of UK anti-discrimination legislation, based on an assessment of the experience of those affected by the legislation. Account has been taken of the requirements of EU law and international human rights treaties which the UK has ratified, as well as relevant experience in other EU member states, the USA, Canada, Australia, New Zealand, and South Africa.

The specific objectives were to develop an accessible legislative framework for ensuring equality of opportunity, to propose other measures which will promote equal opportunity policies and spur compliance with those policies, and to ensure that the UK is in full compliance with its obligations under EU law and international human rights law.

Methodology

We sought to consult as widely as possible with those who have experience of the anti-discrimination legislation. The purpose of this was to provide feedback, perspectives and suggestions from a variety of sources, to help the review balance competing views and interests, to identify the strengths and weaknesses of the legislation, to note any interactions with other legislation, programmes and policies, and to give interested parties a stake in the review. We have sought to identify the widest possible areas of consensus on which realistic reform proposals can be based.

The principal methods used were the following.

(1) *Targeted case studies* of employers in Great Britain, Northern Ireland, and the USA. The findings from these case studies, and an account of how they were selected, will be found in Appendix 1, which is a revised version of the findings which appeared in *Options for Reform*.

(2) *An Initial Consultation Paper* distributed in May 1999 to over 1000 organisations and individuals describing the project and inviting responses to the issues and questions raised in the paper. Eighty-four written submissions were received. These ranged from trade unions, employers' organisations, local government bodies, race equality organisations, disability groups, lawyers' groups, charities and other voluntary sector bodies as well as individuals.

our general recommendations to those of the Task Force. Our working paper No.4 also deals with these issues.

Note on terminology

As far as possible, gender-neutral language has been used, but where statutes use a particular term, such as "Chairman" of an employment tribunal, we have followed this (but see our recommendation in this respect in para.4.11). We have referred to "sex" discrimination, which is the statutory concept, in preference to "gender" discrimination. When we refer to "ethnic minorities" we are not using this as a synonym for "not-white" or "not-Western", but as describing any group (including Jews, Roma or Gypsy people, the Irish travelling community etc.) distinguished by their ethnic origins. "Black" people refers to those from both Africa and the Caribbean. "Asian" includes those with origins in Bangladesh, India, Pakistan, China, Hong Kong and Vietnam. The term "worker" is used in its wide legal sense, including not only those who are employees under contracts of employment, but also jobseekers and anyone who works for another, so including agency, casual and self-employed workers.

CHAPTER ONE

WHY A NEW FRAMEWORK IS NEEDED

A. Challenges to the present framework

(1) Outdated legislation

1.1 The prevailing framework of anti-discrimination legislation in Britain was conceived three decades ago. It deals with only race, sex and disability, and ignores other arbitrary exclusions from work and society, such as age, religion or belief, and sexual orientation. In our consultations and case studies the current legislation was widely criticised for being outdated, fragmented, inconsistent, inadequate, and at times incomprehensible.

1.2 The Sex Discrimination Act (SDA) came into force, with the Equal Pay Act (EqPA), at the end of 1975, and the Race Relations Act (RRA), replacing an Act of 1968, was passed in 1976. Each of these Acts has been amended on several occasions. Their essential feature remains a negative prohibition on discrimination, rather than a positive duty to promote equality. There are separate commissions – the EOC and CRE – with responsibility for enforcing each Act. These Acts formed the model for the Disability Discrimination Act (DDA) in 1995, but with the significant additions of a general defence of justification of direct discrimination and a positive duty to make reasonable adjustments for disabled persons, and the absence of the concept of indirect discrimination. In April 2000, another separate commission – the DRC – came into being to enforce this legislation.[4] There are numerous differences between each of the Acts, and between the powers of the various commissions.[5]

1.3 Meanwhile, in Northern Ireland, the Fair Employment Act 1976 (FEA) applied the British model to the problem of discrimination between the Protestant and Roman Catholic communities. This was unsuccessful in removing entrenched practices. A significant change came with a new FEA in 1989. This shifted the emphasis from the elimination of unlawful discrimination on grounds of religion or political opinion to the reduction of structural inequality in the labour market, whether caused by discrimination or not. Positive duties on employers were introduced to monitor and review the composition of the workforce and to take affirmative action, under the supervision of an enforcement agency, the FEC. The evidence (reviewed in paras. 3.30-3.36 below) indicates that in its first ten years this legislation had a significant impact in reducing inequalities in the workplace. Another innovation in Northern Ireland, resulting from the Good Friday Agreement of 1998, was the enactment of a positive duty on public authorities to promote equality of opportunity not only between the Protestant and Roman Catholic communities, but also between persons of different racial group, age, marital status or sexual orientation; between men and women generally, between persons with a disability and without, and between persons with dependants and without.[6] The three separate commissions dealing with religion, race and sex respectively were merged, from October 1999, into a single equality

---

[4] Set up under the DRCA, amending the DDA.
[5] See chap.2 and Appendix 2, below.
[6] Northern Ireland Act 1998, s. 75.

commission (ECNI) which also took on responsibilities for disability discrimination, and for monitoring the positive duty on public authorities. However, the new commission continues to work under four separate legislative regimes – for religious, race, sex and disability discrimination. The ECNI functions alongside the new Northern Ireland Human Rights Commission, whose remit is wide enough to cover general equality issues.

1.4   These developments in Northern Ireland were bound to raise questions about the continuing emphasis in Britain on negative duties not to discriminate and the fragmentation of legislation and institutions. Indeed, following the Stephen Lawrence inquiry, which highlighted institutional racism in the Metropolitan Police, the Government has introduced a positive duty on public authorities in the current Race Relations (Amendment) Bill, and has committed itself to do the same in respect of gender and disability when legislative time permits.[7]

1.5   The inspiration for British and Northern Irish legislation in the 1960s and 1970s was found in the USA and Canada. The Street Report of 1967 made a study of the workings of anti-discrimination in North America, and contained detailed proposals for a "second generation" Race Relations Act to replace the limited first Act of 1965.[8] This Report had some influence on the shape of the Race Relations Act 1968, but it was not until the "third generation" legislation - the SDA and RRA - that its most important advice was heeded, particularly by strengthening the commissions and the enforcement provisions.[9] The White Papers which preceded the 1975 and 1976 Acts, drafted by Anthony (later Lord) Lester, marked a major turning point. The resulting legislation provided a right for individuals to bring proceedings for compensation for unlawful sex and race discrimination in industrial (later employment) tribunals, or for damages in designated county and sheriff courts in non-employment cases, while at the same time entrusting strategic enforcement in the public interest to the EOC and CRE. The Acts also imported the novel American concept of adverse impact or indirect discrimination.

1.6   The third-generation legislation did not copy the American concept of affirmative action plans (introduced by President Kennedy in 1961 in respect of government contractors) to increase the representation of minorities and of women in the workforce. The exception, as we have seen, was Northern Ireland, in response to the deteriorating political situation there and to the campaign in the US to persuade corporations, state legislatures and municipal governments with investments in Northern Ireland to adopt the "MacBride Principles" which encouraged employers to adopt affirmative action.[10] No similar political imperative existed in Britain. Pressures are now growing, however, for the UK as a whole to move towards a fourth generation of legislation prescribing positive duties on public authorities, employment and pay equity plans, and contract compliance regimes. Several models now exist, apart from fair employment legislation in Northern Ireland, such as employment and pay equity legislation in Canada, affirmative action for women in Australia, and recent employment equity legislation in South Africa. Although the political and social situations in those countries differ from those in the UK, the processes which lead to status discrimination and structural inequality are comparable.

---

[7] Equality Statement, Cabinet Office, 30 November 1999.

[8] Street et al (1967). The other members of the committee under Professor Harry Street's chairmanship were Geoffrey (later Lord) Howe and Geoffrey Bindman. See generally on the earlier legislation, Hepple (1970); Lester and Bindman (1971).

[9] Home Office (1974); Home Office (1975).

[10] McCrudden (1999a), p. 1706.

(2) The law of the European Union

1.7   The third generation legislation has developed under the strong influence of EU law. Article 119 of the EC Treaty, contained a directly applicable right for women and men to equal pay for equal work. (Following the Treaty of Amsterdam this is now embodied in revised form in Article 141 of the EC Treaty.) It was complemented by a series of directives, the most important of which is the Equal Treatment Directive 76/207/EC, implementing the principle of equal treatment in relation to access to employment, vocational training, promotion, working conditions and termination of employment. Many of the extensions of the rights of women resulted from the test case strategy adopted by the EOC, and from infringement proceedings brought by the European Commission. A dynamic relationship has grown up between EC law and domestic UK sex discrimination law, with the former exposing gaps in the coverage of UK law, and concepts from the UK, such as unintentional indirect discrimination, helping to shape EC law. EC directives and recommendations on sex discrimination have widened the gap between the law on this and other forms of discrimination which were not within the scope of the EC Treaty.[11]

1.8   The Treaty of Amsterdam has now inserted a new Article 13 into the EC Treaty, empowering the Council to "take appropriate action to combat discrimination based on sex, racial or ethnic origin, religion or belief, disability, age or sexual orientation." Two draft directives (proposed on 29 November 1999) are currently under discussion. One – the so-called "vertical" directive - covers only employment and occupation but deals with direct and indirect discrimination on all the grounds mentioned in Article 13, except sex, which is already covered in other directives. The second – "horizontal" – directive covers not only employment but also education, social security, the provision of goods and services and cultural activities, but is limited to discrimination on grounds of race and ethnic origin.[12a] The two overlapping directives are not entirely consistent, and will, if enacted, result in different standards in respect of the "new" grounds of discrimination compared to those applying to equal treatment between men and women. The EC proposals are modelled on the negative duties and the individualistic, adversarial approach of third-generation British legislation, rather than the fourth-generation positive duties and affirmative action legislation. Whatever future legislation emerges from the EU, UK legislation will have to be brought into line with it.

(3) Devolution

1.9   Constitutional changes in the UK are already beginning to have a significant effect on equality issues. One of these changes is devolution, which may increase fragmentation of policy and executive decisions within the UK, since Scotland, Wales, and Northern Ireland now have some scope to develop their own equal opportunities policies. All the devolved bodies are subject to the basic ground rule that they cannot act in a way which is incompatible with the ECHR. This includes the Article 14 prohibition on discrimination in relation to convention rights. However, there are important differences as to the extent of devolution on equality matters. Under the Scotland Act 1998 the Scottish Parliament has powers to legislate on all matters except those designated as reserved matters. Subjects that are reserved matters include equal opportunities, in particular the EqPA, the SDA, RRA and DDA.[12] However there is an exception for:

---

[11] See chap.2 and Appendix 3, below.
[12] Scotland Act 1998, Schedule 5, Part II L2.
[12a] This Directive was adopted by the Council on 6 June 2000. Member States will have three years to implement it.

The encouragement (other than by prohibition or regulation) of equal opportunities, and in particular of the observance of the equal opportunity requirements.

Imposing duties on-

(a) any office-holder in the Scottish Administration, or any Scottish public authority with mixed functions or no reserved functions, to make arrangements with a view to securing that the functions of the office-holder or authority are carried out with due regard to the need to meet the equal opportunity requirements, or

(b) any cross-border public authority to make arrangements with a view to securing that its Scottish functions are carried out with due regard to the need to meet the equal opportunity requirements.

The Act defines equal opportunities as "the prevention, elimination or regulation of discrimination between persons on grounds of sex or marital status, on racial grounds, or on grounds of disability, age, sexual orientation, language or social origin, or of other personal attributes, including beliefs or opinions, such as religious beliefs or political opinions". The Scottish Parliament has set up a standing committee on equal opportunities whose aim is to "consider and report on matters relating to equal opportunities and upon the observance of equal opportunities within the Parliament."[13]

1.10   Under the Government of Wales Act 1998 the Welsh Assembly may exercise the powers of making delegated legislation where these are transferred to it by ministerial order. There is a duty on the Assembly to-:

...make appropriate arrangements with a view to securing that its business is conducted with due regard to the principle that there should be equality of opportunity for all people.[14]

By Standing Order 14 the Assembly has set up an Equal Opportunities Committee. The Order states that the committee:

...shall audit the Assembly's arrangements for promoting in the exercise of its functions and the conduct of its business the principle that there should be equality of opportunity for all people. The committee shall also have particular regard to the need for the Assembly to avoid discrimination against any person on grounds of race, sex or disability.

1.11   The Northern Ireland Assembly has far more extensive powers on equality issues than the Scottish Parliament and Welsh Assembly. Broadly speaking, it can legislate on matters relating to the Equality Commission and the positive duty on public authorities only with the permission of the UK Secretary of State (so-called "reserved matters"). But it will have direct legislative responsibility for the existing bodies of law on fair employment, sex equality race relations and disability discrimination in Northern Ireland (so-called "transferred matters"). The hybrid nature of the arrangements can be seen from the fact that the Secretary of State retains policy responsibility for the positive duty on public authorities and has a number of specific functions in relation to equality schemes, but can agree to the Assembly legislating on these matters. Moreover, the ECNI is funded by the Assembly but is under the departmental oversight of the Department of Economic Development. The ability of the Assembly to legislate on the substance of anti-discrimination law, including amendments to present legislation, is subject to some safeguards. Any legislation on equality matters may be made subject to cross-community support, the Assembly cannot legislate in a way which is incompatible with rights under the ECHR or under EU law, nor can it legislate in a way that discriminates directly on grounds of

---

[13] Standing Order Rule 6.9.
[14] Government of Wales Act 1998, s.48.

religious belief or political opinion. The Secretary of State may decide not to submit for Royal Assent an Assembly measure that is incompatible with the UK's international human rights obligations.

1.12   Despite these safeguards, the possibility exists for the Northern Ireland Assembly to legislate on some equality matters in a way that makes the protections against discrimination either stronger or weaker than those in the rest of the UK. Although the Scottish Parliament and Welsh Assembly have fewer powers in this respect, they clearly have scope for developing new equal opportunities policies in relation to matters within their remit. The committees they have established are already taking a pro-active stance on equality issues. The Greater London Authority and other specified London authorities have also been placed under positive duties to promote equality of opportunity,[15] and may be expected to develop extensive policies of their own.

(4) The Human Rights Act 1998

1.13   Another major constitutional change affecting equality is the HRA, already binding in Scotland, Wales, and Northern Ireland, and to come into force in England on 2 October 2000. The Act provides for the enforcement in UK courts and tribunals of rights secured by the ECHR. Article 14 of the ECHR requires Convention rights to be secured "without discrimination on any ground such as sex, race, colour, *language, religion, political or other opinion,* national *or social* origin, *association with a national minority, property, birth or other staus.*" (The italicised grounds are not covered by current UK legislation, except for religion and political opinion in Northern Ireland.) Although this is not a free-standing right to equal treatment, there may be a violation of Article 14 in conjunction with another Article of the ECHR even if there is no violation of that other Article taken alone. Among the relevant Articles are Article 3 (inhuman and degrading treatment), Art.6 (right to a fair trial), Article 8 (right to private and family life), Article 9 (right to freedom of thought, conscience and religion), and Article 2 of the First Protocol (right to education).

1.14   Many discriminatory acts which fall outside the scope of current anti-discrimination legislation are likely to be challenged under the HRA, for example immigration decisions taken on grounds of ethnic origin, discriminatory treatment on grounds of sexual orientation, failure to accommodate the religious beliefs of employees, and decisions which discriminate indirectly on grounds of marital or family status. Although the HRA applies only to public authorities (including bodies exercising functions of a public nature), this includes the courts and tribunals. Anti-discrimination legislation must be judicially interpreted, so far as possible, so as to be compatible with Convention rights. If this cannot be done in respect of primary legislation, the court must make a declaration of incompatibility; offending subordinate legislation must be declared invalid.

1.15   One of the weaknesses of Article 14 of the ECHR is that there is no free-standing right against discrimination on one of the prohibited grounds. It is ancillary to other Convention rights. A draft Protocol No.12, currently under consideration by the Council of Europe, will provide an independent right not to be discriminated against by a public authority in respect of "any right set forth by law". The prime objective is to impose a negative obligation on public authorities

---

[15] Greater London Authority Act 1999, s.33.

not to discriminate, but it may be inferred from the duty on Member States to "secure" the right, that there will be a positive obligation to provide legal redress against discrimination on all the prohibited grounds, even those not currently covered by UK legislation. This could be done by legislation. If not, it would be left to UK courts and tribunals to grant remedies against public authorities in respect of the proscribed grounds, once the new Protocol has been incorporated through an amendment to the HRA.

1.16   The new human rights culture also takes its inspiration from international treaties which the UK has ratified but not yet fully implemented. These obligations include the placing of a duty not to discriminate on all public authorities on grounds similar to those in the ECHR, and also a positive obligation on public authorities to take affirmative action to diminish the conditions which cause or help to perpetuate discrimination.[16] This reflects a growing international consensus in favour of positive measures to reduce inequality.

(5) Summary

1.17   There are thus numerous challenges to the present framework – dissatisfaction with the fragmentation and inconsistencies between four separate anti-discrimination regimes in the UK, and three separate commissions in Britain; demands for the legislation to be made more comprehensible and user-friendly; international, European and domestic pressures to extend the grounds of unlawful discrimination; the commitment of government to impose positive duties on public authorities; the relative success of fair employment legislation in Northern Ireland in reducing structural inequality; the continuing need to keep in line with EU law; the pressure from devolved legislatures and executives in the UK; and the building of a new legal and political culture of equality based on the ECHR and international human rights treaties. These legal and political challenges cannot be met without an understanding of the wider social changes which have occurred since the 1970s.

B. The changing face of disadvantage and discrimination

(1) Social structure and attitudes

1.18   During the three decades of third-generation legislation, the patterns of social exclusion and discrimination have changed considerably. First, there is the phenomenon of an ageing population, which has brought questions of age discrimination against older people into prominence. There are also increased risks of discrimination against young people from the ethnic minorities. Population growth in the UK has, like all post-industrial economies, been slow for the past thirty years because of low fertility rates. Fewer children are being born, and the birth rate has declined from 28.6 in 1900-2, to 12.3 in 1997. Mortality rates have also declined, bringing about the phenomenon of demographic ageing. Life expectancy for women is now 79.5 and for men 74.3. The ageing of the population is expected to continue into the next ten years, so that by 2011, 25% of women and 21% of men will be aged 60 and over.

1.19   However, the ethnic minority population in Great Britain has a much younger age structure than the population as a whole, reflecting the fact that past immigration was mainly of the

---

[16] See Choudhury, Working Paper No.2.

young, with higher fertility patterns. In 1994, only 4% of the Pakistani/Bangladeshi population were over the age of 60 compared with 19% of the white population. Overall, there will be fewer young people leaving education and entering the labour market. In contrast, there will be a "boom" in the numbers of young people from the ethnic minorities, because of the younger age structure of these groups. They will have a rejuvenating effect on the overall demographic profile, and reduce the effect of the ageing of the population. For example, in the United Kingdom, the average age of people from all ethnic minority groups in 1995 was 27, compared with 38 for the white population. In contrast, disability increases with age, so that nearly half (48%) of the disabled population in 1997-98 was aged 65 or over. Nearly one in five (18%) of the working age population is disabled.

1.20 Secondly, the social status of women has changed, and the traditional model of families dependent on the male income has been replaced by many more complex and individual structures. Marriage rates have declined and the average age at marriage has increased. Divorce rates have also increased. In 1997, the marriage rate was 57% and 8% of the adult population were divorced. The proportion of single parent families has trebled. Many women are the heads of household. In education, girls achieve better grades than boys. In 1996-97, at age 16, 51% of girls and 41% of boys gained five or more GCSE passes at grades A* to C, and at A level, 32% of girls and 26% of boys gain two or more A level passes or equivalent.[17] In 1996-97, women comprised 52% of full time undergraduates in all higher education institutions, double their proportion in 1960-61. However, there are marked differences in the subjects studied. More girls study arts subjects, (English, languages, history and social studies), and biological sciences, and more boys study mathematics and sciences (chemistry, and physics) at A level. There is a similar pattern in higher education, with the biggest disparity in engineering and technology, which has six times more men than women.

1.21 Thirdly, the ethnic minorities are no longer the "newcomers" or a "small minority" as described in the 1975 White Paper on racial discrimination. Some ethnic minority groups have higher educational levels than those for whites. Whilst 5% of white men have a degree or equivalent, 7% of African-Asian origin, and 12% of Chinese origin, and 7% of Indian origin people have degrees. These trends are evident too in entrance to university. In 1996, 9.4% of applicants for universities were of Asian origin, and 3.4% were Black. Ethnic minorities are particularly strongly represented in informatics and mathematical sciences. More generally, the UK is no longer, if it ever was, a society with a "majority" white and "minority" non-white population. It is a multi-ethnic, multi-cultural society, in which there is a plurality of groups and communities, some enjoying more power and influence than others. Today there is growing emphasis on cultural diversity and, at the same time, the need to bind together the constituent groups on the basis of shared values such as human rights and equality.[18]

1.22 These developments have had and will continue to have a significant impact on disadvantage. In particular, expectations have grown. People from the groups which have experienced discrimination and disadvantage, on grounds such as race, sex, disability, and sexual orientation, have been exposed to publicity and arguments from governments and others in employment and public life, about the need for equality and the right to it. If they do not experience it in reality, they will increasingly question and challenge public rhetoric and demand results.

---

[17] Equal Opportunities Commission (1999a).

[18] This theme is developed in *The Future of Multi-Ethnic Britain: the Parekh Report*, prepared by the Commission on the Future of Multi-Ethnic Britain (forthcoming).

(2) The labour market and unemployment

1.23   Demographic ageing, described above, will have a growing impact on the labour market, in the UK and other EU member states. The working population is a smaller proportion of the total population, and by 2015, the working population will have fallen significantly: for every 100 persons leaving the labour market, only 90 will be entering it. In the past 20 years the proportion of men aged between 50 and 65 who are not working has doubled. A third of men and women in this age group are unemployed. A recent Cabinet Office report found that most people leaving work early do not do so voluntarily, that early exit contributes substantially to poverty, and that this age group experiences growing exclusion. The drop in work rates among the over-50s costs the economy about £16bn a year, and £3-5bn in extra benefits and lost taxes.[19]

1.24   Women are an increasing proportion of the labour force. In the past thirty years their participation in the labour market increased by 50%. In 1998, women in Britain were 44% of all those of working age in employment, an increase of 2% in ten years. In future, women's participation will increase whilst men's will reduce in all age groups. Women will constitute the main resource for employment growth. Many of these will be mothers. Fifty-nine per cent of mothers in the UK were economically active in 1991, an increase of over 20% since 1971. However, despite the increase in women's participation in employment, women are still over-represented in certain industries and occupations. They are also much more likely to be part-time: 44% compared with 8% of men. Around 86% of women work in service industries, compared with 60% of men. Some 53% of women work in three occupational groups, clerical/secretarial, personal and protective services, and sales. For men these occupations account for only 19% of employed men. Men are over-represented in craft and related jobs, as plant and machinery operatives, and are still the majority in managerial and administrative professions, although the proportion of women has increased from 24% in 1984 to 32% in 1998.

1.25   Ethnic minority people are also more concentrated in certain sectors and occupations, with variations between the different ethnic groups. Caribbean, Indian and Pakistani men are over-represented in manufacturing, notably in the motor industry, and, for Pakistanis, textiles. 17% of African-Asian men are employed in banking and finance, and 10% of Caribbean men are in public administration. Ethnic minority men have a more restricted distribution within industry than white men. Ethnic minority women are also concentrated in certain sectors, such as Caribbean women in hospitals and health care and public administration, and women from all groups in retail and finance.

1.26   The most significant factor, and the most persistent, is the ethnic minority unemployment rate. According to an analysis by the Office of National Statistics (ONS), overall unemployment rates for both men and women from the ethnic minorities were about twice those for white people with the same level of qualifications, and this pattern exists across all age groups and among those with qualifications, including graduates. The gap is smaller for men without qualifications, and greater for some ethnic minority groups (Pakistani/Bangladeshi men and Black African men and women) whose unemployment rates are three times that of whites. The rate for Indian men was the best, only slightly higher than for white men. Unemployment rates for ethnic minorities in the top four social classes were more than twice those for whites, smaller among the partly skilled and least among the unskilled.

---

[19] Cabinet Office (2000), chap.3.

1.27   Another analysis by the Employment Service produces a similar picture.[20] This is based on extensive data on New Deal participants, enabling better monitoring than in any other programme. New Deal is a national programme for young unemployed people aged 18 to 24. In all, 15% of participants are from the ethnic minorities. The analysis shows that all ethnic minority groups on New Deal are better qualified than whites are, which should therefore be an indicator of better employability than whites. But ethnic minorities have a lower rate of job outcomes (entering a job) than white participants. When recording effects and geographic differences are taken into account, ethnic minority participants are achieving 3% fewer job outcomes than white participants. This is in spite of the fact that the Employment Service submits ethnic minority participants to jobs more often than white participants. The analysis tentatively concludes that discrimination might be a factor. It seems hard to avoid the conclusion that discrimination *is* a factor, given the fact that this analysis has allowed for all the known variables.

1.28   Disabled people too have persistently higher unemployment rates than the overall rate. Their unemployment rate is nearly twice that of those of working age (11% compared with 6%), and for men the gap is wider (13% compared with 6%). Looked at another way, almost half of the economically inactive were disabled. People with disabilities are more likely than those without a disability to be self-employed or in part-time work. The proportion of disabled people in employment varies according to the type of disability. People with mental health problems were less likely to be in work than people with physical or sensory impairments.

(3) The gender pay gap

1.29   The Equal Pay Act had a marked initial impact between 1970, when it was enacted, and 1975, when it came into force, as employers changed their pay structures in readiness for the new regime. The hourly rates of pay of women rose from 63% to 71% of men's pay between 1970 and 1975. However, women's relative pay was still only 72% in 1983, just before the law was extended to cover work of equal value. Following the introduction of equal value claims, women's relative pay settled in the range 73-75%. It narrowed to 80% by 1994, and has remained around that level since then, but the difference in hourly earnings between women who work part-time and men who work full-time has not altered significantly. In 1998, female part-timers earned 59% of the hourly earnings of male full-timers, exactly the same proportion as in 1978, despite the widening of the judicial interpretation of the legislation to cover indirect discrimination against women working part-time.[21]

1.30   Equal pay legislation is only one element in the many complex factors which determine women's relative pay. Research commissioned by the Cabinet Office in 1999 came to the conclusion that the level of a woman's educational achievement has the biggest single impact on her lifetime's earnings, but the hours she works, how many children she has and when, and whether she divorces all have significant impacts on her lifetime earnings.[22] The UK is eleventh in the league table of women's relative pay in 15 EU Member States, behind countries such as Belgium and Luxembourg, whose legislation was described by the European Commission in 1994[23] as being less comprehensive and detailed than that in the UK. Among

---

[20] Moody et al (2000).
[21] EOC (1999b), p. 4. They earned 73% of the hourly earnings of women working full-time in 1998.
[22] Rake, (2000).
[23] EC, COM (94) 3, 23 June 1994.

the reasons for the UK's poor showing relative to other EU States, is the different structure of female employment in the UK, but Eurostat reports that even when women's earnings are recalculated to remove structural differences "there still remains an hourly earnings difference between a man and woman with comparable educational background, in the same occupation and industry, of 13% in Sweden, 22% in Spain, 23% in France and almost 25% in the UK".[24]

1.31   Another reason that has been suggested for the continuing gender pay gap is the decline of centralised collective bargaining. A recent analysis by Aileen McColgan[25] shows that there is a relatively small gender wage gap in most EU States where there is a high level of collective bargaining coverage. But this does not guarantee equality as is shown by Austria, where 98% of workers are covered by collective agreements, but women's relative pay was around 74%, even lower than that in the UK. A more significant factor, as shown in a study of OECD countries[26] and of Australia,[27] appears to be the presence of centralised pay determination. Women traditionally did best in systems with not only a high level of collective bargaining but also a centralised bargaining or pay awards system. In the UK the coverage of collective bargaining has declined, and where it does exist it is enterprise-based.

1.32   The underpayment of women is due, in part, to occupational sex segregation and to the accompanying under-valuation of those jobs done predominantly by women. This means that some form of comparison has to be made between predominantly female and predominantly male jobs, and adjustments then have to be made to reduce the pay gap. Another part of women's underpayment is the result of industrial and workplace segregation, in particular the location of many women in relatively small, low-paying workplaces. The introduction of the national minimum wage has been of particular benefit to women workers. The Low Pay Commission has reported[28] that in the year to April 1999 the gap in the average hourly pay of women relative to men narrowed by one percentage point, the largest amount for almost a decade.

(4) Discrimination

1.33   There can be no doubt that the third generation legislation in the UK has broken down many barriers for individuals in their search for jobs, housing and services, and that the SDA and RRA have driven underground those overt expressions of discrimination which were current 25 years ago.[29] The law has fulfilled the promise of the Race Relations Board in its first annual report[30] of providing an unequivocal declaration of public policy, giving support to those who do not wish to discriminate but who feel compelled to do so by social pressure. It has done more than provide a means of redress for minority groups, women, and disabled persons. It has also had an important educative or persuasive function. This was strengthened by bringing situations of indirect discrimination within the ambit of the law. Many organisations were led by this to examine and redefine those practices which might unintentionally have an adverse impact on minorities and women. They have been obliged to remove some of the barriers to equal opportunities. However, many barriers remain.

---

[24] Eurostat, *Statistics in focus*, Population and social conditions, No.15/97.

[25] McColgan, (1999).

[26] Whitehouse, (1992).

[27] McColgan (1999).

[28] Low Pay Commission (2000), para. 3.14.

[29] See the selected examples of allegations of racial discrimination in employment in Hepple (1968), pp.201-216; and in respect of women in Home Office (1974), para. 1-16.

[30] Race Relations Board (1968), para. 65.

1.34   The data on occupational distribution and unemployment levels suggests that the barriers to participation at work are different for different groups. The main barriers facing women are occupational segregation, concentration in low paid work, part-time work, unequal pay, pregnancy discrimination, and harassment. According to the EOC, thousands of complaints of discrimination received each year are on these grounds. A survey by the EOC of women who had contacted them confirmed that pregnant women are facing difficulties in all types of occupations and companies.[31] These include being dismissed or threatened with dismissal when they first told their employer about being pregnant, or before they took their maternity leave, or as a result of reorganisation during maternity leave, or demotion by way of displacement on return. Complaints about treatment on return from maternity leave now constitute around one-third of all complaints received by the EOC. Discrimination on grounds of sexual orientation have also come into prominence. Common examples are abuse and harassment at work and denial of access to benefits received by heterosexual workers and their partners, such as travel concessions and insurance schemes.[32]

1.35   Discrimination against ethnic minorities, or indeed against anyone who is "not like me", is perhaps now more based on avoidance, or on giving preference to other more socially or culturally familiar candidates, rather than on a conscious decision to exclude, although the latter still occurs. Candidates from the same social, cultural or religious background are more favourably considered, because the decision-maker feels more comfortable with them. The effect however is the same as old style racism, as the persistently higher unemployment figures (above) indicate. Discrimination occurs if a person acts on a stereotype and assumes that all members of a group share a common characteristic, without considering the individual's qualities. Although stereotypes have always been a cause of discrimination, the commonly held ones have changed and are more complex. Examples of current stereotypes include beliefs that people from some ethnic groups are good at finance, or that some do not have a strong work ethic, or have an aggressive approach to conflict resolution at work. There is an assumption that women from a Muslim background are not interested in a career, and so a Muslim woman may not be considered for promotion. Racial discrimination is now covert and more complex. Many reported instances involve insensitive behaviour, racial harassment and lack of awareness of minority faith requirements such as wearing the hijaab. Twenty years ago it was commonplace for women and black and ethnic minority employees to have to tolerate jokes and banter about their sexuality, or origins. Now women and ethnic minority employees are more likely to challenge such behaviour.

1.36   The problem goes beyond "discrimination" in the narrow sense of unfavourable actions by individuals. There are also attitudes, policies and practices within institutions which cause disadvantage. The Stephen Lawrence Inquiry highlighted this in its widely-quoted definition of "institutional racism":

[Institutional racism is] the collective failure of an organisation to provide an appropriate and professional service to people because of their colour, culture or ethnic origin. It can be seen or detected in processes, attitudes and behaviour which amount to discrimination through unwitting prejudice, ignorance, thoughtlessness and racist stereotyping which disadvantage minority ethnic people. It persists because of the failure of the organisation openly and adequately to recognise and address the existence and causes by policy, example and leadership. Without recognition and action to eliminate such racism it can prevail as part of the ethos or culture of the organisation. It is a corrosive disease.[33]

---

[31] EOC (1999c), p. 13.
[32] TUC (2000).
[33] Stephen Lawrence Inquiry (1999), para. 6.34.

While this analysis is particularly pertinent to racism, it could also be applied to the ways in which institutions treat women, disabled people and older workers. Members of the disadvantaged groups do not enjoy fair participation and fair access.

1.37   Similarly, in the provision of services, lack of awareness and insensitivity to the needs of others who may not have the same requirements as oneself, leads to assumptions being made. Disabled people face physical barriers such as steps into premises, which affect those with a mobility impairment, or lack of information in alternative forms for blind or hearing-impaired people. Disabled people also face stereotypes about their capabilities, and may be patronised or excluded from activities on the assumption that they cannot contribute. Age discrimination in recruitment, training and promotion and the attitudes of employers is, according to a recent Cabinet Office report, "one of the key causes of declining economic activity among older people."[34]

C. Changed social and employment practices

1.38   The equality legislation and related codes of practice have had a significant impact on employment practices, and the number of employers with equal opportunities policies has risen steadily since the 1980s. A 1995 survey[35] into the implementation of the race equality Code of Practice in large companies indicated that most had a formal policy covering racial equality, and about half of these said that they had a plan to implement their policy. About half the respondents with a plan stated that they monitored its effectiveness, and the same proportion carried out race equality training, and had procedures to deal with racial harassment. Another study for the government in 1995[36] which included samples of organisations of all sizes, showed that of employers who were described as "active", only one-third were taking specific steps to implement an equal opportunities policy, and this became a diminishing proportion if one looked specifically at what was being done, and many of the steps being taken were "soft" such as promoting a better company image by including equality statements in advertisements. Both studies confirmed that large employers, particularly in the public sector and in services and finance, were doing the most.

1.39   More recently, according to the 1998 Workplace Employee Relations Survey (WERS),[37] two-thirds of workplaces stated that they were covered by formal equal opportunities policies. Large companies were most likely to have a formal written policy. Most of those with no policy claim to have one which is not formally written, and most small organisations without a policy believe that it is unnecessary because they employ few people from disadvantaged groups. Only 3% of organisations had had grievances about discrimination, the lowest proportion being small employers.

1.40   However, when the survey asks about more specific aspects of an equal opportunities policy the proportions taking action become lower. Fewer than 20% include equal opportunities in employee training, a little under half discuss equal opportunities at workplace level consultative committees, rising to 68% where there are union representatives. A large majority (almost 84%) has not attempted to measure the effects of the policy. (Figure 1).

---

[34] Cabinet Office (2000), p. 38.
[35] CRE (1995).
[36] Coussey (1995).
[37] We acknowledge the use of data made available by the ESRC Data Archive at the University of Essex.

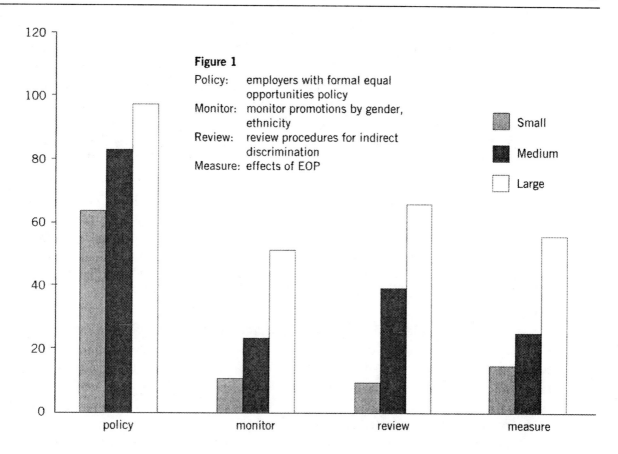

Figure 1
Policy: employers with formal equal opportunities policy
Monitor: monitor promotions by gender, ethnicity
Review: review procedures for indirect discrimination
Measure: effects of EOP

Small
Medium
Large

1.41 Implementation of equal opportunities policies is also much weaker in manufacturing, electrical, hotels, and construction than in finance and the public sector. (Figure 1.2)

Figure 1.2

Sector	Proportion with formal equal opportunities policy
Manufacturing	7
Electrical	0.32
Construction	3.5
Wholesale	17.2
Hotels	8
Transport	65
Financial	78.5
Public	99.6
Education	92
Health	83

1.43 Organisations with a formal policy employed proportionately more people from the ethnic minorities. Organisations with higher proportions of female employees are more likely to have equal opportunities policies. Another survey[38] in 1999 of 140 subscribers to *Equal Opportunities Review*, and some of the top 100 FTSE companies, found that two-thirds of

[38] EOR (1999b), p. 14.

respondents had equal opportunities policies, and 89% of these said that they carried out ethnic monitoring of recruitment. These results suggest that procedures are becoming more transparent. A survey by Pearn Kandola[39] suggests that the most frequently taken diversity initiatives in the UK are the introduction of a formal induction process (95%), and using open selection criteria (93%). Sharing information and consulting employees were also frequently cited initiatives. Whilst these actions will help create a more open workplace culture, they will do little or nothing to overcome the barriers to the employment of a more diverse workforce.

1.44   As the WERS confirms, small employers are less likely to have formal equal opportunities polices, and less likely to collects statistics on the sex or ethnic origin of the workforce; or to check procedures for discrimination. A survey[40] for the Department for Education and Employment in 1996 showed that small employers claimed to offer equal opportunities, but regarded acceptability to the existing workforce as important for recruitment, and there was evidence of widespread stereotyping into men's and women's work. One of the main influences on small employers was a desire to keep within the law.

1.45   No strategy for equality and diversity can be sustained unless managers are involved and understand and accept the aims and goals of the programme. In any examination of what has been effective in employment, it is important to recognise that structural changes have occurred since the 1970s when the Codes of Practice for sex and racial equality were drafted. Many organisations have devolved decision making to managers to simplify management structures, focus on core business functions, and cut overheads. This has been made easier because of technological developments, which were referred to by employers as a reason why a new focus was needed. The consequences of devolved decision making were examined in a study with case studies of the private and public sectors.[41] This found that there were some key conditions which had to be present in order to ensure that change was sustained. These included: active involvement and leadership from senior management; explicit core values to include equality; a clear link made between equality and the organisation's essential functions; external pressure for equality, from advocacy groups, customers, trade unions, complaints and litigation, publicity; access to information on progress with a hierarchy of organisational and local targets and benchmarks; participation by managers and ethnic minority staff in solving problems and meeting challenges, and deciding on action.

D. Towards a new framework

1.46   The conclusion might be that in the past five years most organisations have adopted equal opportunities policies, and increasing numbers are also implementing concrete measures and monitoring the policy's effectiveness. However, there have been few systematic attempts locally or at a national level to assess whether equal opportunities policies have resulted in fairer participation and access. There have been no recent studies of levels of discrimination to assess whether there has been a reduction. The continuing high levels of unemployment found among ethnic minority people, including those with higher and better qualifications than their white counterparts, suggests that equal opportunities policies have yet to make a significant impact on participation in the workplace, for these groups. For women, discrimination on grounds of pregnancy and the more subtle types of exclusion at higher levels continue.

[39] EOR (1999a), p. 33.
[40] Coussey (1996).
[41] Bedington et al (1997).

1.47 The main initiatives being taken under equal opportunities policies tend to be passive and separate from each other. There is little sense that many organisations have a sustained and co-ordinated strategy to improve diversity in the workforce or pursue equal opportunity policies in the delivery of services. This requires a commitment to change that goes beyond many of the practices which according to the surveys quoted, are standard ingredients of company equal opportunities policies. It requires an acceptance of participation by community advocacy organisations which has not been a common feature in the private sector, and participation by managers in implementing the policy and a system to measure progress, which according to the WERS survey, only 16% of employers have ever done. It also requires a culture which embraces diversity and equal opportunity as a measurable business goal.

1.48 Looking at the reviews of experience we can begin to map some elements which appear to be essential components of an effective anti-discrimination model. Equal opportunities policies, stimulated by codes of practice which set broad standards, have been important for changing corporate behaviour. The continuing gap between white and ethnic minority unemployment rates, even for the highly qualified for some groups, the persistence of pregnancy discrimination and the pay gap, suggests that voluntary equal opportunities policies have not been sufficiently focused on achieving an increase in representation. The more processes and practices become objective, the more complex and subtle are the means by which decision-makers exclude people from disadvantaged groups.

1.49 There is no single cause of inequality. There are underlying long-run trends towards greater income and labour-market inequality.[42] Structural barriers perpetuate poor schools and training, low achievement, unemployment and deprivation. A concerted strategy against social exclusion is needed. An essential part of this is eliminating the inequalities faced by women, people from ethnic minority backgrounds, older workers, and disabled persons.

1.50 The present third-generation framework is unable to achieve this for several reasons. First, it adopts a fragmented, inconsistent and incoherent approach to different manifestations of inequality of opportunity. The harmonisation of legislation and institutions is an essential first step to a concerted and integrated approach. This has to be inclusive, based on common principles and concepts and framed against the background of the principle of equal treatment in EU law and of human rights embodied in the HRA. In particular the traditional notions of direct and indirect discrimination have to be supplemented by the application of principles of substantive equity, and the grounds of unlawful discrimination widened. These issues are considered in chapter two.

1.51 Secondly, the current framework was designed largely to deal with a model of organisations with hierarchical, vertically integrated and centralised bureaucracies. This is a top-down rule-making approach which focuses on individual fault-finding and depends on retrospective investigation of an act alleged to be motivated by an unlawful ground of discrimination. This tends to breed negative, defensive and adversarial responses. But today organisations cannot survive and prosper unless they are flexible and adaptable to market changes and technological innovation. Organisations are flattening their hierarchies, giving more authority to lower-level managers, and demanding a high quality workforce, with the active participation of all stakeholders, including workers, customers and clients. Equality of opportunity increasingly depends, not simply on avoiding negative discrimination, but on training and improving skills,

---

[42] DfEE (2000), chap.2.

developing wider social networks, and encouraging adaptability. The present framework places too much emphasis on state regulation and too little on the responsibility of organisations and individuals to generate change. In chapter three, we consider incentives and sanctions to develop organisational responses of this kind.

1.52   This focus on organisational change does not, however, mean that the law should lose the important role, identified by the Race Relations Board in 1968, of providing for "the peaceful and orderly adjustment of grievances and the release of tensions." On the contrary, procedures and remedies for individuals need to be made more effective to deal with the increasingly subtle and complex nature of discrimination. This is considered in chapter four.

CHAPTER TWO
HARMONISING LEGISLATION
AND INSTITUTIONS

A. A Single Statute?

(1) Defects of the present framework

2.1   The first and most obvious defect of the present framework is that there is *too much law*. At present, there are no less than 30 relevant Acts, 38 statutory instruments, 11 codes of practice, and 12 EC directives and recommendations directly relevant to discrimination (Appendix 2). Nearly every year there are amendments or fresh rules. To this is added the weight of an ever-expanding case law, with many thousands of decided cases being available through law reports, the Internet and commercial digests. The statutes are written in a language and style that renders them largely inaccessible to those whose actions they are intended to influence. Human resource managers, trade union officials, officers of public authorities, and those who represent victims of discrimination find difficulty in picking their way through it all.

2.2   Specialist lawyers can also be mystified. In 1983 Lord Denning complained that the "tortuosity and complexity [of the Equal Pay Act 1970] is beyond compare" and that the 1983 Equal Value Regulations were such that "no ordinary lawyer would be able to understand them. The industrial tribunals would have the greatest difficulty and the Court of Appeal would probably be divided in opinion".[43] That prediction has been amply borne out over the years, to the extent that the EOC has described the present framework for equal value claims to be "so complex as to be unworkable." The Bar Council's Sex Discrimination Committee told us that "it is entirely unsatisfactory that at present, if she or he is to know their rights, a lay person is expected to be familiar with several domestic statutes, with Art.119 [141] of the EC Treaty, with the Equal Treatment Directive, the Equal Pay Directive and other directives, and with complex principles of EC law which permit domestic law in certain circumstances to be overridden by EC law." To this list could now be added the Human Rights Act 1998 and the ECHR. Many examples could be given of the difficulties which courts and tribunals have had in interpreting the obscure wording of both the RRA and the SDA, on questions such as whether a comparator is needed in cases of pregnancy discrimination and harassment, the mental element in direct discrimination and victimisation, establishing the pool and adverse impact in cases of indirect discrimination, the meaning of "detriment", and the justification defence, vicarious liability and responsibility for contract workers. The recent DDA has already been the subject of conflicting interpretations, for example on the question whether a person must have knowledge of a disability in order to be said to have discriminated for a reason relating to that disability.

2.3   The complexity and inaccessibility of all this anti-discrimination legislation and case law were identified by our respondents as being among its greatest weaknesses. Regional chairmen of

---

[42] DfEE (2000), chap.2.
[43] HL Deb., 6th series, vol. 445, cols. 901-902.

employment tribunals whom we interviewed regarded this as a major cause of the protraction of legal proceedings. Those representing complainants and respondents (including experienced lawyers) said this was a major barrier to speedy, inexpensive and fair dispute resolution. The most unfortunate result of this mass of legislation and case law is a psychological one. Employers in our case studies (Appendix 1) said that without clear and tangible rules it was difficult and costly to bring about changes in the attitudes and practices of managers. People have come to think that eliminating discrimination and promoting equality is a matter of detailed rules imposed and interpreted by external agencies which they must follow. There is too little reliance on the responsibility of organisations and individuals to change themselves.

2.4   The second main defect is that the law is *inconsistent* and inherently unsatisfactory. In Appendix 3 we set out the main differences between the SDA, RRA, DDA and FETO. We may limit ourselves here to a few examples-

- the DDA, unlike the SDA and RRA does not include the concept of indirect discrimination
- the SDA and RRA, unlike the DDA, do not include the concept of "reasonable adjustment"
- the British legislation, unlike the FETO in Northern Ireland, does not include a positive duty to secure "fair participation" in employment
- the SDA and RRA make it unlawful to discriminate only in respect of "access" to existing opportunities or benefits (e.g. to a job share), while the DDA is not limited in this way
- the RRA places a duty on local authorities to promote racial equality (currently being extended to all public authorities), but there is no similar duty in respect of sex or disability
- the RRA and FETO cover only partnerships of six or more partners, while the SDA covers all partnerships
- the SDA allows recovery of compensation for unintentional indirect discrimination, while the RRA does not
- there are inconsistencies between the powers of the EOC, CRE and DRC, and the ECNI has different powers in respect of different types of discrimination.

2.5   There are gaps and anomalies between the EqPA Act and the SDA, which are set out in Appendix 3. A number of inconsistencies have been resolved only by judicial interpretation, such as the application of the concept of indirect discrimination to equal pay claims, and differences between the test of objective justification under the SDA and "material factor" in the EqPA. But important differences remain, for example-

- the SDA permits a comparison with a hypothetical male, the EqPA does not
- claims for payment of money or for a matter regulated by the "equality clause" in a contract of employment can be brought only under the EqPA, while non-contractual claims can be brought only under the SDA
- the SDA includes discrimination against married persons, the EqPA does not
- the SDA and EqPA have different time limits for bringing claims

2.6   Although important changes have been made in the SDA so as to bring it into closer conformity with EC law, there remain a number of significant respects in which the SDA and EqPA appear to fall short of the standards demanded by EC law. In Working Paper No.1 for this project, Professor Evelyn Ellis pointed out that the obligation placed on the judiciary to interpret domestic law so far as possible in such a way as to make it accord with EC law, the so-called principle of "indirect effect", enables national law to adapt itself to the EC law without the need for specific legislative amendment. Nevertheless, she has identified no less than 15 differences where, subject to two possible exceptions, judicial adaptation appears to be impossible and the statute requires to be amended. These matters are summarised in Appendix 3.

They include coverage of discrimination on grounds of marital or family status, amendment of the definition of indirect discrimination, changes in the burden of proof, and improvement in the remedies.

2.7   The inconsistent and unsatisfactory nature of the existing legislation is a result of its history. Successive anti-discrimination statutes have each concentrated upon a particular target. Notwithstanding the similarities between the SDA, RRA and DDA, and the attempts of the courts to interpret them as a harmonious code, the legislation now present a mass of inconsistent detail, with major gaps in coverage.

(2) How to harmonise

2.8   The Government is already committed to harmonising the provisions of the SDA, RRA and DDA.[44] We canvassed a number of options for achieving this. The most radical would be a single Equality Act. This is the model which can be found in several countries, such as Australia, Canada, Ireland, New Zealand and the United States. An alternative would be to follow the EOC's proposal that the SDA, EqPA and other relevant laws, including EC law, should be replaced by a single Sex Equality Act, but to retain a similarly structured law on racial discrimination, and another on disability discrimination. Presumably, if new grounds of unlawful discrimination were added these would each be the subjects of a new Act or they would be included with an analogous Act (e.g. religion with race, sexual orientation with sex etc.).

2.9   Most of our respondents were in favour of a single equality statute. The most important advantage was seen to be that it would recognise the indivisibility of the concept of equality. Sharing common ground would encourage links among groups facing discrimination, while at the same time focussing the attention of employers and service providers on the need for an inclusive approach. A single statute would make it easier to deal with cases of multiple discrimination, where a person is unfairly treated but does not know the reason. We were told by the Committee on the Administration of Justice that in Northern Ireland, where there is now a single equality commission, the continued existence of four separate and inconsistent statutes is undermining the creation of a one-stop shop for businesses. The unified ECNI considers that a single statute would "ultimately be the most logical target". Women, members of ethnic minorities and disabled people would generally enjoy the same rights and remedies. In their submission to us, Justice argued that there are common concepts and definitions which apply to all forms of discrimination, and that these should be incorporated into one statute. Justice suggested that there could then be separate and distinct chapters, or separate statutes, dealing with issues which are specific to certain forms of discrimination. Others pointed out that if new grounds of unlawful discrimination were added, these would fall under the general equality principle, without the need for major legislative changes. Changes necessitated by treaty obligations, e.g. under EC law and additional protocols to the ECHR, would benefit all groups, and inconsistencies between different statutes or a hierarchy of rights would be avoided.

---

[44] Cabinet Office, Equality Statement (30 November 1999); but contrast the Northern Ireland Office (1998), White Paper which stated that it was not proposed to bring together the separate statutes as they apply in that province. The Better Regulation Task Force (1999), para. 3.1, was not persuaded of the need for a major legislative overhaul either in relation to the individual regimes or in bringing them together.

2.10   There were, however, some reservations. The CRE argued that:

> A separate Race Relations Act is useful for campaigning and education purposes as well as law enforcement. To move to a single equality statute would blur the focus on specific types of discrimination. For so long as institutional racism persists it must be tackled directly, and general concepts of equality and diversity will not have the same sharp impact.

In our view, this reservation confuses a "general" concept with a unified one. The same concept of equality can be applied to each ground of discrimination without undermining specific action against particular grounds of discrimination. RADAR, which works on behalf of disabled people, expressed concern about merging all areas of discrimination under a single equality statute, "because disability discrimination is still not an equal partner in comparison with other legislation." This is really aimed at the way in which an equality statute is enforced rather than the substance of the law, namely whether the focus on particular forms of discrimination should be entrusted to different agencies (see para.2.86 below).

2.11   Another objection was expressed by the Bar Council's Sex Discrimination Committee which thought there was a danger that:

> ...if there were one portmanteau statute, the need to accommodate the differences which exist between the legislation which exists relating to different types of discrimination in the one Act would be unwieldy and confusing.

In our view, this is wrong. First because it presupposes that the different concepts (such as reasonable accommodation and justification) in the different statutes cannot be harmonised, and secondly because it envisages consolidation of the present mass of detail, rather than simplification. An analogy may be drawn with health and safety legislation where in 1972, the Robens Committee recommended:

> A comprehensive and orderly set of revised provisions under a new enabling Act. The new Act should contain a clear statement of the basic principles of safety responsibility. It should be supported by regulations and by non-statutory codes of practice, with emphasis on the latter. [45]

2.12   The first overriding consideration is to reduce the weight of anti-discrimination law, and to render it more comprehensible to those affected by it, so as to encourage the active promotion of equality, rather than dependence on external enforcement of a mass of detailed rules. The second consideration is to remove those inconsistencies which are not appropriate and necessary to eliminating a particular form of discrimination. This will promote the inclusive approach to fair participation that it is central to our recommendations. We believe that this can be done by a single Equality Act which contains a clear statement of the basic principles of non-discrimination and equality, and the framework of regulation. It will need to be supplemented by statutory regulations on specific subjects, and also by codes of practice. All these documents need to be written in plain language a way which facilitates comprehension. They should be well publicised, and available in Braille, on tape and other media taking into account the needs of disabled people.

---

[45] Robens (1972), para. 469. In practice, however, it was EC legislation which had a far more profound impact than the Robens' recommendation in achieving this goal: see Hendy and Ford (1995), p. 14.

Recommendation 1

- There should be a single Equality Act in Britain
- This Act should be supplemented by regulations and by regularly up-dated codes of practice on specific subjects
- The Act and other documents should be written in plain language so as to facilitate comprehension, and should be available in forms which take into account the needs of disabled people

B. Principles

2.13   There was general support for the basic principles of a new framework which were set out in our Options Paper. We have reformulated these in the light of comments received.

2.14   The first principle is that *the goal of legislation and other measures is to eliminate unlawful discrimination and to promote equality regardless of sex, race, colour, ethnic or national origin, religion or belief, disability, age, sexual orientation, or other status.* We elaborate on the meaning of "equality" in paras. 2.34-2.40, and on the grounds of unlawful discrimination in paras.2.57-2.84. The emphasis on promoting equality in addition to eliminating discrimination is integral to the objective, set out in chapter one, of a positive, inclusive approach which encourages the assumption of responsibility by organisations and individuals to achieve change.

2.15   The second principle is that *there must be clear consistent and easily intelligible standards.* We have already explained our view that simplification of the legislation is an essential step to change the present dependency on the external enforcement of detailed rules. The more complex or vague standards are, the easier it is for organisations to avoid them or make them self-serving. Our case studies (Appendix 1) show that clearly written codes, such as that under the DDA in relation to goods, facilities and services, aid compliance. On the other hand, inconsistencies between the codes on racial discrimination and sex discrimination, as well as the failure to update these codes, has diminished their effectiveness. We have proposed (above) a single equality statute, and this will need to be accompanied by revision of regulations and codes of practice, particularly the latter.

2.16   The third principle is that *the regulatory framework must be effective, efficient and equitable, aimed at encouraging individual responsibility and self-generating efforts to promote equality.* One of the dilemmas of policy-makers is to know how to judge whether a particular instrument has been "successful", or in the narrower concept used by economists, "optimal". The evaluation criteria we have chosen have been used in the area of environmental regulation.[46] A measure is said to be effective if it achieves the stated policy goal. The goal here is to eliminate unlawful discrimination and to promote equality. This is measurable by setting objectives to promote fair participation and fair access and monitoring progress towards achieving them. The Law Society's Employment Law Committee pointed to the risk that attempts at measurement can develop the attitude that so long as sufficient boxes have been ticked, nothing more needs to be done. What we have in mind, however, is not mechanistic, but based on a specific objective which is performance-related. The objective should be derived from good practice exemplified in codes of practice. This methodology is now well-known, for example in the field of health and safety. Measurement involves working towards clear targets with the advice where appropriate, of the enforcement agency.

[46] Gunningham (1998), pp. 25-31.

2.17   In assessing efficiency, we need to have regard to the administrative costs of a particular measure, and to administrative simplicity avoiding unnecessary bureaucracy. Also important is the extent to which the measure provides an incentive to the organisation to change. For example, taken as an end in itself, monitoring the composition of the workforce could be viewed as an unreasonable administrative cost on business; however, if effectively linked to producing a more diverse workforce by means of an employment equity plan, the initial set-up costs of monitoring are likely to be outweighed by the advantages to the business of developing a more diverse workforce (see para. 3.36).

2.18   The third element of this principle is equity or fairness. The regulatory framework aims at fair participation of under-represented groups and so distributes advantages to members of those groups. But this may result in a loss of benefits for some previously advantaged groups, and there may be uneven impacts upon different targets of regulation (e.g. large employers may be able to absorb the initial costs more readily than small ones). Since this is always politically contentious, the redistributive measures adopted will depend on what is politically acceptable.

2.19   This last consideration makes it crucial to build into the regulatory framework opportunities for public participation in the making and application of standards. This may not be "efficient" because it is likely to cause delays and consume resources, but it will increase the acceptability, and broaden the social basis, of any particular measure. For this reason we put forward as a fourth principle that *there must be opportunities for those directly affected to participate, through information, consultation and engagement in the process of change*. We make detailed proposals for consultation with interest groups in chapter three.

2.20   The fifth principle is that *individuals should be free to seek redress for the harm they have suffered as a result of unlawful discrimination, through procedures which are fair, inexpensive and expeditious, and the remedies should be effective*. This is necessary not only to allow for the redress of grievances and the peaceful and orderly resolution of disputes (see para.1.52), but also because an individual complaint may spark action in an organisation even where the enforcement agency has not been involved. Recommendations for making procedures and remedies more effective will be found in chapter four.

Recommendation 2

The framework should be based on the following five principles-
- the goal of legislation and other measures is to eliminate unlawful discrimination and to promote equality regardless of sex, race, colour, ethnic or national origin, religion or belief, disability, age, sexual orientation, or other status
- there must be clear consistent and easily intelligible standards
- the regulatory framework must be effective, efficient and equitable, aimed at encouraging personal responsibility and self-generating efforts to promote equality
- there must be opportunities for those directly affected to participate, through information, consultation and engagement in the process of change
- individuals should be free to seek redress for the harm they have suffered as a result of unlawful discrimination, through procedures which are fair, inexpensive and expeditious, and the remedies should be effective

C. The concepts of equality and discrimination

2.21 The goal of eliminating unlawful discrimination and promoting equality has to be translated into clear legal concepts. In our Working Paper No.3 Professor Sandra Fredman considered the conceptual issues in some detail. She analysed the basic notion of equality as having two main dimensions: equality as consistency and substantive equality. Under the first of these dimensions we discuss (a) direct discrimination (including pregnancy discrimination); (b) knowledge, intention and motivation; and (c) victimisation. Under the second, we consider (d) indirect discrimination; (e) equality of opportunity; and (f) fair participation and fair access.

(1) Direct discrimination

2.22 The basic notion of equality, namely that likes should be treated alike, is based on the principle of consistency. This concept of equality is found in the form of the right to equal pay for equal work for men and women in the EqPA and in Article 141 of the EC Treaty; in the form of direct discrimination in the SDA,[47] RRA,[48] and FETO,[49] and in a slightly different formulation in the DDA.[50] It is also central to the principle of equal treatment in the various EC equality directives[51] and in the draft directives under Article 13 of the EC Treaty. Equality as consistency has two main characteristics: first, it requires a comparator whose relevant circumstances are not materially different from those of the complainant; and secondly, the principle is satisfied by consistent treatment regardless of whether the individual benefits substantively as a result. The need for a comparator has led to considerable difficulty in cases where there is no appropriate comparator. In cases of discrimination on grounds related to pregnancy, harassment, and victimisation, no appropriate comparator can be found. In equal pay claims, the need to find a comparator employed by the same employer has meant that job segregation cannot be adequately dealt with. Fredman points out that "the need to find a similarly situated comparator still creates powerful pressures to demonstrate conformity with the male or white or able-bodied norm".[52] Equally problematic is the second characteristic of equality as consistency, namely that the principle is satisfied regardless of whether the individual benefits as a result. More specifically, it is a defence for the respondent to show that the comparator would have been treated equally badly. Similarly, the principle can just as well be satisfied by removing a benefit from one group (levelling down) as by extending the benefit to the other group (levelling up).

2.23 There clearly remains a role for this bedrock principle of consistency, but it needs to be strengthened in two ways. First, several of our respondents agreed with Fredman that the principle needs to be modified in certain circumstances where a comparator is not appropriate. In particular, subjecting a woman to any disadvantage or detriment for a reason related to *pregnancy* or childbirth should be a substantive wrong, not tied to discrimination.[53] We also make proposals (below) for prohibiting *harassment* in a way which is not dependent upon

---

[47] s.1(1)(a); SD(NI)O, art.3(1)(a).

[48] s.1(1)(a); RR(NI)O, art.3(1)(a).

[49] Art.3(2)(a).

[50] s.5(1)(a).

[51] See esp. Council Directive 75/117/EEC, art.1; Council Directive 76/207/EEC, art.1(1). See too, Council Regulation 1612/68/EEC, art.7 on equality of treatment of workers who are nationals of Member States.

[52] Working Paper No.3, para. 3.5.

[53] See the analogous provisions of ERA 1996, s.99 which make dismissal on these and other grounds connected with maternity automatically unfair.

comparisons. The question of pay comparisons between men and women is considered in paras. 3.53-3.60. Secondly, the principle that likes should be treated alike should be interpreted in a way which furthers the explicit aims of the legislation, namely to enhance the dignity, autonomy and worth of every individual and to improve the position of relatively disadvantaged groups. It would be incompatible with these aims to allow levelling down, or to claim that a comparator would be equally badly treated. We make recommendations in this respect in paras. 2.41-2.42.

Recommendation 3

- The concept of direct discrimination should be interpreted in accordance with the overall purposes of the legislation, as set out in Recommendation 8 below
- Adverse treatment of a woman for a reason related to pregnancy or childbirth should be a substantive wrong, without any requirement for comparison with the treatment of another person

(2) Victimisation

2.24   Moreover *victimisation* needs to be redefined. At present it is a species of discrimination,[54] so requiring a comparator who would not have been unfavourably treated in comparable circumstances for doing one of the "protected acts" (e.g. instituting legal proceedings). It has been extremely difficult to prove victimisation where the respondent says "we treat all trouble-makers the same whether they complain about discrimination or anything else."[55] In seeking a new approach, the draft directives under Article 13 of the EC Treaty are not of much assistance. The CRE and the Discrimination Law Association pointed out that Article 9 of the draft "horizontal" directive on racial discrimination is defective because it requires conscious motivation by the alleged victimiser. This would be retrogressive for the UK because in *Nagarjan v London Regional Transport,*[56] the House of Lords held that conscious motivation is not a necessary ingredient of unlawful victimisation. Article 10 of the "vertical" draft EC directive (relating to employment and occupation), is slightly more satisfactory because it refers simply to a "reaction" to a complaint or other legal proceedings. However, even this may lead courts and tribunals to ask *why* a protected act was an important cause of the adverse treatment. That is a motivation which, according to *Nagarajan,* is irrelevant since the purpose of the victimisation provisions is "to give persons victimised on account of their reliance on rights under the Act effective civil remedies, thereby also creating a culture which may deter individuals from penalising those who seek to enforce their rights under the Act."[57]

2.25   Following the reasoning in *Nagarajan,* but omitting the need for a comparator, we would recommend that victimisation be defined as any adverse treatment for a reason related to a protected act. The test would be whether but for doing the protected act the person alleging victimisation would have been treated in this way. The legislation should also codify the *Coote v Granada Hospitality (No.2)*[58] decision by making it clear that the protection applies to ex-employees.

---

[54] SDA, s.4; SD(NI)O, art.6; RRA, s.3; RR(NI)O, art.4; DDA, s.55; FETO, art.3(4).
[55] See comment in EOR (1999c) p. 52.
[56] [1999] ICR 877.
[57] per Lord Steyn at p. 895.
[58] [1999] ICR 942.

Recommendation 4

- Victimisation should be defined as any adverse treatment of a person (including an ex-employee) by reason that such person has brought proceedings, given or collected evidence or information, made an allegation, supported another person, or done any other act under or by reference to the equality legislation; it should not be necessary to show that the person victimised has been less favourably treated than in those circumstances other persons are or would be treated

(3) Knowledge, intention and motivation

2.26   The *Nagarajan* decision confirms that conscious motivation on the part of the discriminator is not a necessary ingredient of unlawful discrimination. We invited views as to whether the legislation should codify this by stating that knowledge, motivation and intention is not relevant to direct discrimination. The Bar Council's Sex Discrimination Committee agreed that these matters are not a necessary ingredient in the vast majority of cases, but said that they could be relevant in some circumstances, such as sexual harassment. The case law on sexual harassment indicates that lack of intent is no defence, and that the question is not whether the harasser subjectively knew that his or her conduct was unwelcome but whether a reasonable person would understand that the victim rejected the sexual advances.[59] This seems to us to be consistent with the general principle. In any event, we recommend (paras. 2.50-2.56) that harassment should be a wrong distinct from discrimination.

2.27   A more difficult problem is whether knowledge of a specific disability, whose material features fall within the statutory definition of disability, is required for a person to be said to have acted for a reason that relates to the disability. There are conflicting decisions of the EAT on this, the most recent deciding that lack of specific knowledge does not mean that the respondent did not act for a disability-related reason, but it can be relevant on the question whether the respondent was justified.[60] A requirement of specific knowledge of the disability would be a disincentive on say, an employer to inquire into the reasons for a disabled person's absence.[61] The test of whether there is a disability is an objective one, for the tribunal and not the employer to determine, otherwise "there will be difficulties with credible and honest yet ignorant or obtuse employers who fail to recognise or acknowledge the obvious".[62] It would be helpful if this were to be clarified by legislation. However, we see no need to change the law in relation to automatically unfair dismissals for pregnancy, under section 99 of the ERA 1996. The EAT has held that the employer must "either have the knowledge of, or a belief, in the pregnancy."[63] In the case of disability discrimination there is a defence of justification,[64] and lack of knowledge of the disability may be relevant to this. Similarly, the duty of reasonable adjustment does not apply "if the employer does not know, and could not reasonably be expected to know, that the person has a disability."[65] On the other hand a dismissal for a reason related to pregnancy is automatically unfair however long after the pregnancy it occurs. If the employer's knowledge were not relevant to this, it would mean that an employer dismissing for absenteeism would always be at risk of a finding of automatic unfairness, with no possibility of justifying the reasonableness of the dismissal in the circumstances.

[59] *Reed v Stedman* [1999] IRLR 299, EAT.
[60] *H.J.Heinz Co v Kenrick* [2000] IRLR 144, EAT; cf. *O'Neill v Symm & Co. Ltd* [1998] IRLR 233.
[61] EOR (2000), p. 49.
[62] per Lindsay J [2000] IRLR at p. 147.
[63] *Del Monte Foods Ltd v Mundon* [1980] IRLR 224, EAT.
[64] We propose, below, para. 2.45, that the general defence of justification should be replaced by specific exceptions.
[65] DDA, s.6(6)(b).

Recommendation 5

- The definition of discrimination should make it clear that intention or conscious motivation is not a necessary ingredient
- For the avoidance of doubt, the legislation should declare that specific knowledge of the disability as such or as to whether its material features fall within schedule 1 of the DDA, is not a necessary ingredient in establishing discrimination on that ground

(4) Indirect discrimination

2.28   This concept was first developed in the USA by way of case law under Title VII of the Civil Rights Act 1964. This was translated into the specific and complex language of the SDA, [66] RRA, [67] and FETO.[68] Indirect discrimination occurs where the same "requirement or condition" is applied to both sexes or different racial groups (or in Northern Ireland religious groups), but the proportion of one sex or racial group (or religious group), who can comply with it is "considerably smaller" than the proportion of the other sex, racial group (or religious group) who can comply. The concept is results-oriented in that "it is not the equality of treatment meted out to the individual that ultimately matters, but the fact that it has a disparate impact on an individual because of his or her membership of the disadvantaged group."[69] There is a defence that the requirement or condition was justifiable irrespective of the sex, racial (or religious) group of the person to whom it is applied.

2.29   The European Court of Justice has developed the concept of indirect discrimination in the context both of discrimination against nationals of Member States, and sex discrimination. This case law has been codified in Article 2(2) of the Burden of Proof Directive 97/80/EC which reads:

> For the purposes of the principle of equal treatment…indirect discrimination shall exist where an apparently neutral provision, criterion or practice disadvantages a substantially higher proportion of the members of one sex unless that provision, criterion or practice is appropriate and necessary and can be justified by objective factors unrelated to sex.

This definition has to be incorporated into UK law, in respect of sex discrimination, by 22 July 2001.

2.30   The European Commission has confused matters by proposing a different definition of indirect discrimination under the draft Article 13 directives. This definition is fundamentally flawed in suggesting that there can be such discrimination where the apparently neutral provision etc. "is liable to adversely affect [an individual] person or persons...". The US case law, from which the concept derives, as well as the settled case law of the ECJ in relation to nationality and sex discrimination, as codified in article 2(2) of the Burden of Proof Directive, makes it clear that the adverse impact must be on members of a group, not simply an individual. In *O'Flynn v Adjudication Officer* [70] to which the Commission's explanatory memorandum refers but appears to misinterpret, the ECJ states (para.20) that the provision must be "intrinsically liable to affect *migrant workers* more than national workers and if there is a consequent risk that it

---

[66] s.1(1)(b); SD(NI)O, art.3(1)(b).
[67] s.1(1)(b); RR(NI)O, art.3(1)(b).
[68] Art. 3(2)(b).
[69] Fredman, Working Paper No.3, para. 3.10; and see McCrudden (1982); Hepple (1983).
[70] Case 237/94, [1996] ECR I-2617.

will place the former at a particular disadvantage." It is also clear that a disproportionate impact must be established. This normally involves statistical evidence of some sort, but, as the Commission points out, this is not always available or reliable. The *O'Flynn* case (para. 21) recognises this, but does so in the specific context of a rule which made payment of funeral expenses incurred by a migrant worker subject to the condition that the funeral take place within the territory of the UK. This was not really neutral but was "intrinsically liable" to disadvantage migrants because, as AG Lenz (para. 27) pointed out, by linking payment of the benefit to an occurrence taking place on the territory of the UK, it created a territorial condition which obviously disadvantages nationals of other Member States.

2.31   We do not consider that an extension of the definition, beyond that contained in article 2(2) of the Burden of Proof directive is necessary. The directive overcomes the need, under current UK law, to show a "requirement or condition," and it also clarifies the test of proportionality which must be applied when establishing objective justification. It sets out the test of a "substantially higher proportion" who can comply for making the relevant comparisons. The English courts have shown themselves capable of deciding whether there is a disparate impact without elaborate statistical evidence, taking judicial notice of social facts. For example in *Edwards v London Underground (No.2)* [71] the Court of Appeal found that disparate impact against single parents was inherent in the application of a rostering system although only one of the 21 female train drivers could not comply with it whereas all 2023 male drivers could comply. Moreover, the House of Lords (by a majority) in the *Seymour-Smith* case[72] interpreted an ambiguous ECJ ruling by finding that "the obligation is to avoid applying unjustifiable requirements which have a considerable disparity of impact,"[73] and that a persistent and constant disparity cannot "be brushed aside and dismissed as insignificant or inconsiderable" [74] Accordingly, we propose that UK legislation should follow the Burden of Proof Directive, so applying a consistent definition to all grounds of discrimination. This would also replace the "material factor" defence under the EqPA.

2.32   At present, the concept of indirect discrimination is not included in the DDA, which defines discrimination in two ways: (1) less favourable treatment, and (2) a failure to comply with a duty to make reasonable adjustments. Professor Doyle (Working Paper No.4) points out that it is not clear that all indirect discrimination will be caught by either of these two definitions. The Disability Rights Task Force did not support the inclusion of indirect discrimination, despite their advocacy of harmonising the DDA with other anti-discrimination legislation. In their submission to us, RADAR argued that:

...inclusion of a concept of indirect discrimination would promote better practice amongst employers and service providers making them identify and remove barriers in advance rather than providing individual solutions to individual problems which the current duty to make reasonable adjustments under the DDA ensures.

The draft directives under Article 13 of the EC Treaty apply the concept of indirect discrimination to all prohibited grounds of discrimination. We can see no justification for a separate approach to disability, nor to other grounds which may be added to domestic legislation in future, such as religion or belief.

---

[71] [1999] ICR 494.
[72] *R. v Secretary of State for Employment, ex parte Seymour-Smith (No.2)*,[2000] ICR 244. For critical comment on the ECJ judgement, Case C-167/97 [1999] 2 AC 554, see Barnard and Hepple (1999).
[73] Per Lord Nicholls, at p. 257.
[74] Per Lord Nicholls, at p. 259.

2.33   If the concept of indirect discrimination is to be applied to discrimination relating to disability ,
        and on grounds of religion or belief then it is necessary to reconcile this with the duty to make
        reasonable adjustments. We propose that the approach taken by the Ontario Human Rights
        Code, s.11(2) should be followed. This has been adapted to the UK in the form set out in the
        recommendation below.

Recommendation 6

- Indirect discrimination should be defined as the application of an apparently neutral provision,
  criterion or practice which disadvantages a substantially higher proportion of the members of a
  "designated group" in comparison with other groups unless that provision, criterion or practice
  is appropriate and necessary and can be justified by objective factors unrelated to any of the
  grounds of unlawful discrimination
- The concept of indirect discrimination should be applied to all prohibited grounds of discrimination, including disability
- A provision, criterion or practice should not be regarded as appropriate and necessary in the
  case of indirect discrimination which disadvantages disabled persons or persons of a religious
  group, unless the needs of that group cannot be reasonably accommodated without causing
  undue hardship on the person responsible for accommodating those needs, having regard to
  factors such as financial and other costs and health and safety requirements
- The "designated groups" should be those covered by the legislation (see below,
  Recommendation 14)

(5) Equality of opportunity

2.34   The concept of indirect discrimination is important, but it does not go far enough in achieving
        equality of outcomes. Professor Fredman points out that if no exclusionary criteria can be
        identified or if appropriate comparisons cannot be made or an economic justification made
        out, no action need be taken. Moreover, the remedy will usually be individual compensation,
        rather than remedial action to remove the offending practice. Both direct and indirect discrim-
        ination are limited in that they do not require any action to be taken unless it can be proved
        that an individual respondent was responsible for the discrimination, and that the complainant
        was a direct victim of that discrimination. On the other hand, a positive duty to promote
        equality, because it is pro-active, sidesteps many of the limitations of the direct and indirect
        discrimination provisions. The law identifies those in the best position to promote equality
        (e.g. public authorities and employers), and the duty is triggered by visible patterns of under-
        representation.

2.35   A positive duty to promote equality leaves open the question what equality itself entials. One
        possibility is the concept of "promoting equality of opportunity". This is the basis of the
        positive duty imposed on employers under the FETO in Northern Ireland.[75] A person of any
        religious belief has equality of employment opportunity with a person of any other religious
        belief if he or she "has the same opportunity...as that other person has or would have [in the
        employment context], due allowance being made for any material difference in their
        suitability."[76] Section 75 of the NIA also refers to "equality of opportunity" between persons of
        different religious belief, political opinion, racial group, age, marital status or sexual orienta-

---

[75] FETO, art. 5; art. 5(4) sets out the kinds of opportunity encompassed by the duty.
[76] Art. 5(2).

tion; between men and women generally; between persons with a disability and without; and between persons with dependants and without.

2.36 This concept tends to treat persons from the different groups as competitors in a race, and seeks to enable them to have similar starting points. But it is not always clear whether the promotion of equality of opportunity is a narrow procedural obligation, or a broader substantive one. The procedural view of equal opportunities involves the removal of obstacles or barriers, such as word-of-mouth recruitment or non-job-related selection criteria. This opens up more opportunities but does "not guarantee that more women or minorities will in fact be in a position to take advantage of those opportunities" because their capacities have been limited by the effects of social disadvantage.[77] Anti-discrimination provisions are only one aspect of a broader framework for the promotion of equality. Other positive measures are required to ensure that affected groups are able to benefit from equal opportunities. These would include provision such as training, child-care facilities, family leave, flexible working and so on.

(6) Fair participation and fair access

2.37 A more results-oriented approach defines equality in terms of fair (sometimes referred to as full) participation of groups in the workforce, and fair access of groups to education and training, and to goods, facilities and services. It aims to overcome the under-representation of disadvantaged groups in the workplace and to ensure their fair share in the distribution of benefits. This may mean special measures to overcome disadvantage. Thus in Northern Ireland, the White Paper which preceded the 1989 FEA made "affirmative action" a cornerstone of the legislation. This was defined as "special measures taken to promote a more representative distribution of employment in the workforce and designed to give all sections of the community full and equal access to employment opportunities."[78] In FETO "affirmative action" is defined as meaning-

action designed to secure fair participation in employment by members of the Protestant, or members of the Roman Catholic, community in Northern Ireland by means including-
(a) the adoption of practices encouraging such participation; and
(b) the modification or abandonment of practices that have or may have the effect of restricting or discouraging such participation.[79]

The definition of "equality of opportunity" in FETO includes a general exception for lawful affirmative action. So if the adoption of a particular affirmative action practice conflicts with equality of opportunity, the affirmative action prevails.

2.38 The FETO does not define "fair participation". The FEC (predecessor of the ECNI) adopted an interpretation which involves redressing imbalances and under-representation in employment between the two communities in Northern Ireland. The aims are to secure greater fairness in the distribution of jobs and opportunities between the two communities and to reduce the relative segregation of the two communities at work.[80]

2.39 A similar emphasis on outcomes is to be found in the Canadian Employment Equity Act, the purpose of which is stated to be:

---

[77] Fredman, Working Paper No.5, para. 3.13.
[78] Northern Ireland Office (1988), para. 3.20.
[79] FETO, art. 4(1).
[80] House of Commons, Northern Ireland Affairs Committee (1999), paras. 36-65.

to achieve equality in the workplace so that no person shall be denied employment opportunities or benefits for reasons unrelated to ability and, in the fulfilment of that goal, to correct the conditions of disadvantage in employment experienced by women, aboriginal peoples, persons with disabilities and members of visible minorities [the designated groups], by giving effect to the principle that employment equity means more than treating persons in the same way but requires special measures and the accommodation of differences.[81]

The Act requires employers to implement employment equity, by identifying and removing employment barriers against persons in the designated groups, and by instituting such positive policies and practices and making such reasonable accommodations as will ensure that persons in designated groups achieve a degree of representation in each occupational group and in the employer's workforce that reflects their representation in the Canadian workforce or those segments of the workforce from which the employer may reasonably be expected to draw employees.[82] This obligation does not require the employer to take a measure that would cause undue hardship to the employer, or to hire or promote unqualified persons.[83]

2.40   In our proposals for changing organisational policies and behaviour (chap. three) we have used the concepts of "fair participation" and "employment equity" with similar aims in mind to those of FETO in Northern Ireland and the Canadian Employment Equity legislation. We have avoided using the words "affirmative action" as such, because of the connotations which this has wrongly acquired of requiring quotas or reverse discrimination. We have preferred the Canadian concept of "employment equity plans" and "pay equity plans" in relation to employers. We have also recommended the concept of "fair access" in relation to the duty on public authorities .

Recommendation 7

- Anti-discrimination measures should be augmented by positive duties to promote equality which do not depend upon proof by individual complainants that a respondent is "at fault"
- Positive duties should be aimed at securing fair participation of under-represented groups in the workforce, fair access to education, training, goods, facilities and services, and a fair distribution of benefits

(7) Interpretative principles

2.41   There was general support among our respondents for a statement of interpretative principles which would help those applying the legislation to promote its purposes, particularly where gaps have to be filled or ambiguities resolved. The basic value is that of protecting the dignity, autonomy, and worth of every individual. The EC Code of Practice on sexual harassment[84] is explicitly based on the notion of protecting "the dignity of women and men at work". The Code of Practice in the employment field under the DDA[85] promotes the autonomy of individuals by stressing the importance of talking to each disabled person about what the effects of the disability might be or what might help. By outlawing gender- or race- based stereotypes or assumptions, the law recognises the inherent worth of every individual.

---

[81] Employment Equity Act 1995 [Can.], s.2.
[82] s.5.
[83] s.6.
[84] Commission Recommendation 92/131/EEC and Code of Practice on the protection of the dignity of women and men at work.
[85] SI 1996/1396.

2.42   It was also generally agreed that there should be a principle of non-regression, of the kind found in the draft directives under Article 13 of the EC Treaty. We have argued earlier (para. 2.23) that the application of the principle of equality should not be used to level-down standards, or to argue that a person from a comparator group would have been "equally badly" treated. The interpretative principles should also include the removal of barriers and the encouragement of positive policies and practices of the kinds described above (paras. 2.34-2.40). Some of our respondents suggested that it would be helpful when interpreting the legislation (e.g. in relation to harassment) to include a specific provision along the lines of section 75(2) of the NIA, namely the promotion of good relations between different groups.

Recommendation 8

The purposes of the legislation should be explicitly stated in the legislation and should be defined as-

- the protection of the dignity, autonomy, and worth of every individual
- the promotion of equality and the elimination of discrimination so that no person should be denied opportunities or benefits for reasons related to one of the prohibited grounds
- the application of the principle of equality in a way which does not require a reduction in the level of protection already afforded to any person
- the identification and removal of barriers against persons in designated groups
- the encouragement of positive policies and practices and such reasonable adjustments as will ensure that persons in the designated groups achieve fair participation in employment, fair access to education, training, goods, facilities and services and a fair distribution of benefits
- the promotion of good relations between persons of different racial or religious group or belief, age, marital status or sexual orientation, between men and women generally, and between persons with a disability and persons without

For these purposes the "prohibited grounds" and "designated groups" are those covered by the legislation (below). In the context of employment, "fair participation" means a degree of representation in each occupational group and in the employer's workforce that reflects their representation in the workforce or those segments of the workforce from which the employer may reasonably be expected to draw employees. "Fair access" and "fair distribution" applies to both the public and private sectors.

D. Justification of discrimination

(1) Direct discrimination

2.43   We sought views on whether a general defence of justification to direct discrimination should be allowed. At present all direct discrimination is unlawful unless it is covered by one of the specific legislative exceptions (e.g. genuine occupational qualification, positive action, pregnancy and confinement benefits). By contrast the two forms of disability discrimination in DDA s.5 are subject to a much more general defence of objective justification. Under the ECHR, the European Court of Human Rights has accepted a defence of justification:

A difference of treatment is discriminatory if it has no objective and reasonable justification, that is if it does not pursue a legitimate aim or if there is not a reasonable relationship of proportionality between the means employed and the aims to be realised.[86]

---

[86] *Abdulaziz* [1985] 7 EHRR 471.

However, the new draft Protocol No.12 to the ECHR makes no reference to justification, apparently on the grounds that justifiable distinctions are not discriminatory in the first place. Although there have been some suggestions that a general defence of justification would be allowed under Article 141 of the EC Treaty and the equality directives, there is no definitive ruling on this point, and it has been strongly argued that such a development would be both misconceived and undesirable.[87]

2.44   Only two individuals among our respondents favoured a general defence, on the ground that this would provide a "safety valve" in extreme cases and would win support from managers for the legislation because it would make it easier for them to raise considerations which at present are not covered by specific exceptions, such as dress codes. Everyone else who made submissions on this issue thought that a general defence would create uncertainty and confusion in an area where the present law works well, and that it would undermine the principle of equality. In the specific case of dress codes, the courts have recognised that if an employer enforces a common standard of smartness or conventionality there can be differences in the content of the code as between men and women.[88] We do not recommend any change in the law.

(2) Disability discrimination

2.45   If the present approach is retained then the question arises whether disability law should be harmonised with other forms of direct discrimination by allowing a defence of justification in only specified circumstances. Recently, the President of the EAT noted that the threshold for justification under DDA s.5 is "very low", and that "the remedy for the lowness of the threshold, if any is required, lies in the hands of the legislature, not the courts."[89] There is at present little evidence as to how the justification defence is working and it was apparently this which led the Disability Rights Task Force to do no more than recommend that the matter should be kept under review.[90] RADAR, and other organisations representing disabled people, favour a genuine occupational qualification (GOQ) defence similar to that in the draft "vertical" directive under Article 13 of the EC Treaty, in place of the present justification defence (below). In our Working Paper No.4,[91] Brian Doyle points out that in defining disability discrimination it is necessary to recognise that, unlike sex or race, disability can make a difference to the way in which a disabled person is treated. He suggests that DDA s.5 might be amended so as to omit the reference to justification, but to permit the respondent to "justify" the otherwise adverse treatment of a disabled person by reference to rational grounds, such as a GOQ. This defence could explicitly list the grounds upon which otherwise less favourable treatment might be defended, in a way similar to the provisions in Part III of the DDA s.20(4). This might include cases where the treatment is necessary in order not to endanger the health and safety of any person (including the disabled person), or where there would be undue hardship (e.g. unreasonable costs) on the employer. We favour this approach which would create greater certainty by giving more specific guidance to employers. The overall principle is that disabled people are not different from other people in any critical way. The only question is whether a disabled person is qualified to perform the essential functions of the job, with or without reasonable adjustments.

---

[87] Ellis (1998), pp.134-136; Hepple (1994), p. 48.
[88] E.g., *Smith v Safeway plc* [1996] IRLR 456, CA.
[89] *H.J.Heinz Co v Kenrick* [2000] IRLR 144, EAT, p. 146.
[90] Disability Rights Task Force (1999), pp. 74-75.
[91] p.4.

Recommendation 9

• The general defence of justification of discrimination in employment in the DDA should be amended so as to permit discrimination only on specified rational grounds such as that the individual would not be able to perform the essential functions of the job, with or without reasonable adjustment, or to protect the health and safety of any person, including the disabled person

(3) Genuine occupational qualification

2.46   The SDA[92] and RRA[93] contain specific lists of GOQs. There are different views as to whether the present lists are too narrow or too broad. An alternative approach would be to follow the wording of the draft directives under Article 13 of the EC Treaty, or Article 70 of FETO. In our view, a general defence of this kind would be preferable to the present outdated lists. Specific examples could be given in a code of practice, such as the requirements of a religious institution to impose a condition of religious affiliation for certain posts. Our recommendation below adapts the wording of Article 70 of FETO which we consider to be clearer than that in the draft directive.

Recommendation 10

• The specific lists of genuine occupational requirements in the SDA and RRA should be replaced by a general defence that the essential functions of the job required it to be done by a person of a particular ethnic or national origin, religious or other belief, sex, or age
• This should be amplified by examples given in a code of practice

(4) Reasonable adjustments

2.47   The DDA imposes obligations to make reasonable adjustments in relation to disabled persons. In our Working Paper No.4, Professor Brian Doyle identified a number of problems which arise in relation to the provision of goods, facilities and services. The Disability Rights Task Force recommended that this approach to the employer's and service provider's duty and factors to be considered in assessing reasonableness should continue.[94] They asked that the factors contained in the code of practice (which attempted to remedy some of the defects in ss.19-21 of the DDA) should be placed in legislation. We endorse the proposals made by the Task Force and by Professor Doyle. We discuss the relationship between the concept of indirect discrimination and reasonable adjustment (above, para. 2.33).

Recommendation 11

• The proposals by the Disability Rights Task Force in relation to the statutory duty to make reasonable adjustments should be implemented

(5) Positive action

2.48   The SDA and RRA do not permit "reverse discrimination" in favour of women or members of ethnic minorities.[95] However, as an exception to the general non-discrimination principle,

---

[92] s.7; SD(NI)O, art. 10.
[93] s.5; RR(NI)O, art. 8.
[94] Disability Rights Task Force (1999), recommendations 5.5 and 5.6.
[95] See Fredman, Working Paper No.3, paras. 4.1-4.6 for a comparative discussion.

certain positive measures to encourage workers and potential workers and to provide training for workers from under-represented groups are permitted.[96] Our case studies (Appendix 1) indicated that these provisions are little used, and are out of date in at least two respects because they are based on a model of training which has changed. Positive action has to be for "particular work". This is no longer an appropriate concept because employer's training programmes are linked to giving people specific competencies which may be needed for a variety of positions. Secondly, the provisions do not allow positive action to be taken for categories such a New Deal and Work Experience trainees because they are not deemed to be employees.

2.49   The provisions are also out of date because they have been overtaken by developments in EC law, which permit wider and more flexible use of positive action. Article 141 of the EC Treaty now provides-

With a view to ensuring full equality in practice between men and women in working life, the principle of equal treatment shall not prevent any Member State from maintaining or adopting measures providing for specific advantages in order to make it easier for the under-represented sex to pursue a vocational activity or to prevent or compensate for disadvantages in professional careers.

Similarly, the draft directives under Article 13 of the EC Treaty allow Member States to maintain or adopt measures intended to prevent or compensate for disadvantages concerning persons to whom any of the discriminatory grounds apply. These provisions appear to codify recent rulings of the ECJ which have, for example, allowed a woman to be preferred over an equally-qualified man, where women were significantly under-represented, provided that reasons specific to the individual male candidate were taken into account.[97] We recommend that the law in the UK should be brought into line with what is permitted under EC law. Indeed, we regard this as essential if proper effect is to be given to the Government's proposals for a positive duty on public authorities to promote equal opportunities. It is also a necessary element in our proposals for employment equity (paras. 3.37-3.40) and pay equity (paras. 3.45-3.50). We are not recommending reverse discrimination, nor that unqualified persons should be recruited or promoted. However, more flexibility is required if fair participation and fair access are to be achieved.

Recommendation 12

- There should be a general exception for positive action intended to provide specific advantages for persons from designated under-represented groups to pursue a vocational activity or to prevent or compensate for disadvantages in professional careers
- Codes of practice should give examples of such positive action taking into account current models of training
- For this purpose the "designated groups" should be racial or ethnic groups, women, and disabled persons

E. Harassment and bullying [98]

2.50   The Protection Against Harassment Act 1997 creates both a criminal offence and a civil wrong of "harassment". This was intended primarily to give the courts more effective powers to deal

---

[96] SDA, ss. 47-48; SD(NI)O, art. 48-49; RRA, ss. 35-38; RR(NI)O, art. 37.
[97] Case C-409/95, *Marschall v Land Nordrhein-Westfalen* [1998] IRLR 39.
[98] This section draws on Hepple (2000, forthcoming).

with stalkers, but it is also apt to cover those who target others on racial or other grounds. The Act avoids the need to prove any intention to harass. The defendant is liable if he or she knows or ought reasonably to know that the conduct amounts to harassment (which is not further defined). The issue with which we are concerned is whether a specific wrong of harassment and bullying at work is also required. A great deal of empirical evidence exists to show that many women, homosexuals, and members of ethnic minorities suffer harassment at work.[99] This helps to intimidate and shut out these groups, as well as undermining their dignity and right to private life. The anti-discrimination legislation in the UK does not specifically outlaw harassment on grounds of race, sex or disability, in contrast to the recent Irish Equality Act and statutes in several other jurisdictions. The approach adopted by the draft directives under Article 13 of the EC Treaty is to deem harassment to be discrimination, and to define it as follows:

Harassment of a person related to any of the discriminatory grounds and areas [covered by the Directive] which has the purpose or effect of creating an intimidating, hostile, offensive or disturbing environment.

2.51   The present UK law on discriminatory harassment is a judicial gloss on the statutes.[100] It has been developed with the help of the European Commission Code of Practice on measures to combat sexual harassment[101] and EOC and CRE codes of practice on the elimination of discrimination and guidance issued by those Commissions on sexual and racial harassment. The reliance on discrimination law has a number of undesirable results. The first of these is that there must be "less favourable treatment." This involves a comparative approach. So in *Stewart v Cleveland Guest (Engineering) Ltd*,[102] it was held that a woman could not complain of the display of pictures of nude women at the workplace because a hypothetical man might also have complained so making the display gender-neutral. This ignores the gist of the complaint about pornographic displays at the workplace, namely that they create a hostile working environment by undermining the dignity of women. If men also object this does not change the effect on women. Sometimes, the EAT has been willing to accept that sexual harassment is sex discrimination *per se* without any need to make reference to how a man would have been treated in similar circumstances,[103] but so long as harassment remains tied to the concept of discrimination this difficulty will persist. Moreover, the exclusion from statutory protection of certain types of arbitrary discrimination, such as on grounds of sexual orientation, has left some vulnerable groups unprotected.[104]

2.52   A second consequence of the reliance on discrimination legislation is the need to show a "detriment". Although this has been broadly interpreted as going beyond so-called *quid pro quo* harassment (e.g. denying promotion to a woman who refused sexual favours),[105] abuse or an insult will not amount to a detriment unless "a reasonable worker would or might take the view that he had thereby been disadvantaged in the circumstances in which he had thereafter to work".[106] The conduct must be considered in relation to a particular victim: sexual innuendoes

---

[99] Houghton-Jones (1995); Fredman (1997), pp. 320-330.

[100] The law on constructive unfair dismissal, and the law of contract, may also give protection where the conduct amounts to a breach of the duty of mutual trust and confidence: see generally, Deakin and Morris (1998), pp. 330-335.

[101] Issued in accordance with the Resolution of the Council of Ministers, O.J. C157, 25 June 1990, p. 3.

[102] [1994] IRLR 440, EAT; see too *Balgobin v London Borough of Tower Hamlets* [1987] IRLR 401, EAT, (requiring woman to continue to work with alleged harasser is not less favourable treatment because a man alleging homosexual advances would have been treated similarly).

[103] E.g. *British Telecommunications plc v Williams* [1997] IRLR 668, EAT; *Strathclyde Regional Council v Porcelli* [1986] IRLR 134, Court of Session (harassment would not have happened had she been a man).

[104] *Smith v Gardner Merchant* [1996] IRLR 342, EAT.

[105] *Strathclyde Regional Council v Porcelli* [1986] IRLR 134, CS.

[106] *De Souza v Automobile Association* [1986] IRLR 103, CA.

directed by A to B might be acceptable, but would not be if they came from C. It is the individual who must reasonably object to the conduct or speech in question.[107] Unlike the Protection from Harassment Act, however, there need not be a course of conduct: a "detriment" on a single occasion is sufficient, provided it is serious.[108] If lewd conduct takes place in the sight or hearing of a woman, or racist jokes are told, it is the repetition of this behaviour after objection has been made, that shows that the conduct was directed against the complainant.

2.53   These limitations on discriminatory harassment have led to proposals that harassment and bullying at work on specified prohibited grounds should be a separate wrong, or an aggravated form of a general wrong of harassment and bullying. A Private Member's Dignity at Work Bill, introduced in the House of Lords in 1996 by Lord Monkswell, proposed to confer the right to dignity at work on all employees and contract workers. It defined a breach of that right as any of the following: persistent or recurrent behaviour which is offensive, abusive or demeaning; verbal or physical intimidation; persistent or recurrent behaviour which is malicious or insulting; penalties imposed without reasonable justification; or changes in duties and responsibilities to the employee's detriment and without reasonable justification. Remedies were provided through industrial tribunals. The Bill, supported by the Campaign against Bullying at Work, was said by its promoters to be needed in view of surveys which showed an alarming incidence of bullying at work.[109]

2.54   The forms of conduct which may constitute discriminatory harassment range across a spectrum from rape and physical assault at one end, to racist and sexist jokes, offensive symbols and displays, and disparaging remarks at the other. The test, as proposed in the draft EC directive (above), is whether the conduct "has the purpose or effect of creating an intimidating, hostile, offensive, or disturbing environment". This is similar to that in the Commission Recommendation 92/131/EEC on the protection of the dignity of women and men at work, except that instead of referring to a "disturbing environment" the Recommendation refers to a "humiliating work environment for the recipient." We consider that the formulation in the Recommendation is more appropriate than that in the draft Directive because it stresses the basic values of the dignity and right to privacy of the individual. To outlaw a "disturbing" environment, on the other hand, is at risk of leading to very broad prohibitions on speech or conduct that might violate article 10(1) of the ECHR (freedom of expression).[110]

2.55   One option would be to enact a statutory "non-harassment" clause as a mandatory term of every contract of employment (like the equality clause for equal pay). This might be regarded as an example of the more general contractual duty of co-operation or mutual trust and confidence. The drawback is that this would not protect jobseekers. Harassment and bullying should therefore be made a statutory employment tort either on a stand-alone basis or in combination with a contractual clause. The elements of this tort should be as set out in our recommendation below.

2.56   It is a matter for consideration whether it should be necessary for the victim to prove that the unlawful harassment and bullying was on one or more of the prohibited grounds such as race,

---

[107] *Wileman v Minilec Engineering* [1988] IRLR 144, EAT.

[108] *Bracebridge Engineering Ltd v Darby* [1990] IRLR 3, EAT.

[109] The Institute of Personnel Development survey conducted by the Harris Research Centre showed that one in eight people claimed to have been bullied at work over the previous five years; a survey by the University of Salford showed that 51 per cent of their sample of 1,000 people had experienced bullying; and a survey by the MSF union said that 30 per cent had been bullied: Lord Monkswell, H.L.Deb., vol.576 , col. 755, 4 December 1996. A survey for the TUC Women's Conference 1999 showed that many women are harassed or bullied for gender-related reasons.

[110] This issue is discussed by Hepple (2000 forthcoming).

gender, religion, disability, sexual orientation etc., or whether these grounds should simply be a factor which would result in an award of aggravated or exemplary damages. The argument for a general wrong is that it would avoid the need to prove the motivation of the harasser: the consequences of the harassment rather than the motivation of the harasser would be decisive. This would be an inclusive approach, protecting all employees (as Lord Monkswell's Bill proposed in 1996), but would recognise the special harm cause by harassment on the impermissible grounds. We favour this alternative.

Recommendation 13

- There should be a statutory tort of harassment and bullying at work
- The elements of this tort should be that: (1) the act or other conduct is unwelcome and offensive to the recipient; (2) it could reasonably be regarded as creating an intimidating, hostile, offensive or humiliating work environment; and (3) the recipient has suffered or is likely to suffer some harm whether physical, psychological or emotional (including anxiety and injury to feelings)

F. Grounds of discrimination

(1) General considerations

2.57   There was widespread support from our respondents for the extension of the law to cover discrimination on a wider set of grounds. At present discrimination legislation is limited to discrimination on grounds of sex, gender reassignment, marital status of married persons, race, colour, ethnic or national origins, nationality, and disability. Discrimination on the grounds of religious belief and political opinion is prohibited only in Northern Ireland. Over the past few years attempts have been made, through private member's bills and amendments to government legislation, to extend the grounds of prohibited discrimination to cover age, religion or belief and sexual orientation.

2.58   Recently, there have been two significant developments. First, the Human Rights Act 1998 incorporates the ECHR into UK law. Article 14 of the Convention prohibits discrimination in relation to convention rights on the grounds of sex, race, colour, language, religion, political or other opinion, national or social origin, association with a national minority, property, birth or other status. Although wider in coverage than domestic legislation, it is limited in that it applies only to the rights specified in the Convention which must be applied without discrimination on the specified grounds. In recognition of this the new draft Protocol No.12 proposes to extend the non-discrimination principle to all rights "set forth by law" as well as requiring that no one be discriminated against by a public authority. Even if the Protocol is not adopted, the HRA opens the prospect of the courts developing remedies against public authorities for discrimination on wider grounds than those covered by domestic legislation, and possibly also giving it indirect effects in actions between individuals.

2.59   A second significant step towards broadening the grounds of discrimination legislation came in Article 13 of the EC Treaty, as inserted by the Amsterdam Treaty. Article 13 makes clear that the European Council has power to make directives to tackle discrimination on the grounds of sex, racial or ethnic origin, religion or belief, disability, age or sexual orientation. The European Commission has produced two proposals for framework directives, one dealing with discrimination on all the prohibited grounds (other than sex which is covered by existing directives) in employment and occupation, and the other dealing with discrimination on grounds of race or ethnic origin only in a wider area. If enacted the directives may be directly effective vertically against public authorities in the UK, and the UK will also be required to enact legislation to give them horizontal effect between private individuals and bodies.

2.60   The patchy and inconsistent coverage of existing and proposed instruments is set out in the Table below.

Table 2 Coverage of gounds of Discrimination

	RRA	SDA	DDA	FETO	EC Treaty	ECHR
Age					*	
Association with a National Minority						*
Belief					*	
Birth						*
Colour	*					*
Disability			*		*	
Ethnic Origin	*				*	
Gender Reassignment		*				
Irish Traveller Community	* (NI)					
Language						*
Married Person's Marital Status		*				
Nationality	*					
National Origin	*					*
Other Opinion						*
Other Status						*
Political Opinion				*		*
Property						*
Race	*					*
Racial Origin					*	
Religion					*	*
Religious Belief				*		
Sex		*			*	*
Sexual Orientation					*	
Social Origin						*

2.61   We pointed out in our options paper that two approaches can be taken to the scope of unlawful grounds. The first is generalised and open-ended and regards all forms of arbitrary discrimination as inter-connected. Discrimination is seen to occur whenever some in-group receive better treatment than anyone outside that group, either because of conscious or unconscious hostility towards or stereotyping of outsiders, or as a form of group solidarity. The second approach treats discrimination as atomised, involving different treatment of someone seen as having a specific characteristic (e.g. Black, Muslim, female, with a disability, homosexual etc.). The generalised approach is reflected in legal provisions which prohibit any unfair discrimination, treating specified grounds only as examples. The atomised approach is reflected in current UK legislation which specifies particular grounds to the exclusion of others. Article 13 of the EC Treaty has taken a similar approach.

2.62   There was general support among our respondents for the first, generalised approach, following the ECHR which protects "other status". This would allow a flexible approach, particularly in cases of cumulative or multiple discrimination, where the precise ground is unclear, and would allow the courts to develop discrimination law in response to changing social *mores*- for example attitudes to gender reassignment and homosexuality have changed radically since the SDA was enacted. There was thought to be little danger of the courts going too far, since "other status" is only a residual category which must be interpreted consistently with the specific stated grounds. The South African Promotion of Equality and Prevention of Unfair Discrimination Act No.4 of 2000, deals with this by providing that where a complainant alleges a generic ground of unfair discrimination, then the complainant must prove that discrimination on that ground (1) causes or perpetuates systemic disadvantage; (2) undermines human dignity; or (3) adversely affects the enjoyment of a person's rights and freedoms in a serious manner that is comparable to discrimination on one of the specific grounds. We do not believe that it would be necessary to set out requirements of this kind in UK legislation, but it may be useful to give an indication of what is meant by "other status" in a Code of Practice.

2.63   We do not propose in this Report to canvas the arguments for and against covering each of the specified grounds. Our brief is to point to some of the technical questions which arise should the legislature decide to extend the grounds. On grounds of consistency with the HRA, and with forthcoming EC directives we do however make a general recommendation.

Recommendation 14

• The prohibited grounds of discrimination should be race, colour, ethnic or national origin, sex, gender reassignment, marital status, family status, sexual orientation, religion or belief, disability, age, or other status

(2) Specific grounds

(a) Age

2.64   Many EC countries have legislation against age discrimination, as do the USA, Canada, Australia, New Zealand and South Africa. We have not been able, as part of our research, to evaluate the impact of age discrimination legislation in these countries. There has been some analysis by others which compares states in the USA with and without age discrimination legislation. This estimates that participation rates have improved, especially for the over-60s, as a result of age discrimination legislation.[111] We would urge caution in drawing comparisons between different countries, because of the variety of factors, apart from legislation, which might be responsible for higher participation by people of particular age groups. The case for legislation in the UK must turn on wider considerations. As the Cabinet Office Performance and Innovation Unit, has recently said, "age discrimination legislation would have a positive effect on British culture and would build –as other discrimination Acts have –on a growing sense of public interest and concern about the issue."[112] The Unit recommended that the Government should make clear that it will introduce such legislation if evaluation of the present Code of Practice on Age Diversity shows that it has not been effective. It suggested that further research should be undertaken, and that if plans were developed for any wider, consolidated anti-discrimination legislation, age should be included as an issue.

2.65   There are two particular issues that legislation covering age would need to address. The first is whether the coverage should be limited to persons over a specified age, such as the US Age Discrimination in Employment Act 1967 which extends only to those of at least 40 years of age. We were told by the EEOC in Washington DC, that they come across many instances of

---

[111] Neumark and Stock (1997).
[112] Cabinet Office (2000), p. 60.

unfair discrimination against younger people and would prefer the law not to have an arbitrary threshold. The Irish Employment Equality Act 1998 covers persons from the age of 18 to the age of 65. This may be the appropriate model as regards the threshold for the UK, since there is special legislation to protect children (under 16) and young persons (16-18). The cut-off point, however, raises the issue of a compulsory retiring age. This was abolished in the USA from 1986 and in New Zealand from 1999, and also in most Australian states. There are powerful demographic arguments for removing a compulsory retirement age, but the issues are complex, particularly in relation to pension benefits, and need detailed consideration.

2.66   The second issue is the specific exceptions which should apply. Article 5 of the draft EC Article 13 framework directive provides-

The following differences in treatment, in particular, shall not constitute direct discrimination on grounds of age, if they are objectively and reasonably justified by a legitimate aim and are appropriate and necessary to the achievement of that aim:-

(a)   the prohibition on access to employment or the provision of special working conditions to ensure the protection of young people and older workers;

(b)   the fixing of a minimum age as a condition of eligibility for retirement or invalidity benefits;

(c)   the fixing of different ages for employees or groups or categories of employees for entitlement to retirement or invalidity benefits on grounds of physical or mental occupational requirements;

(d)   the fixing of a maximum age for recruitment which is based on the training requirements of the post in question or the need for a reasonable period of employment before retirement.

(e)   the establishment of requirements concerning the length of professional experience;

(f)   the establishment of age limits which are appropriate and necessary for the pursuit of legitimate labour market objectives

2.67   The draft EC directive covers only employment and occupation. If the law extended to the provision of goods, facilities and services, other exceptions might be necessary. For example in New Zealand, the prohibition of discrimination in the provision of goods and services covers banking, grants, loans, credit or finance as well as services provided by doctors and other professionals. There are, however, exceptions for the provision of insurance, where different treatment is based on reliable information relating to life expectancy, accidents or sickness; in the organisation of sporting events for certain groups; in the provision of group travel based on age and in the membership of clubs. Furthermore, it is not unlawful to provide goods, services or facilities at a reduced rate to people of a particular age. In relation to accommodation there is an exemption for institutional accommodation such as a retirement village. In our view the guiding principle in the UK should be that set out in the opening paragraph of Article 5 of the draft EC directive, and that exceptions should be specific and as limited as possible, so as not to undermine the general principle of equality and non-discrimination.

Recommendation 15

•   Legislation against age discrimination should apply to all persons aged 18 or over

•   There should be research and consultation on the question of prohibiting compulsory retirement ages

•   The guiding principle for specific exceptions should be that they are objectively justified by a legitimate aim and are appropriate and necessary to the achievement of that aim

(b) Association with protected groups

2.68   The ECHR lists "association with a national minority" as a prohibited ground. Several of our respondents argued for more general clarification of the law to cover not only discrimination against those within a protected group, but also those who face discrimination because of association with such persons. The RNID for instance argued that:

Legislation should protect people associated with disabled people e.g. the partner of a person with HIV or AIDS, the carers of disabled people and those providing services and/or accommodation to disabled people. We see the merits in having a general piece of legislation protecting any person with caring responsibilities (including parents) and those associated with groups covered by discrimination legislation.

To achieve this aim we would propose that all anti-discrimination legislation should adopt wording similar to that of the RRA which prohibits less favourable treatment on "racial grounds". This is different from the wording of the SDA which states that less favourable treatment must be on the grounds of "her sex" or "his or her marital status". The difference in wording here is significant. In *Showboat Entertainments Centre Ltd v Owens*[113] it was held that the dismissal of a white man because he refused to carry out a racially discriminatory instruction by his employers to exclude young blacks from the entertainment centre was on "racial grounds" notwithstanding that the discrimination was not directed at his race or colour.

Recommendation 16

- Legislation should be framed so as to prohibit discrimination on the specified grounds, without the need to show that the victim belongs to the protected group

(c) Disability

2.69   In our Working Paper No.4 Brian Doyle set out a number of aspects of the definition of disability and disabled person in the DDA which need to be reviewed. The Disability Rights Task Force has now made a number of proposals.[114] One of these, supported by several of our respondents, is that there should be protection for people with HIV infection but who do not have any symptoms of AIDS. At present this is not treated as a "disability".

Recommendation 17

- The recommendations of the Disability Rights Task Force on the definition of disability and disabled person should be implemented

(d) Ethnic origin: traveller communities

2.70   At present limited protection from discrimination is provided to some traveller communities by the RRA. Gypsies were found to be an ethnic group within the terms of the RRA in the case of *CRE v Dutton*.[115] In Northern Ireland the Race Relations (NI) Order 1997 specifically refer to the "Irish traveller community". This was defined as "the community of people so called who are identified (both by themselves and others) as people with a shared history, culture and traditions including, historically a nomadic way of life on the island of Ireland". In their response to our consultation paper Save the Children (Scotland) argued for legislation to make explicit reference to the coverage of gypsy/traveller communities by anti-discrimination legislation:

Our experience shows that despite legal judgements and the policy of the CRE, the majority of central and local government officials refuse to acknowledge the position of gypsy/travellers as coming within the definition of an ethnic group as described in the Race Relations Act 1976. For the debate to move forward we consider that there must be commitment, at a senior political level, to gypsy/travellers being expressly included in any amendments to the Race Relations legislation to prevent further avoidance of the issue.

[113] [1984] IRLR 7, EAT.
[114] Disability Rights Task Force (1999), chap.3.
[115] [1989] IRLR 8, CA.

2.71   Rather than define discrimination against gypsies, Roma people, and Irish traveller communities as a separate ground of discrimination, we would propose that the legislation should make it clear that discrimination against them constitutes discrimination on the grounds of race or ethnic origin. This also has the advantage that any duty to promote racial equality (under the Race Relations (Amendment) Bill) would include not only Roma and gypsies but also Irish traveller communities.

Recommendation 18

- The legislation should declare, for the avoidance of doubt, that discrimination on the grounds of membership of Roma, gypsy or Irish traveller communities constitutes discrimination on grounds of race or ethnic origin

(e) Genetic discrimination

2.72   The advances in scientific technology have raised fears of the development of a new form of discrimination in the future based on genetic information. The Human Genetics Advisory Commission has examined the implication of this technology in relation to both insurance[116] and employment.[117] The Commission concluded that a permanent ban on the use of genetic tests in insurance would not be appropriate, but made a number of other recommendations to limit the use of such tests. The Commission also took the view that it would not be in anyone's best interests to ban the use of genetic test results for employment purposes completely.

2.73   There are a number of international measures that control the use of genetic testing. The UNESCO Declaration on the Human Genome and Human Rights provides that no one shall be subjected to discrimination based on genetic characteristics if this has the effect of infringing human rights, fundamental freedoms and human dignity. The declaration has no legal force in the UK. The Council of Europe has produced a Convention on Human Rights and Biomedicine. Article 11 of this Convention prohibits any form of discrimination against a person on grounds of his or her genetic heritage. The Convention was adopted by the Council of Ministers on 19 November 1996 and opened for signature in April 1997. It has been signed by 28 countries and ratified by five. The UK has yet to sign the Convention. There is limited protection for some forms of genetic discrimination within the existing sex, race and disability discrimination legislation.[118]

2.74   We sought views as to whether the grounds of unlawful discrimination should be extended to cover genetic testing and information. RADAR, in their response, favours a prohibition on genetic discrimination. In September 1999 they conducted a survey entitled "Genes are us?" which explored public attitudes to a wide range of issues including genetic patenting, cloning, and genetic testing of adults in employment and insurance. Respondents were asked, "should it be illegal for employers to have access to the results of genetic tests?" Out of a total of 452 respondents 91% said yes, 7% said no and 2% gave no answer. Respondents were also asked if it should be illegal for insurers to have access to the tests. Again an overwhelming majority said yes (90%) with 8% saying no and 2% giving no answer. The majority of those responding to the RADAR survey were disabled persons.

2.75   This survey indicates the strong unease among disabled persons about the use of genetic information. In Australia, legislation was proposed in 1998 to protect genetic privacy of individuals

---

[116] Human Genetics Advisory Commission (1997).
[117] Human Genetics Advisory Commission (1999).
[118] Human Genetics Advisory Commission (1999) p. 11.

and to make genetic discrimination unlawful. Genetic discrimination is described as the different treatment of individuals and their family based on genetic differences (presumed or actual) and this is distinguished from discrimination based on having symptoms of a genetic disease. In our view, any proposals for future legislation on this subject in the UK would have to follow an evaluation of the effectiveness of Data Protection legislation in protecting disclosure of genetic information to third parties (e.g. with consent or where necessary for health and safety reasons or as part of a research project), and also monitoring of the arrangements for the collection, storage and analysis of DNA samples. There are many other complex matters which need to be considered, for example the use of genetic tests for forensic purposes, or for establishing paternity. Certain forms of genetic information might lead to practices that were in effect forms of indirect racial discrimination because certain conditions occur only or disproportionately in certain racial or ethnic groups (e.g. cystic fibrosis, sickle cell anaemia). More generally, is it right to single out genetic discrimination for special status, since in most cases there are lifestyle and environmental factors in the emergence of any disease? All these matters need to be explored. It would not be appropriate at this stage to include genetic discrimination in a comprehensive equality statute. We would prefer to allow time for the policy principles developed by the Human Genetics Advisory Commission to be widely discussed. We note that the Commission has recommended that the issues in relation to employment be fully reviewed five years' after their report.

Recommendation 19

- The recommendations of the Human Genetics Advisory Commission on genetic discrimination should be reviewed no later than 2004

(e) Marital and family status

2.76 At present, the SDA covers only discrimination against married persons. Article 2.1 of the EC Equal Treatment directive specifically includes marital and family status as a ground of sex discrimination.

Recommendation 20

- The legislation should specifically prohibit discrimination on grounds of marital status and family status

(f) Religion or belief

2.77 Our Working Paper No. 5 discussed discrimination on grounds of religion or belief in detail. None of our respondents was opposed in principle to the coverage of these grounds. Case law under the RRA has protected Jews and Sikhs as members of ethnic groups, and members of the Protestant and Roman Catholic communities in Northern Ireland are protected as religious groups. It seems anomalous that Muslims in Britain are protected in respect of dress codes only if they can show indirect discrimination, for example by relying on Pakistani national origins on the ground that a considerably smaller proportion of Pakistanis than other national groups could comply with a particular dress requirement, because of their Islamic beliefs. This does not help Muslims who come from a country where Muslims are in a minority.

2.78 The main reservation expressed at our consultation meetings was the difficulty in defining religion or belief, and the problem of distinguishing a "genuine" religion from a cult with harmful beliefs or practices. There was also concern that the law might be abused where there is tension between sects in a particular geographical area, each claiming protection as a religion. In our view, for reasons given in the Working Paper, these questions can safely be left to the courts to resolve on a case by case basis. There is no definition of "race" or "racial group" in the RRA, but this has not prevented the courts from applying these concepts. The ECHR and legislation in several countries provides no definition, but the courts have not been flooded with claims from fringe cults. It is also to be remembered that the HRA provides a guarantee that practices which are contrary to human rights guaranteed by the Convention will not be tolerated. So, one might expect female genital mutilation or forced marriages to fall foul of convention rights such as that against inhuman or degrading treatment.

2.79   The working paper also argues that the definition of discrimination would need to incorporate the concept of reasonable adjustments to meet religious diversity. Our society is at present structured around basic Christian assumptions and therefore already accommodates the needs of Christians, for example Christmas and Easter are recognised as public holidays. In a multi-cultural, multi-faith society, the needs of other religious groups should be met. The duty to accommodate diversity has long been recognised as a central to equality in Canada.[119] As enacted in 1964, Title VII of the US Civil Rights Act prohibited discrimination on the basis of religion, but imposed no affirmative obligation on employers to accommodate the religious beliefs of their employees. Amendments in 1972 to Title VII introduced the idea of reasonable accommodation. Section 701(j) reads:

The term religion includes all aspects of religious observance and practice, as well as belief, unless and employer demonstrates that he is unable to reasonably accommodate to an employee's or prospective employee's religious observance or practice without undue hardship on the conduct of the employer's business.

An alternative to having a general duty to make reasonable adjustments arising from religion or belief is to specify duties on employers, schools and other institutions, in relation to religious practices. This is the approach taken in the Australian Capital Territory's Discrimination Act 1991.

2.80   The working paper concluded that for legislation to provide effective protection from religious discrimination it should cover both direct and indirect discrimination. The latter should include within it a duty to make reasonable adjustments for religious diversity (see para 2.33 above). Codes of Practice can then be used to set out the details of reasonable adjustments. The cost and burdens arising from this duty should be mitigated by the need for such a duty to be reasonable and not to place undue hardship on the employer, school or other institution. Legislation framed this way should ensure sufficient flexibility for the courts to balance the needs of the believer and the employer or institution.

2.81   As with the other areas of discrimination we would recommend the continuation of the model in SDA and RRA in providing a defence of justification only in relation to indirect discrimination but allowing specific exemptions to the prohibition on direct discrimination. The SDA already contains a exemption for religious bodies allowing them to "discriminate in relation to sex where employment is limited to one sex so as to comply with doctrines of the religion or avoid offending the religious susceptibilities of a significant number of its followers".[120] Robert Wintemute suggests that there should be a specific exemption for sexual orientation discrimination by religious institutions similar to that for sex found in the SDA and that it

---

[119] " . . . for the accommodation of differences, which is the essence of true equality, it will frequently be necessary to make distinctions." Mr. Justice McIntyre, Supreme Court of Canada, *Andrews v. Law Society of British Columbia* 10 C.H.R.R. D/5719 at D/5742.

[120] SDA, s. 19.

should not be extended to cover all employees of religious institutions (other than ministers of religion), such as teachers, secretaries, caretakers, doctors and nurses in schools run by religious institutions.[121] The Association of Muslim Lawyers has suggested that an exception be allowed for the appointment of Directors to Islamic Centres, Imams in mosques, certain teachers in Muslim schools, and anyone employed in the UK but required to work in places where only Muslims are permitted, such as Mecca and Madina in Saudi Arabia.[122] The Australian Human Rights and Equal Opportunities Commission Act 1986 (Cth) provides that discrimination does not include any distinction, exclusion or preference in respect of a particular job based on the inherent requirements of the job; or in connection with employment as a member of the staff of an institution that is conducted in accordance with the doctrines, tenets, beliefs or teachings of a particular religion or creed being a distinction, exclusion or preference made in good faith in order to avoid injury to the religious susceptibilities of adherents of that religion or that creed.[123]

2.82   The working paper concludes that religious discrimination legislation requires its own set of exemptions. The exemptions should cover admissions to religious educational institutions, employment by non-profit making religious bodies where the duties of the employment involve participation by the employee or worker in the teaching, observance or practice of the relevant religion. There may also need to be exceptions allowing discrimination in the relation to access to land or a building of religious significance against people who are not of a particular sex, age or religion where the restriction is in accordance with the doctrine of the religion concerned and is necessary to avoid offending the religious sensitivities of people of the religion. Further areas requiring specific exceptions include the disposition of land and the provision of accommodation by religious organisations. Before legislation in enacted there should be consultation and discussion on these and other areas where there may need to be exemptions from the prohibition on religious discrimination.

Recommendation 21

- The legislation should prohibit direct and indirect discrimination on grounds of religion or belief
- There is no need for a statutory definition of "religion or belief" bearing in mind that practices which are contrary to human rights, as guaranteed by the HRA, will not be lawful
- Employers, schools and other institutions should be under a duty to make reasonable adjustments to accommodate a person's religious observance or practice provided that this can be done without undue hardship on the employer's business or the conduct of the school or other institution
- There should be specific exception for employment for the purposes of an organised religion (1) as a cleric or minister of that religion, or (2) in any other occupation where the essential functions of the job require it to be done by a person holding or not holding a particular religion or belief, or (3) where employment is limited to one sex or to persons of a particular sexual orientation, or who are not undergoing or have not undergone gender reassignment, if the limitation is imposed to avoid offending the religious susceptibilities of a significant number of its followers
- A similar exception should apply to an authorisation or qualification for purposes of an organised religion

---

[121] Wintemute, Working Paper No.7
[122] Association of Muslim Lawyers (1999), p. 5.
[123] s. 3(1).

(g) Sexual orientation

2.83   Our Working Paper No. 7, by Robert Wintemute highlights some of the issues that would arise if legislation were to be extended to cover sexual orientation discrimination. The paper argues that exceptions permitting direct sexual orientation discrimination should be kept narrow. They could include equivalents of the provisions in the RRA relating to employment in a private house and personal services promoting welfare. They should not include exceptions for small dwellings or small private associations

2.84   Prohibition of sexual orientation discrimination also raises questions regarding the treatment of same-sex partners by employers in relation to employment benefits, by owners of rented accommodation in the public and private sectors with regard to applications by same-sex couples, and by service providers (e.g., hotels, tour companies, airlines, restaurants) who might limit a particular service, or offer it at a discounted price, to different-sex couples. In relation to employment the issue can be characterised as one of "equal pay", in that employees with same-sex partners are paid less for the same work than heterosexual employees with different-sex partners, if different-sex partners (married or not) receive employment benefits but same-sex partners do not. In *Grant* v. *South-West Trains*,[124] the European Court of Justice rejected a claim that such a distinction violates existing EC sex discrimination law, but implicitly held that it could be discrimination based on sexual orientation. We would support the proposal in the working paper for the legislation to state expressly that distinctions between same-sex partners and unmarried different-sex partners are direct sexual orientation discrimination (the *Grant* v. *South-West Trains* situation), but that distinctions between same-sex partners and married different-sex partners are neither direct nor indirect sexual orientation discrimination. Requiring employers, owners of housing, and service providers to treat all unmarried partners equally, without regard to sexual orientation, should be politically much less controversial than requiring them to treat same-sex partners in the same way as married different-sex partners. This exception would have to be co-ordinated with any proposed prohibition of marital status discrimination, and any exceptions to such a prohibition, and would not necessarily affect any employment benefits, such as survivor's pensions, or housing rights, such as succession to tenancies, that are governed by other primary legislation.

Recommendation 22

- Legislation should prohibit direct and indirect discrimination on grounds of sexual orientation
- There should be specific exceptions for (1) employment for purposes of a private household; (2) employment where the holder of the job provides persons with services promoting their welfare, and those services can most effectively be provided by a person of a particular sexual orientation; (3) accommodation in small premises provided by a resident owner or occupier; and (4) membership of small private associations
- Distinctions between same-sex partners and unmarried different-sex partners should be treated as direct discrimination on grounds of sexual orientation, but distinctions between same-sex partners and married different-sex partners should not be treated as either direct or indirect discrimination on grounds of sexual orientation

---

[124] Case C-249/96, [1998] ECR I-621, para. 47.

G. Harmonising or merging the Commissions

2.85   The Government has indicated its intention to strengthen the powers of the EOC and CRE and to align them with those of the DRC (as set out in the DRCA 1999).[125] The Government also intends to legislate to remove barriers to the equality commissions working together on common issues and to enable them to produce joint guidance. It is to be noted that the commissions are already engaged in collaborative projects, information exchange, joint lobbying and influence work. There are regular meetings of senior and specialist teams, and more collaboration is projected. The DfEE is planning a pilot project on a "one-stop shop" for advising employers. Although there was considerable scepticism among employers in our survey about this proposal (Appendix 1), we do not intend to anticipate the findings of this pilot. In chapter three we make a number of recommendations about the commissions' role in respect of the positive duty on public authorities and employment equity and pay equity plans. In chapter four we recommend that the commissions should be able to bring representative actions on behalf of a group of claimants, or to intervene in proceedings in the courts and tribunals. In this section we are concerned with two controversial issues relating to the structure of the enforcement agencies.

(1) A single Commission ?

2.86   In our options paper we asked whether there should continue to be single issue commissions in Britain or whether the existing commissions should be merged into a single equality commission as in Northern Ireland or into a broader human rights commission. The arguments for a human rights commission that covered all human rights including those incorporated into UK law by the HRA, were set out by the IPPR in 1998.[126] In the course of a series of seminars organised by the IPPR in 1999 a consensus emerged in favour of a human rights commission broadly similar to those which exist in many other countries. Nearly all the human rights commissions in other countries have responsibility for equality issues. Their functions include the review of legislation, scrutiny of draft legislation, giving advice and assistance to individuals, conducting investigations and inquiries, giving guidance to public authorities, and generally promoting human rights. In Britain, these functions in relation to equality have generally been performed by the equality commissions. In Northern Ireland, there is a separate Human Rights Commission as well as the Equality Commission. We were informed that the two Commissions hope to work closely together and to avoid unnecessary duplication of effort and resources. They are in the process of developing a memorandum of understanding to that end. It remains to be seen whether the co-existence of the two commissions makes for a satisfactory system for protecting equality and human rights.

2.87   There was concern among some of our respondents, such as the ORC Equal Opportunities Group, that "an umbrella Human Rights Commission incorporating all equality agencies ...would become too big and unwieldy and could potentially lose sight of equality issues". Others such as the Law Society's Employment Law Committee, thought that ultimately a single equality and human rights body should be established which would deal with all aspects of discrimination. However, the Law Society added, "this must be properly funded and

---

[125] Equality Statement, Cabinet Office, 30 November 1999.
[126] Spencer and Bynoe (1998).

carefully organised." We support the broad consensus which emerged at the IPPR seminars that there should be an independent and separate human rights commission to deal with broader issues of human rights. As the National Disability Council said in a letter to the Minister of State at the DfEE:

A human rights commission could play a vital role in promoting a culture of respect for human dignity and in protecting rights which are beyond the scope of the equality commissions.

We propose here to deal only with the question whether the existing equality agencies should be merged into a single equality commission, leaving the question of the ultimate relationship between the equality commission(s) and a human rights commission as a matter for the future.

2.88   The CRE told us that they "would support [a merged commission] if we could be satisfied that if would be more effective than the CRE is at present in tackling institutional discrimination". In our view, the main *advantages* of a single equality commission are that the principle of equality is given a higher status, and the agency is not likely to be marginalised as representing sectional interests to the same extent as a single issue commission, particularly if grounds affecting white men such as age and sexual orientation are included. The commission could speak with a single strong voice and give consistent advice. A single commission would assist in identifying and making the connections necessary to tackle multiple discrimination cases, avoiding duplication of resources. Moreover, if discrimination were made unlawful on additional grounds, such as age, sexual orientation, and religion or belief, it would be difficult to create yet further agencies. Administratively, there are likely to be efficiency gains. Employers in our case studies (Appendix 1), especially those with inclusive diversity policies, strongly favoured a single agency. They find it perplexing to deal with separate commissions, each with its own approach. The ORC Equal Opportunity Group said:

On the whole member companies believe that separate agencies are outmoded where a more inclusive approach to diversity is sought. Ultimately employers do not wish to deal with three (or potentially more) equality agencies in the long term and would prefer to see only one agency established.

2.89   The main *disadvantages* are that particular interest groups fear that they will be swamped by other more powerful interests (e.g. ethnic minorities by women or vice versa). This point has been made to us with particular strength by the disability groups who have struggled for many years to establish a DRC. They fear that their gains will be submerged within a generalist body, and that the DRC needs time to establish itself to ensure that it is an equal partner in any future merger. It was argued that the identification of agencies with specific groups, and the perception of them as serving the needs of those groups can provide a source of strength in the inevitable political disputes that arise over funding.[127] The response on this from the GMB expressed this position clearly:

We do not believe there should be combined Commissions. Conceptually, we think it is important that the Commissions remain separate for the foreseeable future. We fear that, even with the best intentions, certain interest groups might operate at the expense of others. We are also concerned that Commissions might be merged solely for economic reasons. If this were to be the case, we think it would mean a devaluing of the work currently being carried out by the separate commissions.

2.90   In our view, these arguments rest on a fundamental misconception about the nature and purpose of an equality commission. The primary objective of the commission is not to represent interest groups or to give them a voice. That is the function of non-governmental organisations and

---

[127] See McCrudden (1999b), at p. 1732.

organised groups such as those promoting racial equality or women's rights, or the rights of disabled persons, and those of other disadvantaged groups. The main objective of the commission is to act as an organ of government promoting change in organisations and, where appropriate helping individuals to assert their rights. The commission's essential role is to promote equality and to ensure that resources are focussed on the most important strategic issues. A single equality commission would be greatly strengthened in promoting fair participation and fair access for members of particular interest groups if it could do so by reference to a broad principle of equality. It would also be able to offer consistent advice and treatment to employers and others. We were told by the Vice-Chair of the EEOC that American experience is that "the more you can bring under one roof the better, because employers and complainants want uniform requirements."

2.91   The success of a single equality commission may be hampered if it has to operate under many different statutes, with distinct powers under each. The ECNI at present has to operate under five different legislative regimes (religion, race, sex, disability, as well as the positive duty on public authorities under the NIA). There is a danger that different interest groups may perceive the Commission as acting differently in respect of the various grounds of discrimination, or as levelling down enforcement. Some of our respondents suggested that ECNI should be allowed to function for a reasonable period to evaluate the impact of merging before any decisions is made regarding restructuring of organisations in Britain. We do not consider that this will provide a fair test, because of the present statutory framework under which the ECNI has to operate. In Britain the first step must be to harmonise the substantive law into a single equality statute. This will then provide a sound basis for a single commission. If the UK were starting with equality legislation today it would have a single commission. In our view this remains a desirable objective, and we believe that the competition between different interest groups can be more successfully resolved through a single commission. A unified commission will also meet the legitimate expectations of employers and others that they will receive consistent treatment in respect of all equality issues. We recommend a single commission for Britain. As with other human rights, it is important that the same standards be maintained throughout the UK. Accordingly, we do not favour separate commissions for Scotland or Wales, although the commission would no doubt wish to have offices and advisory committees in each of those countries and to ensure that they are adequately represented on the commission. We envisage that for the foreseeable future, Northern Ireland will keep its own arrangements.

(2) Structure of a single commission

2.92   If there were to be a single commission, how should such a commission be structured? It may be useful to look briefly at the position in Northern Ireland and in Australia. These countries provide two different models for structuring a single commission. In Northern Ireland, the Report of the Equality Commission Working Group recommended the merging of the existing commissions into the new ECNI in two phases.[128] In phase one the Commission would be separated into directorates dealing with fair employment, race, and sex discrimination. In phase two the Commission's Executive structure would be based on an integrated functional approach. This involves separating the commission into common areas of work, such as information and communication, advisory agencies and training, investigation and regulation, and research. The working group believed that this integrated functional approach would ensure

---

[128] Report of the Equality Commission Working Group (1999).

more effective use of resources, a greater ability to deliver an effective service for the range of customers. A similar approach is taken by the Equality Authority in Ireland.

2.93   In Australia, under the Human Rights and Equal Opportunities Commission Act 1986, a Human Rights and Equal Opportunities Commission was set up. It included a Human Rights Commissioner, a Race Discrimination Commissioner, and a Sex Discrimination Commissioner. These were joined through subsequent legislation by a Privacy Commissioner, and an Aboriginal and Torres Strait Island Social Justice Commissioner. Each Commissioner was responsible for a specific area. The Commissioners, except the Aboriginal and Torres Strait Island Social Justice Commissioner, were able to investigate and determine complaints within their area. Between 1997-99, the HREOC's budget was decreased by the Coalition Government by over 36% on alleged efficiency grounds. The Government also wanted to abolish the specialist commissioners and replace them with generalist commissioners, a proposal apparently motivated by the Commissioners' critical approach to government action. After strong opposition, particularly by women's groups and NGOs, the Government announced its intention to restructure the HREOC (and to rename it the Human Rights and Responsibilities Commission) by abolishing the five specific commissioners and replacing them with three Deputy Presidents. Under new legislation, the Deputy Presidents would have responsibility respectively for: human rights and disability discrimination; racial discrimination and social justice; sex discrimination and equal opportunities. The role of the Deputy Presidents is not the same as that of the previous specialist Commissioners. The key focus of the Deputy Presidents will be on human rights education and assisting business and the community to comply with human rights standards. All complaint investigations and conciliation procedures that arise under separate discrimination statutes go to the President.

2.94   The IPPR, in arguing for a human rights commission, favoured a structure containing identified commissioners with specific responsibilities. Thus an umbrella human rights commission would contain a race equality commissioner and a sex or gender equality commissioner. They acknowledged the advantages of generalist commissioners. This would provide the greatest opportunity for a fundamental review and reallocation of the resources of the existing bodies, enabling the commissioners to concentrate on the issues causing greatest concern. It would also allow cost savings by the sharing of common services. However they favoured having commissioners with responsibilities for specific issues, on the grounds that without specific commissioners those issues would be marginalised. Moreover, in the absence of a specialist commissioner

...the communities or groups predominately concerned with human rights issues, such as race, would not be able to identify a named commissioner accountable for that issue with whom to be in dialogue. The energy and focus of a single issue organisation might be lost within a large, undifferentiated body with numerous roles and functions.[129]

In our view, these questions of structure cannot be resolved through a detailed blueprint. They will need to be debated after the initial decision has been taken to create a single commission, having regard to experience elsewhere.

Recommendation 23
•   There should be a human rights commission for Britain the functions of which will include the review of legislation, scrutiny of draft legislation, giving advice and assistance to individuals,

---

[129] Spencer and Bynoe (1998), p.116.

conducting investigations and inquiries, giving guidance to public authorities, and generally promoting human rights including equality

- There should be a separate single equality commission for Britain covering all grounds of unlawful discrimination
- The internal structure of the equality commission should be the subject of discussion and consultation after the decision has been taken to merge the existing commissions
- The DRC should not be included initially in a merged commission, but this should be reviewed after five years

CHAPTER THREE
CHANGING ORGANISATIONAL POLICY
AND BEHAVIOUR

A. Regulatory strategies

3.1 This Chapter aims to set out a design of "optimal"[130] regulation which can help to reduce, if not eliminate, under-representation, exclusion, and institutional barriers to equality opportunities.

3.2 In our options paper we set out five main strategies of regulation, namely
- *rights and liabilities*, as currently embodied in the right of individuals to bring claims for unlawful discrimination in the courts and tribunals;
- *command and control* by an independent public agency which sets the standards which organisations are required to meet, and enforces them through investigations and legal proceedings;
- *voluntary self-regulation*, which is based on the individual organisation meeting prescribed standards unilaterally without any threat of coercion;
- *enforced self-regulation*, which is aimed at organisations which fail to comply voluntarily;
- *economic incentives* to encourage compliance, such as the award or withdrawal of government contracts and subsidies.

We set out in the options paper the main advantages and disadvantages of each of these approaches. There was general agreement among our respondents that none of these approaches is without strengths or weaknesses and that a combination of them is needed for an effective, efficient, and equitable strategy for changing organisational policy and behaviour. There was a preference among some groups representing employers for *voluntary self-regulation*, while other employers and trade unions recognised the need for *enforced self-regulation*, where voluntary means fail.

3.3 In our view, the consensus for a mixture of strategies is well-founded, because this compensates for the deficiencies of a single approach and takes advantages of the strengths of each. However, it is essential to resist what has been called the "kitchen-sink" or "smorgasbord" approach in which every conceivable policy and legal instrument is thrown in.[131] This rests on the mistaken assumption that more coercion is always necessary, and that resources for regulation are unlimited. Such an approach is in danger of being counter-productive through regulatory overload. Imposing too many bureaucratic requirements on organisations will not only be costly; they are also likely to engender resistance and adversarialism, and will be politically unacceptable. On the other hand, those who advocate entirely voluntary and "best practice" methods, such as the Better Regulation Task Force in relation to company equality policies,[132] seem to ignore the evidence from regulatory research[133] that voluntarism can work only if it is

---

130 We use the concept of "optimal" regulation as explained in paras. 2.16-2.18.
131 Gunningham and Sinclair (1998), p. 398.
132 Better Regulation Task Force (1999), p. 4; a view with which the Government agreed in its response (14 July 1999).
133 Gunningham and Sinclair (1998), pp. 432-433; Grabosky and Gunningham (1998), pp. 300-307.

complemented with other methods such as enforced self-regulation. A comparison can be drawn between age discrimination, where the Government has promulgated a non-statutory code of practice, and disability discrimination, where there are statutory codes of practice which can be used in proceedings under the DDA, as well as being benchmarks for action plans imposed with non-discrimination notices by the DRC. All the employers in our case studies (Appendix 1) said that the voluntary code would be ineffective, and none of them had taken measures to combat age discrimination, although they conceded that it was widespread. On the other hand, they praised the codes on disability because of their practical recommendations, which were backed by the force of law.

3.4   The Better Regulation Task Force held out the promise that if voluntary methods did not work then legislation could be introduced "at a later date". This evolutionary approach was adopted in respect of racial discrimination in employment in the 1960s, when enforcement was left to voluntary bodies in 40 industries.[134] This failed abysmally, because there was no pressure to change entrenched managerial practices. There is no reason to believe that voluntarism on its own can succeed any better today against the new forms of institutional race and sex discrimination and in relation to matters such as age. The trap into which the Task Force and some others fall is to pose one form of regulation (e.g. voluntarism) as preferable to another (e.g. enforced self-regulation). The point is that a voluntary approach may work in influencing the behaviour of some organisations (e.g. a leading edge company whose markets are among ethnic minorities will readily want to project an equality policy), but not others who for economic or social reasons are resistant to change. This has led to a theory of "responsive regulation", the idea that regulation needs to be responsive to the different behaviour of the various organisations subject to regulation.[135] Models of an enforcement pyramid have been developed. At the base, the regulators assume voluntary compliance and promise co-operation. When this fails they climb up the pyramid with progressively more deterrent penalties until there is compliance. In order to work, there must be a gradual escalation and, at the top, sufficiently strong sanctions to deter even the most persistent offender. A related problem is that a method which was expected to be effective on its own, turns out after experience to be a failure. This can be dealt with by sequencing sanctions with an escalation from the first low intervention option to increasingly more coercive methods.[136]

3.5   A crucial element in the design of an enforcement pyramid is to identify the potential participants in the regulatory process. In the equal opportunities field strategic enforcement has traditionally been seen as a dialogue between the commissions and those who are being regulated (employers, service providers etc.). Modern regulatory theory offers two critical insights in this respect. The first is that private forms of social control are often far more important in changing behaviour than state law enforcement, and more can be achieved by harnessing the enlightened self-interest of employers and providers than through command and control regulation.[137] Our case studies of employers (Appendix 1) show that it is well recognised in the UK that there is a strong "business case" for inclusivity and diversity. The second is that the quality of regulation can be improved by bringing into the regulatory process the experience and views of those directly affected. Groups such as trade unions, community organisations and public interest bodies act as watchdogs, educate and inform others, and help individuals to enforce their rights. These considerations suggest that:

---

[134] Hepple (1970), pp.175-202.
[135] Ayres and Braithwaite (1992).
[136] Gunningham and Sinclair (1998), pp. 404-406.
[137] Gunningham (1998), p. 12.

- regulation should build on the self-interest of business and providers;
- interest groups should have opportunities to participate in the regulatory process, through information, consultation and engagement.

The definition of "interest group" will depend upon the specific context, as we shall elaborate when dealing below with the positive duty on public authorities, employment equity and pay equity.

3.6   With these considerations in mind, our broad design for a regulatory enforcement pyramid (illustrated in figure 3.1) is as follows:

Level one: Persuasion, information and disclosure. This includes education and training, monitoring, and disclosure of the results of monitoring to interest groups.

Level two: Voluntary action plans. The organisation would draw these up in accordance with minimum performance standards prescribed by the commission in a code, but would also encouraged to go beyond these to "best practice." Interest groups would have a right to be informed, consulted, and otherwise engaged in the process.

Level three: Commission investigation. If the commission had a belief that there is no monitoring or plan, the commission would be entitled to make inquiries and seek undertakings.

Level four: Compliance notice. If requests for information were not heeded or no suitable undertakings are given, the commission would be entitled to issue a compliance or directions notice which could include an action plan. The respondent would be entitled to appeal against the notice to a court or tribunal.

Level five: Judicial enforcement: If the compliance notice was not observed, the commission would be entitled to institute proceedings in a court or tribunal, which could make an order requiring the respondent to take action within a specified period.

Level six. Sanction. If the judicial order were disobeyed, sanctions could be imposed for contempt of court, or there could be a monetary penalty.

Level seven. Withdrawal of contracts, licences etc. This would be an additional sanction on government contractors etc., who were found liable for persistent non-compliance.

3.7   It will be seen that this pyramid involves three interlocking mechanisms.[138] The first is internal scrutiny by the institution itself to ensure effective self-regulation. The second is the role of interest groups which those regulated are required to inform, consult, and engage in the process of change. The third is the Commission, which provides the back-up role of assistance and ultimately enforcement where voluntary methods fail. These interlocking mechanisms create a triangular relationship between those regulated, those whose interests are affected, and the Commission as the guardian of the public interest. This broad strategy needs to be refined in specific contexts, in particular (1) the positive duty on public authorities; (2) employment equity; and (3) pay equity. Finally, we shall explain the possibilities for using contract and subsidy compliance as a sanction and incentive.

---

[138] We are grateful to Professor Christopher McCrudden who formulated this explanation in respect of the way in which the positive duty on public authorities under the NIA s.75, will work. We believe this provides a sound general basis for regulation, although it will be clear that our enforcement pyramid differs in details from the requirements under s.75, or the requirements of the FETO, particularly in not requiring plans to be approved or monitoring returns to be made automatically to the Commission.

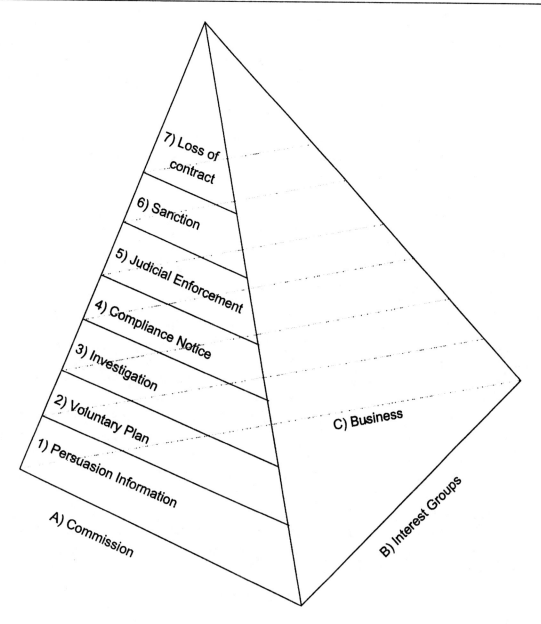

Equality enforcement pyramid (figure 3.1)[139]

B. Duty on Public Authorities to Promote Equality

(1) Purposes

3.8   There was widespread support in the responses for a positive duty to be placed on public authorities to have due regard to the need to promote equality of opportunity. Such a duty exists under section 75 of the NIA, which attempts "to make equality issues central to the whole range of public policy debates."[140] The primary reason for "mainstreaming" is to reduce the risk that these issues become sidelined. The reactive and negative approach of anti-discrimination is replaced by pro-active, anticipatory and integrative methods. It means that public

---

[139] Adopted from Gunningham (1998), p. 398
[140] McCrudden (1999b), p. 11; and McCrudden (1998), on which we have drawn extensively.

authorities are bound to have regard to the need for positive action, to set goals and targets, and to review and implement their action plans. The CRE said that the positive duty would mean that equality could not be ignored while developing policy in other areas. For example, a local authority making arrangements for school allocation in accordance with parental preferences would have to ensure that allocations did not conflict with racial equality principles.

3.9   A second, and related, reason is to encourage greater participation by disadvantaged groups in decision-making. In the words of a submission to us by the Committee on the Administration of Justice: "in moving from a solely anti-discrimination focus to a pro-active equality of opportunity duty, one opens up the door for people to get very directly involved in the decision-making process affecting their lives." There are, however, potential risks in mainstreaming. If the responsibility for equality issues is too widely dispersed across all public bodies, there may be fragmentation of policy; as an inter-departmental policy mainstreaming will have to contend with the ethos of departmental exclusiveness; and there are likely to be political and financial constraints on effective implementation. A public duty has to be designed and implemented sensitively in order to counteract these factors.

3.10   The Better Regulation Task Force[141] was persuaded that there should be such a duty in Britain, but did not believe that this required further legislation. Those with experience in Northern Ireland disagreed. For example, Professor McCrudden said that the "non-statutory, light touch regulatory approach adopted in the PAFT [Policy Appraisal and Fair Treatment] guidelines signally failed to deliver anything but frustration and annoyance outside government." In the absence of a clear legal basis there was uncertainty as to the scope of "equality-proofing", a lack of commitment in some departments, and an absence of enforcement mechanisms. It was for this reason that a statutory scheme was developed under the NIA, s.75. The Government has now accepted that the current Race Relations (Amendment) Bill should be amended so as to place a positive duty on public authorities in respect of racial equality. At the time of writing the details of the amendments are not known. There was also a Government commitment, on 30 November 1999, to extend the positive duty to sex and disability discrimination, when legislative time permits.[142]

(2) Principles

3.11   In a response to our consultation paper Professor McCrudden identified six key principles upon which the duty in Northern Ireland is based:

- a clear positive statutory duty to promote equality of opportunity by public authorities across all areas of government policy making and activities
- the participation of affected groups in determining how this should be achieved
- the assessment of impact of existing and future government policies on affected groups
- consideration of the alternatives which have less of an adverse impact
- the consideration of how to mitigate adverse impacts which cannot be avoided
- transparency and openness in the process of assessment.

These principles accord with the regulatory design which we set out above, and, in our view, should form the basis of any extension of the public duty in Britain.

---

[141] (1999), p. 19.
[142] Cabinet Office, Equality Statement, 30 November 1999.

(3) Scope

3.12   The scope of the duty on public authorities to promote equality of opportunity in Northern Ireland is set out in the NIA :

> 75. (1) A public authority shall in carrying out its functions relating to Northern Ireland have due regard to the need to promote equality of opportunity-
> (a) between persons of different religious belief, political opinion, racial group, age, marital status or sexual orientation
> (b) between men and women generally;
> (c) between persons with a disability and persons without; and
> (d) between persons with dependants and persons without.
>
> (2) Without prejudice to its obligations under subsection (1), a public authority shall in carry out its functions relating to Northern Ireland have regard to the desirability of promoting good relations between persons of different religious belief, political opinion or racial group.

3.13   This may be compared with the present RRA, s. 71 which imposed a duty on local authorities to:

> ...make appropriate arrangements with a view to securing their various functions are carried out with due regard to the need—
> (a) to eliminate unlawful racial discrimination; and
> (b) to promote equality of opportunity and good relations, between persons of different racial groups

The effectiveness of this provision was undermined by the wording which limited the duty on local authorities only to "make appropriate arrangements". This wording proved to be too vague and allowed local authorities to do very little beyond making arrangements. The more recent Great London Authority Act 1999, s.33, also contains a general duty to promote equal opportunity including a duty to report annually on the steps it has taken in pursuance of its duty. In exercising their functions, the GLA and other specified London authorities must have regard to the need:

(a) to promote equality of opportunity for all persons irrespective of their race, sex, disability, age, sexual orientation or religion;
(b) to eliminate unlawful discrimination; and
(c) to promote good relations between persons of different racial groups, religious beliefs and sexual orientation.

This formulation is different from and, in our view, less satisfactory than the approach in the NIA, s.75 because it calls for the promotion of equality of opportunity irrespective of race etc rather than between different groups. The duty to promote equality of opportunity between different groups is more specific and progress towards meeting the duty can be more easily measured. Moreover, the duty to have "regard" is weaker than the duty to have "due regard" to the need to promote equality of opportunity. The latter means that the authority must do more than take equality of opportunity into account. It must give considerable weight to equality, but this does not mean that the duty overrides other clearly conflicting statutory duties with which the body must comply.[143] For reasons explained in paras. 2.34-2.40, we have preferred the term "equality" to "equality of opportuniy".

Recommendation 24

There should be a duty on specified public authorities in the exercise of their functions to eliminate unlawful discrimination and to have due regard to the need to promote equality

---

[143] Equality Commission Working Group (1999), p. 93.

- between persons of different racial groups, religious belief, age, marital status or sexual orientation
- between men and women generally
- between persons with a disability and without
- between persons with dependants and persons without.

(4) Equality schemes

3.14   Under the NIA, s.75 each public authority is required to submit an equality scheme, detailing how it plans to fulfil the duties imposed by section 75, to the ECNI for approval or reference to the Secretary of State. Where a scheme is submitted by a Northern Ireland public authority it is referred to the Secretary of State, who can approve it, or request the public authority to make a revised scheme, or make a scheme for the public authority. The key requirements under the duty are set out in schedule 9 of the Act. This includes a statement of the authority's arrangements:

(a) for assessing its compliance with the duties under section 75 and for consulting on matters to which a duty under that section is likely to be relevant (including details of the persons to be consulted);
(b) for assessing and consulting on the likely impact of policies adopted or proposed to be adopted by the authority on the promotion of equality of opportunity;
(c) for monitoring any adverse impact of policies adopted by the authority on the promotion of equality of opportunity;
(d for publishing the results of such assessments as are mentioned in paragraph (b) and such monitoring as is mentioned in paragraph (c);
(e) for training staff;
(f) for ensuring, and assessing, public access to information and to services provided by the authority.[144]

3.15   In our view it would not be feasible in Britain, in view of the large number of public authorities and the limited resources available to the commission, to require advance approval of equality schemes by the commission. Moreover, the view was strongly expressed to us in Northern Ireland, that the NIA has externalised the responsibility for revising and policing the duty. It was argued that in order to make an impact, mainstreaming must be driven from the centre of government and not left to the commission. Accordingly, we make no recommendation for prior approval, preferring to limit the role of the commission to one of providing assistance to authorities where this is requested, issuing guidance in the form of codes of practice, and securing compliance in the event of failure to make or implement a scheme (below).

3.16   Before submitting a scheme a public authority in Northern Ireland is required to consult representatives of the persons likely to be affected by the scheme and other persons specified in directions by the ECNI.[145] This is similar to the duty placed on public bodies in Wales under the Welsh Language Act when preparing schemes for the use of Welsh, to "carry out such consultations as may be appropriate in order to ascertain views representative of both Welsh-speaking and other members of the public who may be affected by the scheme."[146] As we have pointed out, participation of this kind is a crucial feature of the public duty. Guidelines prepared by the ECNI emphasise that consultation should be an integral part of the policy process, and give advice as to the methods for achieving the widest participation both as to the

---

[144] Northern Ireland Act 1998, Schedule 9 s.4(2).
[145] NIA, s.5 and sched.9.
[146] Welsh Language Act 1993, s.13.

policy areas which should be considered and as the impact of the scheme. Similar commission guidance in the form of a code of practice would be needed in Britain. Judicial review would be available to any group which claimed that they had been excluded from the consultation on irrational grounds

Recommendation 25

Every specified public authority should be required to collect and publish such information as is appropriate and necessary to facilitate the performance of its duty to promote equality, and to publish an equality scheme, setting out its arrangements-

- for assessing its compliance with the duty and for consulting on matters to which the duty is likely to be relevant
- for assessing and consulting on the likely impact of policies adopted or proposed to be adopted on the promotion of equality
- for monitoring any adverse impact of policies adopted by the authority on the promotion of equality, and in doing so to have regard to the aims of the policy, measures capable of mitigating any adverse impact, and alternative policies which might better achieve the promotion of equality

(5) Which authorities and functions?

3.17   The NIA, s.75 defines the public authorities covered by the duty first by automatically including those bodies which are within the jurisdiction of the Northern Ireland Ombudsman, and secondly by allowing the Secretary of State to designate other bodies, including Northern Ireland bodies, such as the Royal Ulster Constabulary, and UK-wide bodies which carry out functions in Northern Ireland, such as the Ministry of Defence. There are distinct advantages in specifying the bodies which are covered, rather than following the precedent of the HRA, s.6(3) which does not define a public authority, except to include a court or tribunal, and also "any person certain of whose functions are functions of a public nature". In response to our options paper, Professor Gillian Morris identified the advantages of specifying authorities:

It will remove the need for litigation to decide whether an authority is subject to the duty. Whilst such litigation will be inevitable in the context of the Human Rights Act, the framework of that legislation is such that all bodies should in any event be seeking to comply with Convention rights. Moreover that approach has been developed against a background of considerable uncertainty as to the nature of the bodies for which the state is responsible under the ECHR...Specifying bodies subject to the duty would concentrate the mind on the need for more consistent and cohesive policies developed at the highest level rather than this being left to individual managers within a service, and to individual organisations which may be uncertain as to whether they are covered by the duty.

3.18   This still leaves the question, which authorities should be specified in Britain? It seems obvious that government departments, local authorities, the Scottish Administration and the National Assembly for Wales and its subsidiaries should be covered. There are also other authorities providing core public services where equality issues are frequently in issue. These include police authorities, health authorities and boards, NHS trusts and primary care trusts, and local education authorities. In our view, these should be automatically included in respect of all their functions. However, there are many smaller public authorities, operating in different parts of the country, where it would not be appropriate to include them in respect of all their functions because to do so would be disproportionate. Accordingly, the Secretary of State should have power, after consultation, to designate other bodies in respect of some or all of their functions.

3.19   As regards the range of functions to be covered, a broad approach is desirable. This would include not only the "core" services provided by the authorities specified, but also other functions such as procurement and employment. We discuss these other functions in paras. 3.61-3.77 below.

Recommendation 26

The duty should apply -

• in respect of all their functions, including procurement and employment, to government departments, the Scottish Administration, the National Assembly for Wales and its subsidiaries, police authorities, health authorities and boards, NHS trusts and primary care trusts and local education authorities

• in respect of specified functions to such other public authorities as the Secretary of State may designate, after consultation

(6) Enforcement

3.20   In Northern Ireland, if the ECNI receives a complaint, made in accordance with certain formalities, of failure by a public authority to comply with an equality scheme approved by the commission or made by the Secretary of State, it is required to investigate or give the complainant reasons for not investigating. The ECNI may also carry out an investigation, without receiving a complaint, in pursuance of its general duty to keep under review the effectiveness of section 75. If, after investigation, the ECNI recommends action by the authority, and considers that such action has not been taken within a reasonable time, enforcement depends upon whether the authority is a Northern Ireland or UK-wide one. In the case of the former, the matter may be referred to the Secretary of State who can issue directions to the authority. In the latter case, the only sanction is for the ECNI to lay a report before Parliament and the Northern Ireland Assembly.

3.21   In our view, mainstreaming of equality of opportunity can best be enforced by building this into the Government's performance management frameworks. Regular monitoring and progress reports form a central feature of this approach. The use of a "basket of indicators" in each public authority, showing progress towards fair participation and fair access over a period of time, would enable the results of equality schemes to be reviewed. This would include information about matters such as employment, service delivery to different groups, and attitudinal studies of comparative perceptions of public services. Inspection and audit should, as far as possible, be by those bodies already responsible for these functions in the public sector, such as the Audit Commission, the National Audit Office, HMIC, OFSTED, and HMIP.

3.22   The commission should have residual powers to enforce compliance, either on receiving a formal complaint, or on its own initiative where it appears that a public authority has failed to take appropriate steps to comply with its duty. The commission should be able to issue a compliance notice, after giving the authority an opportunity to make representations. The notice should state the nature of the alleged non-compliance, the evidence that is required to demonstrate an adequate level of compliance, and the time by which such evidence should be produced. The authority should be entitled to appeal to a tribunal against the notice. If after the time specified in the notice, the public authority has failed to produce the evidence specified, the commission should be able to apply to a tribunal for an order requiring the authority to comply with the notice. We recommend later (para. 4.13-4.17) that all proceedings in respect of discrimination should be started in the employment tribunals, but that the President or a regional chairman should have power to transfer these to a county or sheriff court. In order to concentrate specialisation, we make a similar proposal here.

Recommendation 27

- Performance of the duty should be measured through performance management frameworks which use a basket of indicators on equality showing progress towards fair participation and fair access over a period of time
- Inspection and audit should be carried out, wherever possible, by those bodies which have general inspection and audit functions in the public sector
- The commission should have residual power to issue a compliance notice, after allowing the authority an opportunity to make representations, requiring evidence of compliance to be produced within a specified time
- The public authority should be able to appeal against the notice to a tribunal
- In the event of non-compliance, the commission should be able to apply to a tribunal for an order requiring the authority to comply

C. Employment Equity

(1) Lessons from the USA

3.23   In 1961, President Kennedy issued Executive Order 10925 which introduced the novel concept of affirmative action by requiring government contractors not merely to abstain from unlawful discrimination but also to take positive measures to increase the representation of racial minorities in their workforces. The current Order 11246 issued by President Johnson in 1964, and amended in 1967 to cover sex and religion, outlines the requirements on contractors. There are also affirmative action requirements in respect of persons with disabilities and disabled war veterans.[147] Enforcement is by the Office of Federal Contract Compliance Programs (OFCCP) which issues detailed regulations.[148] The Executive Order is estimated to apply to about 300,000 Federal contractors, employing about 40% of the working population.[149] An equal opportunity clause is inserted in all Federal contracts worth in excess of $10,000. The obligation to develop a written affirmative action program for each of its establishments applies to all Federal contractors and sub-contractors with 50 or more employees bidding for contracts of $50,000 or more.

3.24   All the employers whom we interviewed in the USA said that it was the affirmative action requirements which were the most significant influence on their organisations. This was also the view of those who have professional experience of the OFCCP and the EEOC respectively. The EEOC is largely tied down to individual complaint investigations, with "Commissioner's charges" alleging patterns and practices of discrimination being relatively rare. The OFCCP, in contrast has no fewer than four investigatory methods in race and gender cases: (1) routine compliance reviews; (2) pre-award compliance reviews; (3) individual complaint investigations, and (4) "class-type" complaint investigations. (In disability and war veterans' cases the OFCCP uses only complaints investigations.) The OFCCP is most feared for its compliance

---

[147] 41 Code of Federal Regulations (CFR), s.60-250, s.60-741.
[148] 41 CFR , s.60.
[149] Morris (1990), p. 123.

reviews, which are discussed below. We have studied the American practice to discover the secret of its success. Our conclusion is that its real strength does not come from the passive obligation not to discriminate. It derives from the compulsion on contractors to initiate positive action with a view to achieving fair participation, and from the power of an expert independent body, the OFCCP, to enforce this obligation on the basis of the economic power of withdrawal of contracts.

3.25   Employers are required to file an annual report on a relatively straightforward form (EEO1), and on this will indicate if they are government contractors. The OFCCP may conduct compliance reviews. The scale of these is relatively modest. The OFCCP has only 450 investigators in 6 regions and 40 district offices. As a result only about 2% of Federal contractors are investigated. The OFCCP identifies audit targets bearing in mind a number of considerations. First, and most important, is the Equal Employment Opportunity Data System (EEDS), a computerised listing of all federal contractors and sub-contractors known to have filed EEO1s. The computer breaks down the information provided on EEO1s by regions, districts and industries. The computer places an asterisk by each job category if the contractor employs less than the average percentage of minorities or women than the contractor's "comparator" in that industry and location employs. The OFCCP "red flags" those contractors below average. The district director of the OFCCP must select at least 75% of the audits from the EEDS asterisk listings, and has a discretion as to the others to be selected, taking account of factors such as recency and frequency of review, recent complaint activity against that contractor, and community reaction to the employer. The OFCCP encourages district directors to target contractors who are actively engaged in hiring because this is an opportunity to increase the employment of minorities and women.

3.26   The OFCCP divides its audit into three parts. First they call for the affirmative action plan and other data and do a desk analysis. This is followed by on-site investigation, usually lasting about three days. Then an office analysis takes place. Notice of the results of investigation is given to the employer. The OFCCP completes over 80% of its compliance reviews within 6 months.

3.27   In 20-30% of cases the employer is found to be in full compliance. In cases of serious ("material") violations, the OFCCP attempts to reach a formal conciliation agreement. If the agreement is violated, the OFCCP can directly enforce it. Contractors are said to be reluctant to sign such an agreement, not only because it constitutes proof of violations, but also because the agreement permits the re-opening of the audit and other requirements. Where the violations are minor, the employer is asked for undertakings, previously set out in a letter of commitment, but now usually simply recorded by the OFCCP. If a conciliation agreement is not signed, there is negotiation and conciliation. If agreement is still not reached, the case is reported to the Solicitor of Labor at local level, who has to confirm whether or not a violation has occurred. The next step is for the OFCCP to file a complaint before a Department of Labor administrative law judge who hears the case and makes a "recommended decision", the OFCCP and the contractor can then appeal. That appeal used to go to the Secretary of Labor, but because of lengthy delays it is now referred to the Board of Administrative Review.

3.28   The Executive Order confers authority on the OFCCP to impose sanctions on contractors by declaring them ineligible to receive further contracts and to interrupt progress payments on existing contracts, but, in view of the requirements of due process, such sanctions require the decision of the Board of Administrative Review after the administrative law judge's hearing and recommendations. From 1961 to 1999 only 36 contractors had been debarred. none of them large employers. The threat of debarment has proved to be a sufficient deterrent, but even more important has been the risk of bad publicity.

3.29   Significantly, all the US employers whom we interviewed accepted the need for contract compliance, and said that they would not have been able to sustain the significant increases in the representation of women and minorities which had taken place in their organisations without the compulsory affirmative action requirements. All our respondents agreed that these requirements had resource costs, but said that these did not outweigh the gains. However, we heard several criticisms of the way in which the federal contract compliance system operates. First it was said that the reporting requirements and the way in which the action plan must be drawn up have become – in the words of a retired OFCCP official – a "statistical morass", with more time spent on writing up the plan than implementing it. The requirements were said to be too rigid, not taking account of the diversity of employers and the structure of individual companies. The plan has to contain two main statistical analyses, a workforce analysis and an utilisation analysis. The latter consists of three identifiable statistical subparts, including a division into (a) "major" job groups, (b) an eight-factor "availability" analysis,[150] and (c) goals developed following a determination. Attempts had been made to reduce the eight factors to two, but this had been strongly resisted by civil rights groups although compliance officers believed that this simplification would have made enforcement more effective. It was argued that there was over-reliance on numerical standards, and that more emphasis should be placed in audits on good faith efforts to achieve standards or targets, and outreach and training programs Secondly, it was said that the uniform guidelines on employee selection procedures (1978)[151] had become outdated and were too rigid, for example in defining as an applicant anyone who had ever shown an interest in the job so leading to difficulties in defining the applicant population. Thirdly, there were criticisms from employers and their lawyers about the way in which the OFCCP has moved away from hiring and promotion issues in order to focus on alleged pay discrimination through the theory of "comparable work".[152]

(2) Northern Ireland

3.30   The US experience with affirmative action has been influential in several other countries such as Canada[153] (where the concept of "employment equity" was used), Australia,[154] and recently in South Africa.[155] Of greatest relevance in the UK, is the FEA 1989 which imposed positive duties to achieve fair participation of the Roman Catholic and Protestant communities on certain employers. These obligations, with significant amendments, are now contained in Part VII of the FETO 1998. The first obligation on employers is to *monitor.* The legislation[156] requires private sector employers with more than 10 full-time employees in Northern Ireland to register with the ECNI (formerly the FEC). Registered employers and public authorities are

---

[150] 41 CFR, s.60-2.11(a).
[151] 41 CFR, s.60-3.
[152] E.g. Copus (1999).
[153] Employment Equity Act 1995 (Can.) (which came into force in October 1996).
[154] Equal Opportunity for Women in the Workplace Act 1999, which consolidates with amendments the earlier Affirmative Action (Equal Employment Opportunity for Women) Act No.91 of 1986, following a regulatory review which led the Coalition Government to make the legislation more "business friendly", in particular minimising compliance costs by reducing reporting requirements and focusing on the achievement of reasonably practicable outcomes rather than on specific processes: Commonwealth of Australia (1998), and Government Response (December 1998).
[155] Employment Equity Act , No.55 of 1998.
[156] FETO, arts. 47-54.

required to prepare and serve each year on the commission a monitoring return to enable the composition of the workforce (including part-time employees) to be ascertained, that is the number of employees who belong to the Protestant community and the number who belong to the Roman Catholic community. In addition, these employers are required to serve a monitoring return to enable the composition of applicants for employment to be ascertained. Each public authority and the employer in a registered concern with more than 250 employees also has to serve a monitoring return in respect of those ceasing to be employed.[157] There are detailed requirements as to the information to be contained in a monitoring return, and the methods by which the employer can determine the community to which an employee or applicant belongs. Employers have to retain certain information for three years, and there are criminal offences for failing to serve a return, or giving false information.[158]

3.31   The second obligation on employers is to undertake *periodic reviews* (once every three years) of their employment practices (affecting recruitment, training, promotion or redundancy) for the purpose of determining whether members of each community are enjoying, and are likely to continue to enjoy, fair participation in employment in the firm (see para. 2.38 regarding the meaning of this). Thirdly, where fair participation is not evident the employer must engage in *affirmative action* (see para. 2.37 for the meaning of this). In doing so the employer must have regard to the Code of Practice. The commission must, if requested by the employer to do so, give advice as to the manner in which a review should be carried out.[159]

3.32   Fourthly, the commission has *enforcement* powers.[160] It can request information from the employer, including the matters disclosed by the review and as to affirmative action that has been taken, and it can make recommendations as to the affirmative action to be taken. Where the commission is of the opinion that the employer's monitoring is inadequate, or the employer is not carrying out a satisfactory review, it must use its best endeavours to secure satisfactory written undertakings. If such undertakings are not given, the commission can serve a notice giving directions to the employer; similarly if an undertaking, although given, is not complied with the commission may either serve a directions notice or apply to the tribunal for enforcement of the undertaking. The commission also has power to serve a notice about goals and timetables, against which to measure progress, on an employer who has given an undertaking, or been directed to take action, or has been subject to a tribunal order to take any action.

3.33   Finally, the *sanction of denial of government contracts or financial assistance* may be imposed against defaulting employers (after due notice and an opportunity to appeal).[161] This covers those who are convicted of an offence for failure to register, or to make monitoring returns, or have failed to comply with a tribunal or High Court order. Such an employer may be served with a notice stating that it is not qualified for the purposes of entering into a contract with a public authority to execute any work or supply any goods or services. If the notice is not cancelled after an appeal, no public authority may contract with the unqualified employer,

---

[157] Under the earlier legislation, only employers in public authorities and in registered concerns with more than 250 full-time employees were required to monitor applicants for employment. There was no requirement on any employer to monitor those ceasing to be employed. In addition, the definition of "employee" excluded those working less than 16 hours weekly.

[158] Fair Employment (Monitoring) Regulations (Northern Ireland) 1999, SR 1999, No.148 (replacing old regulations from 1 January 2001).

[159] FETO, art. 55(5).

[160] FETO, arts. 55-61. Under the earlier legislation, the FEC had received 64 formal undertakings, and affirmative action programmes were in place with 137 employers by the end of March 1998: House of Commons Northern Ireland Affair's Committee Fourth Report (1999), para. 48.

[161] FETO, arts. 62-68.

unless the Secretary of State certifies that the work, goods or services are necessary or desirable for the purpose of safeguarding national security or protecting public safety or public order. The commission can enforce this duty against public authorities. Similarly financial assistance may be refused by a Northern Ireland department or withdrawn from a defaulting employer.

3.34   It is too early to review the impact of the amendments made in 1998, but it is clear that the earlier legislation in Northern Ireland has had a significant impact. The House of Commons' Northern Ireland Affairs Committee reported in 1999 that:

> the extent to which employers have complied with the regulatory requirements of the legislation appears to be impressive...The FEC reported a high level of compliance by employers with their statutory duties of monitoring, submitting monitoring returns, and periodically reviewing their employment practices. It also reported that there have been considerable improvements in equality-based employment practices in recent years.[162]

> They reported reductions in employment segregation, in the under-representation of the Catholic community overall and of Protestant and Catholic communities in specific areas, and in the unemployment differential between the communities.[163]

3.35   Our case studies in Northern Ireland (Appendix 1) indicate that the legislation has, in general proved to be acceptable to employers. Our respondents were unanimous in their view that the legislation had made a fundamental difference to equal opportunities. They said that the requirements to monitor and to review employment practices were very important, and that the requirement to take affirmative action had helped them to tackle vested local interests. Employers operating in Britain as well as Northern Ireland contrasted the difference in approach where there was a statutory duty. In Britain "equal opportunities disappeared" as competitive pressures increased. In Northern Ireland, on the other hand, it was "something that had to be done".

3.36   There were, however, some reservations about the costs of compliance. These costs occurred at the outset in setting up the systems, but overall these costs were said to be outweighed by the advantages of monitoring and periodic reviews. At the same time, employers advocated stream-lining of the reporting requirements, for example allowing large corporations to report for the entire group rather than individual concerns. The Northern Ireland Affairs Committee unsuc-cessfully attempted to ascertain the costs of the legislation to employers. They concluded that the evidence was "at best, somewhat anecdotal" and that further research would be necessary before definitive conclusions could be reached.[164] Overall, the Committee found that the earlier legislation had made "an important contribution to improving the degree of fairness of employ-ment in Northern Ireland, even if the precise extent of that contribution cannot be accurately determined."[165]

(3) A scheme for Britain

3.37   There was general support from our respondents for an inclusive, pro-active non-adversarial approach to achieve employment equity or fair participation. The commissions, trade unions and organisations representing those adversely affected by discrimination all favoured a

---

[162] House of Commons Northern Ireland Affairs Committee Fourth Report (1999), para. 48
[163] House of Commons Northern Ireland Affairs Committee Fourth Report (1999), para. 37.
[164] House of Commons Northern Ireland Affairs Committee Fourth Report (1999), para. 50-53.
[165] House of Commons Northern Ireland Affairs Committee Fourth Report (1999), para. 55

positive legal duty on employers in the public and private sectors, in respect of race and sex. There was a difference of opinion among employer respondents as to whether or not this duty should be compulsory. For example, the ORC Equal Employment Opportunity Group, which networks over 35 large private sector companies, informed us that

On the one hand, some companies favour the imposition of a positive duty...[They] recognise that with such a duty in place, employers would be less likely to discriminate or just pay lip service to equality issues. They believe that it would encourage organisations to appreciate fully the business benefits of an inclusive approach to equality...Moreover, it would place an additional accountability responsibility vis-à-vis company shareholders...Those in favour of the imposition of such a duty are, nevertheless uneasy about compulsory monitoring and believe that the cost burden must be considered and in particular, the negative impact on the competitiveness of smaller organisations...On the other hand, those opposing a 'duty', believe that it would lead to more bureaucracy...

3.38   The first lesson which we draw from the North American and Northern Ireland experience is that there will not be significant improvements in the representation of women and ethnic minorities in the workforce without positive action. Unfortunately, positive action has, in the past been taken to mean compulsory monitoring. This focuses the attention of companies on regulatory compliance rather than on the positive action which is needed to change organisational policies and behaviour. Monitoring on its own will not achieve fair participation. The CRE pointed out to us, that "if accompanied by proper analysis of the data and publication of the data, this is a critical first stage in achieving equality of opportunity." While we agree with this, we believe that the legal obligation should be focussed not on compulsory monitoring and reporting to the commission, but rather on a requirement to conduct periodic reviews, and to publicise the results. The objection taken by the Better Regulation Task Force[166] to compulsory monitoring, that this will impose an "additional statutory burden on business", and also the concern expressed by ORC and other employers' groups that there will be disproportionate costs is based on the implicit assumption that the costs of monitoring stand alone and are not part of an action plan which has business benefits. It is to be noted that even the recent deregulatory Equal Opportunity for Women in the Workplace Act 1999 in Australia has retained a statutory duty on employers with 100 or more employees to prepare a workforce profile and analysis, to develop and implement equal employment opportunity for women workplace programmes in consultation with employees or their representatives, and to publish a report about the outcomes. However, the Australian Act does not have an enforcement pyramid of the kind which we regard as crucial.

3.39   It was generally agreed by our respondents that any duty needs to take account of the size and administrative resources of the employer. We canvassed views as to various options. We note that in Australia and Canada there is a threshold of 100 or more employees, in South Africa 50 or more employees, and in Northern Ireland 10 full-time employees The CBI has generally opposed exemptions for small and medium-sized enterprises in respect of employment rights, but argues that any proposals should be built so as to be practical for the majority of businesses and not for only large companies. We have tried to meet this point by making no recommendation for compulsory monitoring, but instead requiring only a periodic review. If there is to be a numbers threshold then, for reasons of consistency in the UK, and in recognition of the arguments for the widest possible coverage of a flexible duty, we recommend that the Northern Ireland threshold of 10 employees should be adopted, but with a statement that in assessing compliance regard should be had to the size and administrative resources of the employer.

---

[166] Better Regulation Task Force (1999), p.23, para. 3(2)(ii). This was supported by the Disability Rights Task Force (1999), paras. 47-48, a recommendation with which RADAR disagreed in their submission to us.

3.40   A second lesson from the USA and Northern Ireland, is the need to avoid unnecessary bureaucratic requirements. Significantly, neither the EOC nor CRE in Britain advocate a requirement on employers to make annual returns to the commission on a prescribed form. Instead, they propose that the information should be reported in the annual report of the company, and to employees, and that it should be supplied to the commission only if requested. The far larger number of employers in Britain (3.7 million businesses) than in Northern Ireland, and the foreseeable lack of resources of the commission in Britain, is likely to mean that the cost of compulsory reporting would not be outweighed by any administrative advantage to the commission. We note that in the USA, the OFCCP uses the data mainly to select for audit those government contractors whose returns show significant under-representation, but that the EEOC uses the data only as a back-up when there is a substantial number of charges against a particular employer. The Vice-Chair of the EEOC told us: "on the whole real stories are more effective than statistics." We have also noted (para.3. 29) the concern in the USA that affirmative action plans have been discredited when turned into a "statistical morass". The main trigger for commission intervention would be complaints from interest groups, in particular employees and their representatives (see below, para. 3.48 about consultation with employee representatives). The sanction for failure to conduct a periodic review would be by allowing this fact to be used as evidence in individual (or representative) proceedings for unlawful discrimination. Those companies which depend upon an "ethical" image may be influenced by adverse publicity, through a power for the commission, after due notice, to "name and shame" a defaulting employer.[167]

Recommendation 28

- Every employer (including an associated employer) with more than 10 employees should be required to conduct a periodical review (once every three years) of its employment practices (affecting recruitment, training, promotion or redundancy) for the purpose of determining whether members of ethnic minorities, women and disabled persons, are enjoying, and are likely to continue to enjoy, fair participation in employment in the undertaking.

- If the employer finds, following such a review, that there is significant under-representation of any group, it should be under a duty draw up and implement an employment equity plan to identify and remove barriers to the recruitment, training and promotion of members of ethnic minorities, women and disabled persons, whether as full-time or part-time employees

- The plan should include provision for such reasonable adjustments as may be necessary to ensure that people from the designated groups achieve a degree of representation in each occupational group and in the employer's workforce that reflects their representation in the national workforce or in those segments of the workforce from which the employer may reasonably be expected to recruit employees

- The employer should not be obliged to take any action which would involve undue hardship to the employer's undertaking, nor to recruit or promote a person who would not be qualified for the job

- This review should be conducted in consultation with interest groups, in particular employees or their representatives, with a view to reaching agreement on the action plan

- The employer should be obliged to disclose information as to the results of the review and of any employment equity plan in the company report, and to employees or their representatives

- The failure of an employer to conduct a periodic review, or, where appropriate, to draw up an employment equity plan, or to disclose information about the review or plan, should be admissible in evidence in any proceedings for unlawful discrimination, and the tribunal should be

[167] See the Australian Equal Opportunity for Women in the Workplace Act, s.19.

entitled to draw an adverse inference from this fact, having regard to the size and administrative resources of the employer

- The commission should have power, after due notice, to publish the fact that an employer has failed to conduct a review or to consult or to draw up and implement an employment equity plan
- The commission should publish a code of practice giving guidance to employers on periodic reviews and employment equity plans
- The commission should have power to require information on the review and action plan, and to make recommendations as to the action to be taken
- Where the commission is of the opinion that the employer's monitoring is unsatisfactory, or the employer is not carrying out a satisfactory review, it should use its best endeavours to secure satisfactory written undertakings
- If such undertakings are not given, the commission should be able to serve a notice giving directions to the employer; similarly if an undertaking, although given, is not complied with the commission should be able either to serve a directions notice or to apply to a tribunal for enforcement of the undertaking
- The commission should also have power to serve a notice about goals and timetables, against which to measure progress, on an employer who has given an undertaking, or been directed to take action, or has been subject to a tribunal order to take any action
- The commission should be able to apply to an employment tribunal to enforce an undertaking or directions, or goals and timetables notice, and the tribunal should have power to make an order specifying the steps to be taken
- In the event of failure to comply with a tribunal order, the tribunal should be able either to certify the failure to the High Court for contempt proceedings, or itself to award a monetary penalty

D. Pay Equity

(1) Introduction

3.41   We have canvassed three main strategies for overcoming the weaknesses in the present law and procedures, relating to equal pay for men and women. The first is that of *pay equity plans*. This concentrates on employers' pay structures and collective agreements, placing a positive duty on employers to provide pay equity, and is designed to remove the gender pay gap over a period of time. The second strategy is that of extending the *basis of comparison and improving the methods of assessing the relative value of jobs*. These are discussed in this chapter. Thirdly, in chapter four we consider *new and improved tribunal procedures* for the enforcement of individual equal pay claims.

(2) EOC and TUC proposals

3.42   The EOC has recommended[168] that:
- employers (with the exception of private households) should be required to monitor their workforce in terms of the gender, job-title or grade, and rates of pay of their employees on at least an annual basis;
- employers should be required to give information obtained via monitoring to employees, employees' representatives and the EOC if it is asked for;

---

[168] EOC (1998b), p. 4.

- the possible penalties for not following these rules should be the subject of detailed consultation; the penalties should be similar to those in other legislation such as the National Minimum Wage Act 1998.

3.43 The EOC has made no proposal for legislation to require pay equity plans following monitoring or for the involvement of workers' representatives in this process. The EOC's code of practice on equal pay provides guidance on how to carry out pay reviews. The equal pay policy in annex A to the code includes a statement that the employer will "discuss and agree the equal pay policy with employees, trade unions or staff representatives where appropriate". However, it does not specifically involve these stakeholders in the monitoring and pay review process. The TUC argues[169] that, in order to develop a partnership between working people and their unions with employers to remove pay inequalities, there should be a statutory duty on employers to inform and consult any trade union recognised either for collective bargaining or for dealing with individual grievances. Where there is no recognised union there should be information and consultation through properly elected independent representatives. Failure to consult would attract the same penalties as under the legislation relating to information and consultation on collective redundancies and business transfers. The TUC proposes that where an employer fails to carry out a pay review, or does so inadequately, an individual, the EOC or a trade union should be able to refer the matter to an employment tribunal, which would be able to impose legally enforceable requirements on the employer to take specified action.

(3) The Ontario Pay Equity Act

3.44 A model of legislation which places a proactive obligation on employers to implement pay equity is the Pay Equity Act 1987 of Ontario. The province of Manitoba and various US municipalities had adopted pay equity programmes some years before Ontario, but the latter was the first jurisdiction to apply such legislation to both public and private sectors. "Pay equity" is defined in the Ontario statute as being achieved when "excluding non gender-related factors which influence pay, work performed by women which is equivalent in value to that performed by men in the same establishment is...paid the same." [170] This is broadly the same as the concept of equal pay for work of equal value in the EC and the UK. However, unlike the Equal Pay Act, the Ontario legislation is not complaints-based, and it places positive obligations on employers to redress systemic discrimination in pay for work performed by women in "female" job classes.[171] Unlike the UK, comparisons are between job classes and not between particular employees. We commissioned Aileen McColgan to write a working paper on the lessons to be drawn for this Act,[172] updating her earlier study.[173] Reference should be made to her paper for a detailed analysis and critique.

(4) Enforcement of pay equity schemes.

3.45 We have proposed (above) that employers should be under a statutory duty to draw up and implement employment equity plans. The case for compulsion is even stronger in respect of

---

[169] TUC (1998), para. 4.8.
[170] Government of Ontario (1985), p. 3.
[171] Pay Equity Act 1987, s.4(1).
[172] Working Paper No.5, November 1999.
[173] McColgan (1997), chap.7.

pay equity than employment equity. Sue Hastings, an expert with much experience in this field, wrote to us:

Unlike issues covered by the sex, race and disability discrimination Acts, such as recruitment, promotion and training, where non-discriminatory policies and procedures are relatively cheap to implement and can be cost-effective through attracting high quality employees in both the advantaged and disadvantaged groups, equal pay legislation is perceived by employers as both expensive to implement and as having only limited compensating gains...Again, unlike the sex, race and disability discrimination Acts, where taking a lead in introducing progressive policies can result in competitive advantage for buyers in the labour market, being the first to implement an equal pay policy is perceived as resulting only in competitive disadvantage through higher labour costs...This is confirmed by the reluctance of employers in many countries whatever the approach to pay equity legislation to move from unequal to equal pay; and their willingness to take litigation to extreme levels to avoid, or at least defer, implementation

This, she says, indicates the need "for a multi-faceted legal approach to equal pay, which helps with the educational and negotiating objectives of the legislation as much as improving procedures for litigation." We agree with this approach, which would support the EOC's "Valuing Women" campaign.

3.46   We propose a three-stage process. The first stage would be for the employer to conduct a periodic pay audit, identifying "male" and "female" job classes within the same employment, evaluating those classes and seeking male job classes of equal value to each female job class. This would follow the Ontario approach in identifying job classes rather than making comparisons between particular individuals. So a predominantly female job class (e.g. home helps, secretaries or nurses) could be compared with predominantly male classes of equal value (e.g. porters, clerks, etc.). The results of the audit would be reported in the company's report, and to employees or their representatives. The commission should also have the power to obtain this information on request. In the event of failure or refusal to conduct an audit or to make disclosure the commission should have power to "name and shame" the employer. In addition, the failure or refusal to conduct a pay audit and provide information is a fact which an employment tribunal should be required to consider, and from which it may draw an adverse inference of pay discrimination, in any individual (or representative) equal pay proceedings, having regard to the size and administrative resources of the employer.

3.47   The second stage would be to draw up a pay equity plan, designed to bring pay rates of female job classes into line with those of comparable male job classes. The plan could provide for such adjustments to be phased in gradually, if necessary over a period of years, having regard to the employer's economic circumstances and the seriousness of the disparity. There would be a code of practice, issued by the commission, with detailed guidance on these matters.

3.48   In keeping with our general approach (para. 3.5), we regard the participation of employees or their representatives as an essential feature of both employment and pay equity. The case for employee participation in general, and collective bargaining in particular, is forcefully made in Aileen McColgan's paper, and also in an important study by the European Foundation for the Improvement of Living and Working Conditions, on *Equal Opportunities and Collective Bargaining in Europe* (1998). Their arguments will not be repeated here. If the arguments are accepted, then a series of technical questions arise. A union may seek recognition for purposes of collective bargaining on pay under the provisions of Schedule A1 to TULRCA 1992 (as inserted by the ERA 1999), and we can see no reason why this should not include questions of pay equity. However, negotiated moves towards pay equity may be frustrated where an employer refuses to negotiate with a union recognised for purposes of pay bargaining on the subject of pay equity. We propose that there should be a provision that when bargaining over pay an employer and recognised union shall have due regard to the need to promote equal pay for men and women doing work of equal value. Moreover, on the analogy of provisions which require consultation on collective redundancies and business transfers, we propose that, in the absence of a recognised union, there should be a duty to consult elected employee representatives on pay equity plans with a view to reaching a workforce agreement. For this purpose we would define "workforce agreement" in a similar way to that in the Maternity and Parental Leave Regulations 1999, sched.1, and in the Working Time Regulations 1998, sched.1. The terms of a collective agreement or workforce agreement relating to equal pay would be incorporated into the contracts of employment of all relevant employees. The minimum (or default) contractual right of an employee to equal pay for work of equal value (as currently embodied in s.1 of the Equal Pay Act) would apply where there was no collective agreement or workforce agreement

3.49   The recognised union, or employee representatives, or the commission should be able to refer to the Central Arbitration Committee (CAC) a dispute concerning a pay equity plan. The CAC would have power to make an arbitration award including a scheme for the phasing in of pay equity. The award would become a mandatory term of the contracts of employment of the relevant employees in place of the minimum (default) right (see para.3.48 above). We believe that it would be appropriate for the CAC, rather than an employment tribunal, to deal with these consultation and negotiation issues, and to make an arbitration award. The CAC has recently been given jurisdiction in respect of recognition claims, and has long experience in dealing with collective pay issues. The CAC's former role (under the repealed s.3 of the Equal Pay Act) to strike out discriminatory provisions in collective agreements and pay structures could also usefully be restored and updated. Moreover, if at some future date, a procedure for extension of pay equity awards were to be instituted (an issue which we leave open), the CAC would be the natural body for this role. It would be essential for the members of a CAC panel to have experience and training in job evaluation and equal pay matters.

3.50   The third stage would be application of the agreement. If the employer failed to comply with the terms of a collective agreement or workforce agreement or CAC award on pay equity, individual employees could bring proceedings in an employment tribunal for breach of this term as incorporated in the individual contract of employment. The commission or a trade union would be able to bring a representative action in certain circumstances (see para. 4.24-25).

Recommendation 29

- Employers with more than ten full-time employees should be obliged to conduct a periodic pay audit (once every three years),covering both full- and part-time employees, and to publish this in the company's report, and to inform employees or their representatives and, on request, the commission
- The failure of an employer to conduct an audit or to disclose, should be admissible in evidence in any proceedings for unlawful discrimination, and the tribunal should be entitled to draw an adverse inference from this fact, having regard to the size and administrative resources of the employer
- The commission should have power, after due notice, to publish the fact that an employer has failed to conduct a pay audit or to disclose
- If, following an audit, the employer finds a significant disparity between predominantly female and predominantly male job classes, it should be obliged to draw up a pay equity plan in negotiation with recognised trade unions with a view to reaching a collective agreement, or where no

union is recognised in respect of pay, after consultation with a view to reaching a workforce agreement with employees or their representatives

- When bargaining on pay, the employer and recognised union should have due regard to the need to promote equal pay for work of equal value for men and women
- The minimum (default) contractual right of an employee to equal pay for work of equal value should apply where there is no collective agreement or workforce agreement on the subject
- There should be the possibility of CAC arbitration in the event of a dispute, and the CAC should have power to award a pay equity plan, which should operate in the same way as a collective agreement or workforce agreement
- Individual employees should be able to bring proceedings in an employment tribunal for breach of a collective agreement or workforce agreement or CAC award relating to equal pay
- The CAC should have power to strike out or amend provisions in collective or workforce agreements or employer's pay structures which are directly or indirectly discriminatory

(5) Relationship of pay equity plan to individual right

3.51 There were different views among our consultees as to the effect, if any, which a pay equity plan should have on claims by individuals enforcing their right to equal pay. Two main views were expressed: (1) the employer should be given a defence as against individual claims in respect of back pay, which arise by virtue of the pay equity process, as distinct from claims that the process is flawed; (2) there should be a moratorium on equal pay claims during the reasonable duration of the audit (perhaps registered with the CAC) and by the incentive of a negotiated phasing-in of any pay increases resulting from the exercise.

3.52 We doubt whether, as a matter of EC law, it would be possible to deny individuals their right to back pay for work of equal value (which on recent authority may be for up to 6 years). At the same time it is necessary to provide an incentive to employers to negotiate pay equity plans because in the long term this is the most effective way of guaranteeing equal pay. An analogy may be drawn with the rights of employees in respect of working-time and also in respect of parental leave, where EC law allows contracting-out through a collective agreement or workforce agreement. It is not clear how far a similar exception would be permitted under present EC law in respect of the right to equal pay. In our view, it would be possible to argue that such an exception is legitimate and it would then be for the tribunal or court in a particular case to determine whether the period of phasing-in was appropriate and necessary. Our proposals for collective agreements, workforce agreements and CAC awards (above) provide a possible solution. Where the collective agreement or workforce agreement is alleged to be directly or indirectly discriminatory against a certain groups of women, they will be able to apply to the CAC to strike out or amend those provisions (para. 3.49).

Recommendation 30

- It should be possible to contract-out of the individual's right to equal pay by collective agreement or workforce agreement in respect of a defined and reasonable period so far as is appropriate and necessary to allow the employer time to absorb the costs of implementation of an agreed pay equity plan
- A CAC pay equity award should operate in the same way as a collective agreement or workforce agreement

(6) Pay comparisons

3.53   In her review of the Ontario legislation, Aileen McColgan found that the problem of "comparatorless" female job classes – stemming from the requirement for job to job comparisons between those employed within the county, territorial district or regional municipality by the same employer - had served to reduce very substantially, the overall impact of the Pay Equity Act.[174] In 1993 amendments were made to the Act to address the problem of predominantly female workplaces. Two new methods of comparison, supplementary to the job-to-job approach were adopted. The first was that of "proportional value" comparisons. These were designed, in effect, to allow female job classes which were rated as (say) 90 percent as valuable as the nearest male comparator, but were paid only (say) 70 percent of the wage to improve their wages.[175] Secondly, "proxy" adjustments required the comparison of wages between different employers, but this could be used only as a last resort on the order of the Pay Equity Commission and was limited to the public sector. Public sector funding for proxy adjustments was made available only in 1999, and then capped at a level far below that needed to fund the adjustments.

3.54   The first lesson which McColgan draws from the Ontario experience is that some method is needed in order to measure the extent to which female jobs are undervalued, but that this should not be limited to those female jobs for which there happens to exist an equivalently valuable male job class. The proportional value approach would avoid some of the difficulties connected with the absence of a male comparator class. Under the Equal Pay Act[176] and EC law[177] a woman's claim can succeed only if her work is of equal value or more than equal value to that of a man's job. It appears, however, that EC law permits an employer to justify a difference in pay for work of equal value only to the extent that the difference is attributable to factors which are not related to sex, and this would in effect require proportional pay.[178]

Recommendation 31

- The principle of proportionality in relation to the defence of objective justification for a difference in pay between men and women should be codified, by providing that a difference in pay for work of equal value is justified only to the extent that the difference is attributable to factors which are not related to sex

3.55   A second lesson from the Ontario experience is that, for those workplaces which are so overwhelmingly female that no comparison can be made, a "proxy" approach could achieve significant improvements in pay for some of the lowest-paid female jobs. The Equal Pay Act provides that a woman can compare her job with that of a man "in the same employment", and this means that they must have the same employer or an associated employer.[179] However, EC law is wider allowing a comparison of those employed in the same "establishment or service". This has been held by the EAT to allow comparisons between public sector organisations which fall outside the scope of the Equal Pay Act because they are not "associated employers" in the company law sense of a company controlled by another.[180] If this ruling were to apply to

---

[174] Working Paper No.5, para. 2.11- 2.12.

[175] For details see Working Paper No.5, paras. 2.13 to 2.19, and McColgan (1997), pp. 312-16.

[176] s.1(2)(c).

[177] *Murphy v Bord Telecom Eireann* [1988] IRLR 267,ECJ.

[178] *Enderby v Frenchay Health Authority* [1993] IRLR 591, ECJ, C-127/92; and see comment in EOR (1993), p. 43.

[179] s.1(6).

[180] *Scullard v Knowles* [1996] IRLR 344, EAT, which appears to have been somewhat restricted in *Lawrence v Regent Office Care Ltd* [1999] IRLR 148, EAT.

pay equity plans, there would need to be an accompanying commitment of public expenditure to fund it.

Recommendation 32

- The definition of "same employment" should be clarified so as to conform to EC law, by including any employment by the same employer or by an associated employer or by any other employer who forms part of the same public service

3.56   The present limitation of comparisons between two or more establishment of the same employer to those at which there are "common terms and conditions of employment" has given rise to many difficulties of interpretation. The House of Lords has forestalled attempts by employers to avoid equal pay by segregating women in different establishments from men,[181] and has now given such a broad definition of "common terms" [182] that it is difficult to see what purpose is served by this requirement. When a comparison is made between different establishments of the same employer, it is still open to the employer to justify objectively a difference of pay, for example on grounds of different geographical location, local market forces and so on.

Recommendation 33

- An employer should be obliged to achieve pay equity at the level of the entire undertaking, rather than within a particular establishment or establishments as at present, subject to the general defence of objective justification

3.57   Our consultations indicate that in this country there would not be general support for proxy adjustments requiring the comparison of pay between different employers. This approach was described to us by a leading equal pay expert as "unnecessarily aggressive and to raise dangers of inadvertently introducing pay anomalies, where proxy pay line comparisons are used for female-dominated groups." She points out that "this could make the approach unacceptable to male employees and to trade unions, who, in my view, are essential to negotiating pay equity." Aileen McColgan[183] has suggested the possibility of an "extension" procedure along the lines of the repealed Schedule 11 to the Employment Protection Act 1975, so as to enable the CAC to extend the benefits of pay equity from those workplaces in which comparisons were possible to those which by virtue of their size and/or predominantly female workforce, were not. While we see merits in an extension procedure as a means of reducing inequality, we do not believe that this can be introduced by way of amendment to equal pay legislation. It raises wider questions as to the extension of pay agreements and awards, which need to be addressed in any future review of employment law.

3.58   We received a number of submissions which expressed concern that public sector bodies could avoid their pay equity obligations when they contract-out services staffed predominantly by women, such as school meals and cleaning. Prior to contracting-out there may well have been a job evaluation comparing the contracted-out jobs with in-house jobs. If that job evaluation has already been completed and the contracting-out amounts to a transfer of an undertaking, within the scope of the Council Directive 77/187/EEC relating to acquired rights on business transfers, then the pay of the transferred workers will be safeguarded. On 7 January 2000, the Cabinet Office issued *A Statement of Practice on Staff Transfers in the Public Sector*. This sets out the

---

[181] *Leverton v Clwyd County Council* [1989] IRLR 28, HL.
[182] *British Coal Corpn v Smith* [1996] IRLR 404, HL.
[183] Working Paper No.5, para. 3.6.

policy that in the public sector, public/private partnerships and contracting exercises (including retendering) will be conducted on the basis that staff will transfer and TUPE will apply unless there are genuinely exceptional reasons for it not to. The Government has also issued draft guidance on *Best Value and Procurement*[184] which states that TUPE will apply to staff transfers under Best Value. Although the situation needs to be kept under review, we see no need to make a recommendation.

3.59 The most obvious methodology for establishing pay equity is job evaluation. Our consultees pointed out, however, that job evaluation is problematic: it was developed to replicate the (discriminatory) market rates of the early 1950s in Britain; it usually reproduces existing organisational hierarchies, imposing new grading and pay structures on this; and management consultants have a vested interested in defending their own off-the-shelf schemes. It was alleged that a number of job evaluation schemes have discriminatory features. However, there is now a great deal of understanding as to how traditional job evaluation schemes may indirectly discriminate against women. The EC code of practice on the implementation of equal pay for work of equal value (1996) provides a particularly significant set of guidelines in this respect. There is evidence that this code is beginning to have an impact on tribunal decisions. Moreover, there are now several important job evaluation systems in the public and private sectors.

Recommendation 34

- The EOC code of practice on equal pay should be revised, simplified, and expanded in the light of recent experience
- There should be encouragement to review existing job evaluation schemes against the EC code, the EOC guidelines on good equal opportunities practice in analytical job evaluation and other sources
- Chairmen and members of employment tribunals (and, if our proposals in Recommendation 29 are accepted members of the CAC), who hear equal value claims, should receive training in the nature of job evaluation schemes

3.60 We have received anecdotal evidence of the abuse of job evaluation schemes. This is said to arise when employers buy "off-the-shelf" schemes from management consultants so as to have a technical defence to an equal value claim. We have had evidence that this is encouraged by section 2A(2) of the Equal Pay Act which allows an employer to raise a preliminary defence that there are "no reasonable grounds" for proceeding with an equal value claim because there is already a completed job evaluation scheme.

Recommendation 35

- Section 2A(2) of the Equal Pay Act should be repealed. An existing scheme should be admissible and relevant evidence in determining whether the work is of equal value, but it should not be conclusive

E. Contract and subsidy compliance

(1) Meaning

3.61 We received a number of submissions, both to our initial consultation exercise and to the consultation paper, supporting the use of contract and subsidy compliance as an incentive to

---

[184] DETR (2000).

promote equal opportunities. The Better Regulation Task Force[185] has urged the Government to promote equality practices among contractors and suppliers to the public sector. There is no agreed or precise definition of what this means, largely because of the many and varied forms which it can take. Broadly speaking, it involves the use of the purchasing power of public authorities, and their power to make subsidies, as a means of promoting social or industrial objectives unconnected with the primary purpose of obtaining goods and services or supporting economic activities on the best possible commercial terms. At one end there are those who favour a requirement to promote equal opportunities, at all stages of the contracting or grants process from approved lists and invitations to tender, through contractual conditions and termination. At the other end, there are those who would restrict its use to that of an additional sanction for persistent or recalcitrant unlawful conduct. Similar techniques are sometimes proposed in respect of licensing and franchising arrangements. The social goals, which may include the promotion of equal opportunities, are sometimes referred to as "secondary" policies, although in some cases the primary purpose of the contract or subsidy may be a social one, such as helping a workplace for disabled persons.[186]

(2) Practice in Britain

3.62   There is a long history of contract compliance to achieve fair labour standards in the UK, starting even before the Fair Wages Resolutions of 1891 which was extended and applied by central government departments until removed by the Conservative Government in 1983.[187] Since 1969 a term has been included in government contracts requiring contractors to refrain from unlawful racial discrimination, and to ensure that their servants, agents and sub-contractors observe this requirement, but compliance with this clause is not monitored and no contract has ever been terminated for a breach of it. Most local authorities had contract conditions relating to working conditions of those employed on procurement contracts, until this was halted by the Local Government Act 1988. In the early 1980s a number of local authorities had utilised contract compliance specifically to promote equal opportunities. The contract conditions were of two types, those which required compliance by contractors with race and sex discrimination legislation and the accompanying codes of practice, and those (relatively limited in number) which went further imposing political conditions, such as not doing business with South Africa. The period for which these operated was relatively short and, not surprisingly, there is no reliable evidence as to their impact, if any.[188]

3.63   Section 17 of the 1988 Act- introduced at the same time as compulsory competitive tendering (CCT)- prohibited local authorities and certain other specified bodies[189] in England and Wales from having reference to "non-commercial matters" in respect of certain procurement functions.[190] The list of "non-commercial matters" included a number of workforce matters, namely, "the terms and conditions of employment by contractors of their workers or the composition of, the arrangements for the promotion, transfer or training of or other opportunities afforded to, their workforce".[191] In the *Islington* case[192] it was held that a contract condi-

---

[185] (1999), pp. 25-26.

[186] Arrowsmith (1995), p. 235 n.1.

[187] Hepple (1970), at pp. 276-81; Bercusson (1978); Carr (1987).

[188] Morris (1990), p. 93.

[189] LGA 1988, sched.2. This includes police and fire authorities.

[190] These functions are listed in LGA 1988, s.17(4), and includes (1) decisions relating to approval for contracts, approved lists for tenders etc; decisions relating to the award of specific contracts; and (3) decisions relating to a subsisting contract.

[191] s.17(5).

[192] *R v London Borough of Islington, ex p. Building Employers' Confederation* [1989] IRLR 382.

tion requiring compliance with obligations under the SDA contravened section 17. There was an exception, under section 18, relating to race relations. This allowed local authorities (1) to ask firms applying for entry to lists of tenderers six approved questions about the steps they take to avoid unlawful racial discrimination and to promote equal opportunities for racial minorities, and assess the answers (the "approved questions arrangement"); and (2) include in a draft contract, or draft tender for a contract, terms or provisions relating to steps designed to achieve equal employment opportunities for racial minorities and to consider the responses of contractors in relation to such terms.[193] This exception was made because of the duty placed on local authorities by section 71 of the RRA to eliminate unlawful discrimination and to promote equality of opportunity between persons of different racial groups. Arguably, although section 18 limits the way in which authorities may exercise their powers, the duty under section 71 of the RRA obliges authorities to consider race relations matters in exercising their procurement function.[194] There are no other exceptions in respect of equal opportunities, although attempts were made during the passage of the DDA to allow contract compliance in respect of disabled persons.

3.64 These restrictions will be modified as a result of the new "best value" regime introduced in England and Wales by the Local Government Act 1999 and in Scotland by voluntary means. This abolishes CCT and subjects most local authorities to new arrangements for the achievement of "best value" in the performance of their functions, including procurement. "Best value" is defined as "arrangements to secure continuous improvement in the way in which its functions are exercised, having regard to a combination of economy, efficiency and fairness".[195] At the time of writing, the Government is proposing to make a statutory instrument under section 19 of the 1999 Act, so as to provide for specified workforce matters to cease to be "non-commercial" matters. Draft guidance on the handling of workforce matters (including equal opportunities) was published in April 2000.[196] The draft guidance in respect of equal opportunities is vague and unsatisfactory. It says that "tenderers can be excluded from the tendering exercise if they have been breaking the law or have been found guilty of grave misconduct" but it does not specify what this means in relation to equal opportunities legislation. The draft guidance goes on to say that pre-qualification inquiries should not be made that exceed what is permitted under European procurement rules, but fails to specify what those rules permit. Authorities are told that where the service requires particular qualities of the staff they should "address these matters in output terms as part of the specification (i.e. how the bidder would meet the needs of a particular community group), not in terms of the composition of the contractor's workforce," but the implications are not spelt out. It is said that nothing in the statutory instrument will affect the ability of best value authorities to ask the approved questions in relation to race relations allowed under section 18 of the 1988 Act, but there is no guidance as to whether similar questions can now be raised in relation to sex or disability discrimination.

3.65 A radical change in present government practice is likely to come from the proposed positive duty on public authorities to promote equal opportunities and to eliminate unlawful discrimination. The Race Relations (Amendment) Bill, currently before Parliament, will impose this duty on specified authorities in respect of racial discrimination. At the time of writing, it is not known whether the functions of the specified authorities will be limited in a way which excludes procurement. We note that no such restriction has been made under the Northern

[194] Arrowsmith (1996), p. 839.
[195] LGA 1999, s.3(1).
[196] DETR (2000), paras. 30-35.

Ireland Act. In view of the ambiguity of the present situation, it is necessary for us to consider the situation in Northern Ireland, the objections and justifications for contract and subsidy compliance, and the limitations imposed by EC procurement rules before making specific proposals.

(3) Northern Ireland

3.66   The FEA 1989 used disqualification from government contracts and grants as a final sanction against an employer who was acting contrary to the provisions of the legislation. These provisions are now contained in sections 62 to 68 of the FETO 1998. The Equality Commission (formerly the FEC) may serve a notice on an employer who is in "default" stating that the employer is not qualified to be considered for contracts awarded by Northern Ireland government departments or to execute work or supply goods or services to them. The employer is in default where it has been convicted of an offence for failing to register or provide returns or has been subject to a penalty for failing to comply with an order of the Fair Employment Tribunal or High Court. The Commission has to bring to disqualification to the attention of public authorities, which are prohibited from contracting with the disqualified party and in some cases must take all reasonable steps to ensure that no work is done on the contract by a disqualified party. The legislation also empowers a Northern Ireland department to refuse to give a disqualified person specific types of financial assistance, or to refuse or cease to make payments under any assistance. There is, however, no provision for terminating existing contracts.

3.67   The House of Commons Northern Ireland Affairs Committee reported that "these provisions appear to have had very little impact in practice".[197] One employer was temporarily disqualified but subsequently came into compliance. Some of those whom we interviewed in Northern Ireland informed us, at the end of 1999, that the provisions have not been regarded as important, because of the wide powers which the Commission has to enforce the reporting and other requirements of the fair employment legislation against all relevant employers. Attention is now focussed on the introduction of the best value regime in Northern Ireland, and also on equality schemes which public authorities will be obliged to prepare under the Northern Ireland Act 1998. It is anticipated that these will include criteria on public procurement. In 1997, the SACHR adapted earlier EOC proposals[198] to recommend broadening the scope of contract compliance, linking access to contracts and grants to the promotion of affirmative action and fair participation measures by employers.[199] The SACHR also proposed significant changes to strengthen the sanctions against defaulting employers. The Government largely rejected these proposals.[200] The House of Commons Northern Ireland Affairs Select Committee has, however, asked the Government to reconsider this.[201]

(4) Objections and justifications

3.68   The Government has rejected proposals for wider use of contract compliance in Britain and in Northern Ireland, on the ground that this "runs counter to the spirit of market liberalisation in

---

[197] House of Commons Northern Ireland Affairs Committee Fourth Report (1999), para. 93.
[198] Equal Opportunities Commission for Northern Ireland (1996).
[199] Standing Advisory Commission on Human Rights (1997), pp. 90-91.
[200] Northern Ireland Office (1998), paras. 5.25-5.27.
[201] House of Commons Northern Ireland Affairs Committee Fourth Report (1999), para. 101

public procurement which has been promoted by the European Union and the UK Government."[202] The Government's policy is "that all public procurement is to be based on value for money having due regard to propriety and regularity".[203] Within this policy and the legal framework for procurement, government departments are able to reject suppliers on grounds of "impropriety", such as conviction of a criminal offence or having committed an act of gross misconduct, to the extent that this is allowed by the EC law (below).

3.69   Objection has also been raised to contract compliance on the constitutional ground that it is not legitimate to impose an obligation on only one group of violators, namely government contractors. This argument has not been accepted in the USA. There it has been held that the Executive Order is lawful on the basis of implied Congressional authority. This authority was more or less assumed on the ground that it is clearly in the interests of economic efficiency that Government has "the largest possible pool of qualified manpower...available for the accomplishment of its projects."[204] In other words, the efficiency argument can be used to argue, as the DETR does in Circular 10/99 (above para.6.4), that a positive and effective approach to equal opportunities is appropriate and necessary in order to get the best from staff and to maximise the potential of the labour market.

3.70   A number of justifications in addition to "value for money" or efficiency have also been put forward.[205] These include the moral ground that the Government should not allow contracts and grants to be used to subsidise discrimination, that contract compliance is a more effective means of combatting discrimination than orthodox complaints-based mechanisms, that it fosters fair competition or a level playing-field by requiring all contractors to observe certain minimum requirements, and that it can produce tangible benefits for companies of the kind identified by US employers in our survey.

(5) Restrictions under EC law

3.71   Contract compliance in respect of equal opportunities does have to work within the important restrictions which result from the EC Treaty and directives on procurement and utilities, as well as from the WTO Agreement on Government Procurement (GPA). For example, in August 1994 the Conservative Government was led to abandon the "Priority Suppliers Scheme" which gave preferential treatment to workshops for disabled persons on the ground that this contravened EC law. A more limited policy was subsequently introduced confined to contracts below the threshold levels prescribed by the directives and which is open to workshops from other Member States. The restrictions are complex and uncertain and it is not possible, within the scope of this report, to analyse them.[206]

3.72   The Government is pressing the European Commission to simplify and clarify the principles under which social policies can be taken into account in the procurement process, consistent with EC law. However, we believe that it can be stated with some certainty that equal opportu-

---

[202] Northern Ireland Office (1998), para. 5.25

[203] Better Regulation Task Force (1999), para.20; cf DfEE (2000), Recommendation 31 which advocates favouring ethnic minority business and local people. including people from ethnic minority communities in government procurement. The legality of this under EU procurement rules is dubious. (see below,para.3.69).

[204] *Contractors Association of Eastern Pennsylvania v Secretary of Labor* 442 F2d 159 (3rd Cir.,1970), *cert den* 404 US 854; Morris (1990), pp. 135-137.

[205] Morris (1990), at pp. 87-90.

[206] See generally, Arrowsmith (1995), at pp. 248-282; (1996), pp. 815-830.

nities policies will meet the requirements of EC law and the GPA provided that care is taken to avoid direct or indirect discrimination between suppliers from other Member States. Arrowsmith[207] points out the risks involved in requiring contractors to adhere to UK legislation and codes of practice. These may favour UK firms which are more familiar with these requirements. It might, therefore, be necessary to limit observance to the employment of workers within the UK. This would apply as well to workers posted to the UK by undertakings established in another Member State.[208] If the proposed EC directives on discrimination, under Article 13 of the EC Treaty, come into force, some of the difficulties will be overcome by requiring adherence to the EC-wide standards.

3.73   A more serious obstacle to contract compliance comes from the procedures imposed by the EC procurement and utilities directives and the GPA which appear to prevent public authorities from debarring contractors on policy grounds unless they have been convicted of an offence involving professional conduct or, short of a conviction, have been guilty of "grave" professional misconduct. (The Northern Ireland legislation satisfies this by making exclusion depend upon a conviction.) Arguably, a finding of unlawful discrimination would constitute "grave misconduct". The directives provide that where an authority gives information in the contract about applicable working conditions, it must require tenderers to state that they have taken these into account. It appears[209] that this allows exclusion of those who have not done so, or who appear incapable of complying with the conditions. It seems clear that the "applicable" conditions would include the standards imposed by legislation and, probably codes of practice. If a positive legal duty to promote equal opportunities were established, then presumably this too would be part of the "applicable" conditions.

(6) Proposals

3.74   The first conclusion which we draw from this analysis is that if a positive duty to promote equal opportunities and to eliminate unlawful discrimination is imposed on public authorities, this should include the "functions" of procurement, grant and subsidy, licensing and franchising. It would defeat the object if a public authority could avoid the positive duty simply by outsourcing. If the positive duty were not applied to all these functions there would not be a level playing field between in-house and outside providers.

3.75   Secondly, the positive duty on public authorities to promote equal opportunities can be reconciled with the legislative requirement of "best value" and the Government's "value for money" approach. Achieving equal opportunities is efficient in the sense that it enables public authorities to ensure the best possible use of the labour market. The costs of compliance must, however, be kept to a minimum by reducing unnecessary burdens on authorities and contractors. This can best be done by including equal opportunities considerations among the core performance indicators and performance standards to be met by best value authorities. The normal system of best value reviews, performance plans, audit and inspections would apply to equal opportunities matters.

3.76   Thirdly, the US experience (paras. 3.21 to 3.27) indicates that the key conditions for effectiveness of a contract compliance strategy are: (1) a requirement that contractors take positive

---

[207] (1996), p. 821.
[208] Under Council Directive 96/71/EC concerning the posting of workers in the framework of the provision of services, art. 3(f) of which expressly includes "equality of treatment between men and women and other provisions of non-discrimination".
[209] Arrowsmith (1995), at pp. 273-274.

action to achieve equal opportunities; (2) a system of compliance review or audit by an expert independent agency; (3) the power to impose sanctions for non-compliance; and (4) due process (i.e. a fair hearing) for contractors whom it is proposed to penalise. On the other hand, a contract compliance strategy is likely to be ineffective if: (1) it is limited to a negative prohibition on unlawful discrimination, particularly if the possibility of any sanction is remote; or (2) over- reliance is placed on numerical standards, rather than on encouraging and assisting contractors to achieve standards or targets, which are flexibly interpreted and applied.

3.77   Finally, the limitations imposed by EC law need to be clarified and simplified. In particular, they are unduly restrictive in appearing to allow disbarment or non-selection of contractors only where there has conviction of a criminal offence or grave misconduct. In any event, it ought to be made clear that failure to observe the requirements of equality legislation and codes of practice can constitutes "grave" misconduct. A contractor who is threatened with disbarment or non-selection or termination on this ground should be provided with a hearing before an employment tribunal before such a sanction is imposed.

Recommendation 36

- The positive duty on specified public authorities to promote equality and eliminate unlawful discrimination should apply to their procurement, grant and subsidy, licensing and franchising functions
- Equality standards should be included among the core performance indicators for the purposes of compliance with the duty to secure best value
- The normal system of best value reviews, audit and inspection should include measures for fair participation and fair access, and in addition, the commission should be able to make inquiries and request information, and, where an authority has failed to take appropriate steps to comply, the commission should be able to apply to a tribunal for an appropriate order
- The "approved questions arrangement", with suitable amendments, should be applied to all grounds of unlawful discrimination
- Contractors should be excluded from approved lists, not invited to tender, not selected against competing bids and be liable to have their contracts terminated, if they have been found by an employment tribunal, after a fair hearing, to have committed gross misconduct, including persistent discrimination or any other serious breach of equality legislation
- The UK Government should press the European Commission for a less restrictive approach to contractual obligations to achieve equal opportunities, and for a clarification and simplification of the EC rules in this respect.

CHAPTER FOUR

MAKING PROCEDURES AND REMEDIES
MORE EFFECTIVE

4.1   In chapter two we stated the principle that *individuals should be free to seek redress for the harm they have suffered as a result of unlawful discrimination, through procedures which are fair, inexpensive and expeditious, and that the remedies should be effective.* This chapter considers the extent to which present procedures and remedies meet this objective and how they could be improved.

A. Specialisation and training

(1) A specialist division?

4.2   Both the CRE and the EOC have, for many years, advocated greater specialisation among chairmen of tribunals, on the grounds that familiarity with the ways in which discrimination occurs and a proper understanding of this complex branch of law is necessary. The CRE proposed in its *Second Review of the Race Relations Act 1976* that a "Discrimination Division" within the (then) industrial tribunal system should be set up to hear both employment and non-employment cases. This would be similar to the Fair Employment Tribunal in Northern Ireland. The EOC recommended in 1998 that sex, race and disability discrimination and equal pay cases should be heard by tribunal chairmen drawn from lists of specialists in discrimination law.[210]

4.3   We commissioned research by the EOC into the extent of experience tribunal chairmen had in hearing sex discrimination claims in Britain in the period between January 1996 and June 1999. The research examined the number of cases heard by each chairman and the percentage of those cases which were successful. Using data from the CRE database, we conducted a similar analysis of tribunal chairmen's experience of hearing race discrimination cases in Britain between 1996 and 1999.

4.4   The analysis indicates that in practice there already is a level of specialisation in discrimination cases by employment tribunal chairmen in England, Wales and Scotland. Fifteen per cent of chairmen heard 40% of sex discrimination cases. Similarly 17% of chairmen heard 50% of the race discrimination cases. At the other end, 54% of chairmen heard less than one sex discrimination case a year. In cases of race discrimination almost 60% of the chairmen heard an average of one or fewer race discrimination cases per year. Thus a small number of chairmen, through hearing such a large proportion of the cases have built up experience and in effect specialisation of hearing discrimination cases.[211] On the other hand, a high proportion of

---

[210] EOC (1998b), p. 12.
[211] These findings are similar to those made by the EOC in its 1998 report, which reviewed some 2000 sex discrimination and equal pay cases decided by tribunals in England from July 1991 to December 1996, see EOC (1998b), p. 12.

chairmen have heard very few race and sex cases. The concentration of relatively few chairmen to some extent reflects the current practice in nearly all English regions that a chairman sitting in discrimination case is either a full-time chairman or a part-time chairman who has completed the national residential training course known as refresher one. This is usually about two years after initial appointment. The course includes extensive discrimination training. There are occasional exceptions for chairmen who already have practical experience in this field. In Scotland, only full-time chairmen sit on these cases. In English regions there would be logistical difficulties in assembling suitable tribunals if only full-time chairmen could be used.

4.5   We examined the data (tables 4.1 and 4.2.) to see if there was a correlation between the experience of tribunal chairmen and the success rate of cases. There were 273 chairmen who heard 1811 race discrimination cases and 281 chairmen who heard 1786 sex discrimination cases in this period. We noted two things of importance. First, the overall success rate in race discrimination cases (15.9%) was just half the success rate in sex discrimination cases (32%). Secondly, generally speaking, though not without exception, fewer cases heard by chairmen with little experience were successful. In race cases, only 8.7% of cases heard by a chairman hearing less than 5 cases were successful, as compared to the overall success rate of 15.9%. In sex discrimination cases, 29.3% of cases heard by a chairman hearing less than five cases were successful compared to the overall success rate of 32%. This is, of course, only one indicator because the quality of the decision is not to be measured by a successful outcome for the applicant. The performance indicator is whether there was a fair hearing in which the tribunal drew legitimate inferences and correctly applied the law. This cannot be measured by these statistics.

4.6   A number of reasons have been advanced for not going further along the path of specialised tribunals. First, it is becoming increasingly rare for a complainant to confine an application to discrimination only. Other claims such as unfair dismissal, breach of contract or redundancy payments are frequently added. A tribunal needs to be able deal with all these issues in the same proceedings. We were told by a group of employment lawyers in Northern Ireland that lengthy delays are caused by the system there of giving priority to the FET which hears fair employment claims (e.g. the FET cannot deal with equal pay claims which have to go to an ET). They could see no point in maintaining a specialist tribunal, and, instead favoured specialisation among all tribunal chairmen. A second reason for avoiding specialist tribunals strongly advanced from within the tribunals is, in the words of the President, that "a diet of hearing only discrimination cases could eventually cause a rather weary approach from the tribunal – the chairmen and members lacking the stimulation of hearing cases involving a wide variety of issues." The Bar Council's Sex Discrimination Committee said that "specialised full-time discrimination chairmen may become jaded or develop a reputation as being routinely pro-employer or pro-employee".

(2) Training of chairmen

4.7   There is, however, general support for the current practice of assigning cases to a chairman who has experience or the requisite training. In responding to the consultation paper the EOC commented that "until chairmen hearing discrimination cases become consistently well trained across Great Britain, individual applicants will receive different 'levels of justice' depending on where they live, a situation which is clearly unacceptable". It is therefore important that training should be conducted primarily at national level. With the majority of cases being heard by a relatively small number of chairmen, refresher training may be more effective and

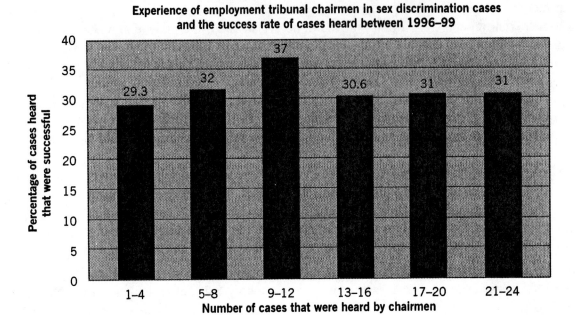

Table 4.1

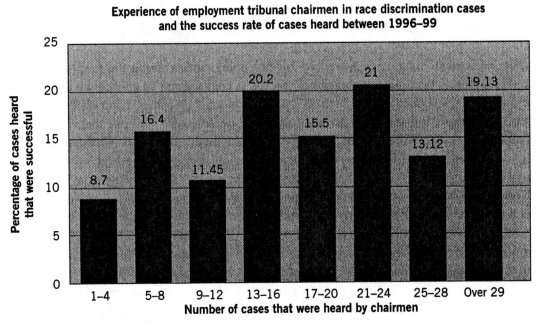

Table 4.2

efficient if focused on these chairmen, while at the same time ensuring that all chairman have the opportunity to acquire skills in this field.

Recommendation 37

- Regular discrimination training should continue to be received on a national basis by all chairmen, but additional refresher courses should be provided for experienced chairmen
- Discrimination cases should be assigned only to chairmen with the requisite experience or specialist training

(3) Lay members

4.8 Discrimination cases are heard by a chairman sitting with two lay members. It is the practice for procedural interlocutory issues, as well, to be dealt with in this way. We raised with respondents the question whether there should be specialist lay members for the hearing of discrimination cases. Some members are designated by the DfEE on appointment as having special knowledge and experience of race relations and it is the normal practice to have one of these members in race cases. In at least one region a specialist disability panel has been informally set up. The view was expressed to us in the English regions that the attitudes of some lay members, even those on the present race panels, present difficulties particularly those members who were involved in personnel management and unions at a time when racist and sexist attitudes were more widespread. This view was not shared in Scotland. The then President of Tribunals in Scotland told us that "to create specialised tribunal members creates disharmony among the body of tribunal members and, in any event, I think it would create dissension among users of the tribunal system because they would find it difficult to understand why special people were chosen for some kind of cases and not for others."

4.9 There is considerable support for the view that it is more important to train lay members in the judicial task than for them to become discrimination specialists. How to approach the judicial task in discrimination cases is a vital aspect of this training. There is now a three-year rolling programme in operation in England and Wales which applies in all regions and includes training in the handling of discrimination claims for all lay members. Lay members will generally be expected to have considerable experience sitting in tribunals before being assigned to a discrimination case. There is also regular training in Scotland. Bearing in mind that resources for training are limited, and that there are some 2500 lay members it would seem sensible that while all members should receive basic training in respect of discrimination, additional training in judging discrimination cases should be concentrated on selected members. This would remove the need for the anomalous specialist race panel. The Disability Rights Task Force has proposed that wherever possible cases involving disability discrimination should be heard by a panel including at least one person with disability expertise.[212] In our view, instead of establishing specialist panels, all the members sitting in discrimination cases should have the requisite experience or training. It is also essential that chairmen should give clear guidance to lay members sitting on a case to put aside any prejudices and stereotyped attitudes, and to deal fairly with the evidence. Any members who show themselves unable or unwilling to do so should not be called to sit again on such cases. All members would benefit from use of the Judicial Studies Board's *Equal Treatment Bench Book*.

Recommendation 38
- The current programme of discrimination training for lay members should be continued and additional resources should be provided for specialist training to a selected number of lay members
- The practice should continue that lay members are not called to sit on discrimination cases unless they have the requisite experience or training
- The specialist race panel should be discontinued
- Chairmen should give clear guidance to lay members to avoid prejudice and stereotyped attitudes, and members who are unable or unwilling to do so, should not be called for discrimination cases

---

[212] Disability Rights Task Force (1999), p. 97.

4.10   Women, ethnic minorities and disabled persons continue to be under-represented on employ-
        ment tribunals. Following the recent round of appointments of tribunal members, 32% are now
        women (up from 29%), 7% from ethnic minorities (up from 5%) and 7% are disabled persons
        (up from 4%).[213] The Government has accepted that tribunals should reflect the composition of
        the workforce they serve as closely as possible. Of the 324 new appointments made in 2000 for
        a three-year period, 54% are women, 17% from ethnic minorities and 18% have experience of
        working with some form of disability. The Home Office has set targets for recruitment from
        ethnic minorities in public services generally, and the DfEE should take a similar approach to
        the recruitment of tribunal members from ethnic minorities and of women.[214] The Disability
        Rights Task Force has made proposals for removing barriers – such as a bar because of blind-
        ness, or the need for assistance - on the service of disabled persons as magistrates and jurors.[215]
        A similar approach should be taken to the appointment of lay members of tribunals.

Recommendation 39

- An equality scheme for the employment tribunals should set targets for achieving a lay membership of not less than 40% women by 2003, and 50% by 2006, and a percentage that reflects
  the proportion of ethnic minority communities in each region by 2006
- Barriers on the service of disabled persons as members of tribunals should be removed, unless
  they can be justified as appropriate and necessary

(4) The title of "chairman"

4.11   Some of our respondents told us that the perception of employment tribunals as being sexist is
        encouraged by the designation of the presiding officer as a "chairman". There was no agree-
        ment as to a suitable substitute. Some thought that "chair" was now generally acceptable, while
        others suggested that it would raise the status of the tribunals if a title such as "employment
        judge (EJ)" were used. The latter is our preference given the judicial nature of the tribunals,
        and the use of similar terms, such as "labour court judge" in other European jurisdictions.

Recommendation 40

- The title of chairman of employment tribunals should be changed to employment judge

B. Jurisdiction: employment appeal tribunal and county and sheriff courts

(1) Transfer of cases to the Employment Appeal Tribunal

4.12   A suggestion for transferring more complex cases to the EAT was first made in the report by
        Justice, *Industrial Tribunals* (1987). The transfers would be to the EAT as a court of original
        jurisdiction: (1) where a significant point of law arises; or (2) where the case has important
        implications extending beyond the interests of the individual parties; or (3) where the evidence
        is highly complex or specialised and raises difficult issues of evaluation. The advantage of this
        would be to utilise from the outset the legal expertise of the High Court (or the Court of
        Session) judge on the complex issues of the law or fact which may arise. This proposal was

---

[213] DTI, News Release, 31 March 2000.
[214] Home Office (2000), p. 45 and Appendix J.
[215] Disability Rights Task Force (1999), pp. 174-175.

revived by some of our respondents. However, it was opposed by the Bar Council's Sex Discrimination Committee, the CRE, the Discrimination Law Association, and the Law Society's Employment Committee. There were concerns that such fast tracking of cases could overburden the EAT or lead to delays in normal appeals. The EOC and some other respondents said that today specially trained and experienced tribunal chairmen are likely to be at least as adept as a High Court judge in this field. We make no recommendation in this respect.

(2) County and sheriff court cases

4.13   Discrimination cases involving goods, services and facilities come under the jurisdiction of the county and sheriff courts. In race discrimination cases the county court judges can sit with the assistance of an assessor.[216] Submissions to our initial consultation paper and comments at consultation meetings indicated widespread dissatisfaction with these courts. Both the EOC and the CRE have in the past proposed transferring their jurisdiction in goods, facilities and services cases to employment tribunals. This was supported in their submissions to us by the Bar Council's Sex Discrimination Committee, the Law Society's Employment Committee, the Discrimination Law Association and the RADAR, the latter organisation claiming that the problems associated with county courts are the "biggest barrier" facing individuals wishing to take up cases under Part III of the DDA. However, in their submission, the CRE suggests that more time should be allowed both for greater experience of bringing Race Relations Act cases under the new civil procedure rules, and to learn from cases under the wider scope of the Act after the current amending Bill comes into force.

4.14   There can be little doubt, as the EOC argues, that the rarity of cases brought to county and sheriff courts since 1975 results "from the formality, cost, and protracted nature of the county court process." Unfortunately, since 1990 the Judicial Statistics no longer reveal the number of race and sex discrimination cases heard in these courts. Between 1977 and 1989, the last year for which such statistics were compiled, the average number of race cases per year in county courts was 24, and for sex discrimination cases the average was 5 cases per year. The monitoring of the first 19 months of implementation of the DDA revealed only 9 county court cases.[217] The recent reforms in civil procedure put a heavy burden on the claimant to spell out the details of his or her case at an early point. This acts as a deterrent to claimants who believe that they have been discriminated against, but need to cross-examine the defendant and to obtain disclosure of relevant documents before they can establish their case, because the reasons for the treatment are only within the defendant's knowledge. By contrast, the complainant in employment tribunal proceedings does not need to set out such details in the originating application.

4.15   Unlike complaints in tribunals, those proceeding in the county and sheriff's courts have to pay court fees, and may face an order for costs or expenses if unsuccessful. In view of the small amounts generally involved in discrimination cases, it is highly unlikely to be attractive to lawyers to offer to take such cases on a conditional fee basis, as is now possible. Non-employment claims are often for less than £3000 and so may be routed into the small claims arbitration procedure of the county court or the sheriff court. This procedure has the advantage that, as in tribunals, parties meet their own costs and it is less formal than the ordinary courts.

---

[216] RRA s.67; RR(NI)O, art. 54(7).
[217] Meager et al. (1999), chap.7.

However, recent research into the operation of the DDA found that those who went through the process found it difficult and stressful.[218] Moreover, discrimination cases frequently raise complex questions of law or fact and may thus be transferred for trial rather than arbitration.

4.16   Another argument for transferring non-employment cases to employment tribunals, apart from questions of procedure, cost and formality, is that all discrimination cases, whether relating to employment or other areas, raise common legal themes and have similar sensitivities as to the drawing of inferences from primary facts. County court judges have relatively little experience and no training in this field. It would be costly and difficult to lay on special training for the relatively few county court judges and sheriffs likely to hear these cases. There may be an increase in the number of cases as a result of a positive duty being imposed on public authorities, and a growing case load from disability cases, now that Part III of the DDA is in force, but there are still likely to be only relatively few judges or sheriffs involved.

4.17   There is usually more in common between employment and non-employment discrimination cases than between these cases and the other county and sheriff courts jurisdictions. At the same time we recognise that some claims of racial or sex discrimination may be part of a set of claims more appropriately dealt with in the civil courts. An example would be a claim of false imprisonment or malicious prosecution against the police where racial discrimination is also alleged. This leads us to propose that while all discrimination claims should commence in the employment tribunals, there should be a power to transfer cases to the county court or sheriff court. Where the tribunal hears a non-employment case, confusion may be avoided by designating it as an "equality tribunal" for this purpose. (There is a precedent in cases where they perform a specialist function under the title of the reserve forces appeal tribunal.)

Recommendation 41

- All discrimination cases should be commenced in the employment tribunals
- Where the matter does not relate to employment, the tribunal should be designated as an "equality tribunal"
- The lay members should be called to hear cases having regard to their knowledge and experience of the relevant field. If necessary, additional members should be appointed with relevant knowledge in respect of education and consumer affairs
- The President of tribunals or a regional chairman should have the power to transfer a matter to the county court, either on application by a party, or on his or her own motion
- Equivalent provisions should be made for the transfer of cases to the sheriff court in Scotland
- The criteria for transfer should include: (1) whether it would be more convenient or fair for the hearing to be held in that court, having regard to the facts, legal issues, remedies and procedure; (2) the availability of a judge specialising in this type of claim; (3) the facilities available at the tribunal and at the court where the claim is to be dealt with and whether they may be inadequate because of the disabilities of a party or a potential witness; and (4) the financial value of the claim and the importance of the claim to the public in general.[219]

---

[218] Meager et al. (1999), p. 273.
[219] These criteria are modelled on Rule 30.3 of the Civil Procedure Rules 1998.

C. Pre-Hearing Matters

(1) Unmeritorious cases

4.18   A tribunal has the discretion, either on the application of the party or of its own motion, to hold a pre-hearing review (PHR) to determine whether the application or arguments of either party have any chance of success. Where the tribunal considers that a party has no reasonable prospects of success it can require a party to make a deposit of £150 to proceed further with the case. The order must include a note warning the party that they may have an award of costs made against them and lose their deposit if they persist. PHRs are rarely used in England and Wales in discrimination cases, and would arise in Scotland only where there was in effect a plea as to the relevancy of a claim (i.e., where the grounds alleged would not entitle the party to any relief or would not constitute a defence). This is because, in the words of the Bar Council's Sex Discrimination Committee, "a person who has been turned down for a job or promotion is not privy to the employer's process of deliberations, and so can only act upon a suspicion that race or sex is the reason for her or his lack of success. Their complaints should not be rejected without an opportunity for cross-examination." The £150 deposit was generally held by our respondents to be an ineffective means of weeding-out unmeritorious claims. The amount was too low to deter the determined vexatious litigant while at the same time being sufficiently high to deter a genuine litigant of limited resources.

4.19   Some respondents thought that consideration should be given to a revival of the old pre-hearing assessments (PHAs) under which a costs warning could be given to a party who was unlikely to be successful. It was believed that this would make it easier for the tribunals to apply a costs sanction if at the end of the case a party was shown to have acted frivolously, vexatiously or otherwise unreasonably. However, the PHA procedure was discontinued precisely because it was not being effectively used in that way, and it was never considered suitable in discrimination cases. Chairmen told us that "try-on" claims not infrequently came from dismissed employees who lacked the two years' qualifying period to complain of unfair dismissal, and are seeking a legal peg on which to hang their grievance. With the lowering of the period to one year, from 25 October 1999, this source of unmeritorious claims will be diminished. In our view, the only realistic measures are for tribunals to make more effective use of interlocutory hearings (IHAs) at which issues can be refined, and parties may realise the weakness of their claim or defence, and by greater use of existing powers to award costs where a party acts unreasonably.

(2) Interlocutory hearings (IHAs)

4.20   An interlocutory (directions) hearing (IHA) may take place on the application of either party or on the initiative of the tribunal, on procedural matters. The hearings allow the tribunal to deal with particulars, discovery, questionnaires, listing of the case, the serving of witness statements and similar matters. All the regions we interviewed in England regularly make use of IHAs in the more complex cases. They are seen as particularly valuable in DDA cases because the parties often do not understand the issues. Parties are required to attend. Some representatives such as the CRE brief the applicant but do not attend because of the resources involved. There are, however, a number of inconsistencies as to how IHAs are used. In some regions they are seen primarily as a means of encouraging conciliation, pointing out the benefits of settlement.

Unfortunately, statistics are not available as to how many cases settle after an IHA, or as to the content of such settlements. In some regions orders are routinely made for the exchange of witness statements, as a means of expediting hearings, but in others such exchanges are seen as inappropriate where the applicant is a litigant in person and may be placed at a disadvantage. Orders for particulars and discovery are regularly made (including details of other applicants for a post etc. where this is material). The position is different in Scotland, where it is not the practice to call IHAs, unless the issue relates to non-compliance with a tribunal order, or exceptionally where the issues are unusually complex and require clarification. It is felt that an unrepresented party may be at a disadvantage at an IHA, and unable to comply effectively with orders of discovery, exchange of statements etc.

4.21   The EOC and some other respondents agreed that greater use should be made of IHAs and suggested that greater use should be made of powers to order discovery. An IHA is particularly helpful if there is a dispute as to which documents should be disclosed. A practitioner has suggested that the rules should provide for automatic disclosure of all relevant documents , rather than the present rules under which a special order has to be sought for discovery of a document other than one on which a party intends to rely. There is, however, a risk that this might over-burden an unrepresented party, for example a disabled person should not be required to provide more than a brief written medical report where disability is in issue. There is also a risk that automatic disclosure of "relevant" documents would be abused by legal representatives who would argue as to what is "relevant". Accordingly, we do not make any recommendation for automatic disclosure. Parties would be helped if there were pro forma questions for directions hearings and standard directions of the kind that are already in use in some regions.

Recommendation 42

- Tribunals should continue to use IHAs where they are satisfied that unrepresented parties will not be at a disadvantage
- The parties should be sent in advance pro forma questions which are to be raised at the IHA

(3) Questionnaire procedure

4.22   Questionnaires[220] are widely used by potential applicants particularly where the CRE, EOC or ECNI is advising them. They help applicants and their advisers to assess the strength of their case, clarify the issues, and facilitate early settlements and withdrawals. The questions and replies are admissible in evidence. We were told that there is widespread ignorance among those who receive questionnaires that if they deliberately or without reasonable excuse fail to reply or are evasive or equivocal, the tribunal is entitled to draw any inference it thinks it just and equitable to draw, including an inference that the respondent acted unlawfully. There was general agreement that it would be helpful if a single and simplified questionnaire were developed that could be used in all types of discrimination cases. In multiple discrimination cases this would remove the need for the applicant to identify the particular form of discrimination that has taken place, and would avoid the need to duplicate forms. It would also save the respondent from having to answer several different questionnaires. This will be very important, if as we recommend, the legislation is extended to cover other grounds of discrimination. The single questionnaire procedure should be extended to cases under Part III (goods and services)

---

[220] Under RRA, s.65; RR(NI)O, art. 63; SDA, s.74; SD(NI)O, art. 74; DDA, s.56; FETO, art. 44.

of the DDA. The questionnaire should explain in clear and understandable form what its purpose is and what the consequences are of failure to respond or an untruthful reply. The questionnaire should also be used to ask the parties whether attempts have been made to mediate the case and if not whether they would like the case to go to mediation.

4.23   It was the view of some of our respondents that the use of the questionnaire procedure should be made compulsory, so as to force the parties to assess the relative strength of their cases before reference to a tribunal, and in order to encourage early settlement. Against this, it was argued that this would place unrepresented parties at a disadvantage. Another suggestion was to give the tribunal discretion, after proceedings have commenced, to require an applicant to serve a questionnaire within a specified time. However, there seems to be little point in this, because once proceedings have commenced there is provision to request particulars and discovery. It was suggested to us that, in any event, reply to questionnaires should be made compulsory. At present, where there is no reply the applicant frequently finds it necessary to duplicate the questionnaire by a series of requests for further and better particulars, with such requests having to be enforced at an IHA. We support this proposal.

Recommendation 43

- A simplified single questionnaire should be used for all types of discrimination claim
- The form should be made available to applicants by the Employment Tribunals Service together with the originating application IT1
- The form should state clearly the consequences of failure to reply or an evasive or equivocal reply
- Respondents should be required to reply within eight weeks of service of the questionnaire, failing which the tribunal should have power, on application or of its own motion, to strike out all or part of the notice of appearance or to debar the respondent from defending altogether, but this should not be done without giving the respondent an opportunity to show cause why such an order should not be made

(4) Class actions and group litigation

4.24   Discriminatory practices affect people by virtue of their membership of a group. As the Committee on the Administration of Justice noted in their response "it is of vital importance that discrimination and anti-discrimination measures not be conceived in a purely individualised way". This group element to discrimination has generated support for allowing class actions in discrimination claims. We received a number of submissions supporting the use of class actions in discrimination cases. We quote from one of these:

At present many sex equality issues have been litigated through representative actions, e.g. part-time workers' pension cases, equal pay claim of speech therapists, where trade unions, pressure groups, law centres etc have co-ordinated the bringing of claims. Thus it would not be a large step to take formally to permit class actions. The advantages of class actions would be that individual applicants would not need to be found to bring the legal proceedings. Furthermore this principle could be widened by permitting trade unions and equality agencies the right to bring actions on behalf of workers in the abstract. A discriminatory rule could then be challenged even where it is not possible to find a worker who has been affected. This is important in challenging embedded institutional practices which may have dissuaded women or ethnic minorities from applying for jobs, as in the rostering arrangement challenged under *London Underground* v. *Edwards* [221]

---

[221] [1997] IRLR 157

4.25   It is possible at present for an employment tribunal, on the application of a party, or on its own motion, to combine proceedings. This can be done in three circumstances. First, where a common question of law or fact arises in some or all of the originating applications. Secondly, where the relief claimed is in respect of or arises out of the same set of facts. Thirdly, where for any other reason it is desirable to order the proceedings to be combined.[222] In county court cases the new civil procedure rules allow for representative actions where numerous persons have the same interest.[223] The new rules also allow the courts to make a group litigation order on the application of the parties or on the court's own initiative.[224] These forms of action continue to require individual applicants to be identified and at least one of them to pursue a case. A class action could remove the need to find an individual applicant through whom the proceedings are to be conducted. It would allow actions to be brought by one of the commissions or a trade union. The CRE in its review of the RRA argued for an amendment to "enable a court or tribunal to consider a complaint where the discrimination affects a number of people who wish to bring a group complaint, without the need for each person separately to bring proceedings".[225] Similarly the EOC has argued that they should be able to bring legal proceedings in the commission's own name.[226] The EOC cited the example of a discriminatory provision in a collective agreement that would be best challenged by a class actions brought on behalf of the members of the class by the EOC.

4.26   The CRE and EOC proposals have some similarities with the power of the EEOC in the USA to bring an action either in their own name or jointly with individuals. The number of these actions is relatively limited but we were told by the EEOC that they are extremely important for publicity, an example being a recent action against a Japanese transnational company operating in the USA in respect of sexual harassment. We were given examples of EEOC actions against major employers which have had a significant effect in opening top jobs for women. The basis of these actions has been a combination of disparate treatment (direct discrimination) and disparate impact (indirect discrimination). Unlike private class actions in the USA, in which injunctive or declaratory relief must be the predominant remedy sought by the class, the EEOC can include compensatory and punitive damages for individuals and this puts pressure on respondents to mediate or settle the claim. While the private class action could not be transposed to the UK, we believe that enforcement would be enhanced if the commission had power to institute proceedings in its own name or jointly with individuals, where there is a common question of fact or law affecting a number of persons, whether identified or not.

Recommendation 44

- The commission should have power to institute proceedings in its own name or jointly with individuals in respect of unlawful discrimination where there is a common question of fact or law affecting a number of persons, whether identified or not
- The commission should be able to claim injunctive and declaratory relief and also an order requiring compensation to be paid to a defined group of individuals
- Individuals who fall within the defined group should be able to register within a specified time, and, if they do so, to enforce any order for compensation to the extent of their own loss or injury

---

[222] The Employment Tribunals (Constitutions and Rules of Procedure) Regulations 1993, (S.I. 1993 No. 2687), Sched.1, rule 18 (there is a similar rule in Scotland).

[223] Schedule 1 RSC Rules - Rule 12; Schedule 2 CCR Rules – Rule 5

[224] Civil Procedure Rules Practice Direction 19B

[225] CRE (1998) p.39

[226] EOC (1998b) p.12

- If our recommendation 50 in respect of exemplary damages is accepted, then in any proceedings brought by the commission the amount of such damages should be paid to the commission

(5) Equal pay claims

4.27 The present procedures for enforcing equal pay claims impede rather than facilitate an individual's access to judicial determination. The equal value procedure generally involves three stages:

- *Preliminary hearing.* Unless the tribunal is satisfied that there are no reasonable grounds for determining that the work is of equal value, the tribunal will usually refer the question whether the work is of equal value to an independent expert. Since July 1996, the tribunal has had a discretion – so far only rarely used – to determine this question itself. At the preliminary hearing the tribunal may also consider the employer's defence that there is a genuine material factor (GMF) justifying the difference in pay.
- *Independent expert's report.* If the tribunal is satisfied that (1) there are reasonable grounds for determining that the work is of equal value (above), (2) the woman's job and the man's job have not already been rated under a non-discriminatory job evaluation scheme (JES) as being unequal, and (3) it does not wish to determine the question of equal value itself, it must refer this question to an independent expert.
- *Final report.* The tribunal will consider the expert's report and hear evidence from the employer and the applicant. The GMF defence may be re-opened at this hearing or raised for the first time.

4.28 This procedure causes inordinate delay. In 1990, the EAT said that the rules "give rise to delays which are properly described as scandalous and amount to a denial of justice to women through the judicial process".[227] In 1993, the EAT said that the whole system " requires a prompt and thorough review. [228] Since then there have been some minor changes in procedure aimed at reducing delay, such as the discretion given to tribunals to determine the question of equal value without referring this to an expert (above). However, these changes appear to have had little effect. In only eight cases up to the summer of 1999 has a tribunal dispensed with the expert. According to the *Equal Opportunities Review* , the average time taken from the tribunal's decision to refer the case to an independent expert until a decision on equal pay in 1998-99 was just over 19 months, and ranged from 11 months to 28 months .[229] In the two years before the rule changes, the average time was 20 months. [230] The median length of time for an equal value case to be completed in 1998-99 was 17 months, just one month shorter than the previous year. These figures hide the full extent of the delay in cases with multiple claimants. Claims by 1,280 women against British Coal have still to be determined 15 years after the first applications were made. Speech therapists' claims against health authorities were concluded only 14 years after they were launched.

4.29 The equal pay procedure has largely failed to deliver pay equity to women. From 1976 to 1998 12,344 equal pay claims were brought in tribunals. Only 20 percent of these were won after a tribunal hearing or settled. Of the cases that went to hearing, only 26 percent were

---

[227] *Aldridge v. British Telecommunications plc.*[1990] IRLR 10 at 14.
[228] *British Coal Corpn. v Smith* [1993] IRLR 308 at 310.
[229] EOR No.88, November/ December 1999, p.16.
[230] EOR No.76, November/December 1997,p.18; EOR No.70, November/December 1996, p.13.

successful.[231] Just over half of the claims during the eleven-year period between 1984 and the summer of 1995, were equal value claims. These involved 8,500 applicants and 640 employers. Approximately one-third of these claims were from British Coal employees or employees in the health service. In this period the tribunals appointed experts in 195 cases involving around 1,900 applicants. In 30 of these the claim was upheld by the tribunal; in 18 the claim was dismissed; 14 cases were ongoing and the remaining cases were withdrawn [232]. There were 2,886 equal pay applications in 1997 and 3,447 in 1998. It is estimated by *Equal Opportunities Review* that just under 1,000 women shared a total of £3.4m in settlement of their equal value claims in 1998–99.[233]Although the settlements were significant for these women, they involved a long and expensive procedure at considerable public cost. They made no impact on the overall gender pay gap.

4.30   We sought views on three options for improving procedures in relation to individual claims. The first was whether greater powers should be given to full-time independent experts subject to strict time limits. The Bar Council's Sex Discrimination Committee doubted whether there was enough work to sustain full-time experts and considered that the present panel of approved experts works well. Experienced chairmen of employment tribunals also doubted whether the situation would be ameliorated by making experts full-time and imposing statutory time limits. In the light of these and other responses to our options paper, we consider that delays could be reduced by more active case management by chairmen of tribunals.

4.31   The second question we raised was whether the independent experts should be removed altogether from the process, leaving it to the parties to call their own experts. Several objections were raised to this. First, it would increase the cost to all parties and aggravate the inequality between the parties, particularly where the applicant does not have union representation and the employer has either in-house staff or external consultants. Secondly, it would increase the adversarial approach. An independent expert's report is more likely to lead to an agreed settlement of the claim. As we noted in the options paper, tribunals have so far been reluctant to exercise their power to conduct their own job evaluations, and it appears that they are unable to do so in the absence of expert evidence. It is unlikely that resources, in the form of legal aid or otherwise, can be made available to help parties employ their own experts. There seems to be no viable alternative to the present system.

4.32   The third question was whether all individual claims should be referred either to the CAC or to an independent expert for arbitration. We have already proposed the CAC-route for what are essentially collective claims under pay equity plans (paras.3.49-3.50). Most consultees who discussed this question felt that this was unlikely to be suitable in individual cases. The Law Society's Employment Committee, however, thought that there may be some scope for alternative dispute resolution (see para.4.59 below). Overall, our conclusion is that there is not much scope for improving the procedures in individual equal pay claims. Significant changes in the gender pay gap can be brought about only through pay equity plans, changes in the basis of comparison of pay and improved job evaluation (see paras. 3.45-3.60). In addition, as proposed in recommendation 35 section 2A(2) of the Equal Pay Act) the no reasonable grounds preliminary defence) should be repealed.

---

[231] EOC, *Employment Tribunal Statistics Equal Pay Cases Only from 1976 to 1998*, EOC 1999.
[232] EOR No.88,p.16. Unfortunately, separate equal value statistics are not available since 1996 because ACAS in Britain and the LRB in Northern Ireland no longer differentiate between the different types of equal pay claim.
[233] EOR No.88, p. 16.

Recommendation 45

- There should be more active case management by chairmen of tribunals in equal pay cases, speedier appointment of the expert, an early meeting between the expert and the parties (under the chairman's management) to establish a strict timetable, with any departure from this being subject to a directions hearing.

D. The Hearing

(1) Length of hearings

4.33   We consulted as to how the length of hearings in discrimination cases could be reduced consistently with the just disposal of the case. There has for long been a managerial concern within the Tribunals Service that these cases generally take longer than other types of tribunal claim. National statistics reveal that in 1998-99 the average length of hearing in SDA cases was 3.57 days, RRA cases 3.44 days, DDA cases 3.0 days, and Equal Pay 4.14 days.[234] There are regional variations but these are not particularly significant. Those respondents who addressed this question doubted whether more could be done than to continue to emphasise the need for firm case management by the chairman. The Bar Council's Sex Discrimination Committee said that in their experience chairmen are far more indulgent towards applicants and their representatives in discrimination cases than in other types of case. On the other hand, there is good reason for these cases taking a relatively long time. They often turn on questions of credibility and require multiple witnesses and a careful examination of evidence covering what may be an extensive a period of time. There have been several statements from judges in the EAT that it is undesirable to allow these hearings to be adjourned for lengthy periods. It seems to be generally recognised by the tribunals that more effective case management, making full use of IHAs to determine the probable length of the hearing, is needed.

(2) Legal help and representation

4.34   High quality advice, assistance and representation is essential to ensuring access to justice. Recent research on the operation of the DDA confirms what is already well-known in respect of other forms of discrimination: a legally-represented applicant in a disability case is more likely to be successful at a hearing than one who appears in person, but an applicant in person is more likely to be successful than if they were represented by a non-legal person such as a trade union or CAB. Tribunals were also most likely to find in favour of a respondent who is legally represented.[235] No current statistics are available as to the extent of representation in race and sex cases, but as a matter of impression tribunal chairmen whom we interviewed reported that at least 75% of applicants and a higher proportion of respondents are represented in discrimination cases. These representatives include not only lawyers but also trade unions, CAB, pro bono units, the Disability Rights Advisory Service, and others.

4.35   The Commissions themselves have the power to provide advice and assistance.[236] It is not possible to make direct comparisons between the EOC and CRE in this respect because of the

---

[234] Information from the Employment Tribunals Service, November 1999.
[235] Meager et al. (1999), pp. 101-103.
[236] RRA, s.66; RR(NI)O, art. 64; SDA, s.76; SD(NI)O, art. 75; DRCA, s.7; FETO, art. 45.

different ways in which they present their statistics. The EOC reported that in 1997-98 it had received 187 formal requests for assistance and gave assistance in 47 of these and advice in 18 cases. In 1998-99 it received 225 applications for assistance and gave this in 81 cases. These figures refer only to cases taken to a tribunal. In addition, in 1998-99 the EOC case workers gave informal advice in 7589 matters.[237] In 1998, CRE case workers gave formal advice and assistance in 972 cases, full representation in 163 cases and limited representation in 101 cases; 92 cases were referred to other organisations. The CRE figures do not include many other occasions on which informal advice is given by telephone, letter or personal visit.

4.36   There have for long been debates as to whether legal aid should be extended to cover representation before employment tribunals. These have now been overtaken in England and Wales by the establishment of the Community Legal Service (CLS) and the Community Legal Service Fund (CLSF), administered by the Legal Services Commission, from 1 April 2000. The CLS brings together organisations offering legal and advice services into local networks. These networks include solicitors, CAB, Law Centres, local authority services, community services, trade unions, and others. Many of these organisations offer services free, or provide a free initial interview, or a fixed fee interview in discrimination cases. Others charge for their services. The CLSF exists to help people who meet certain eligibility rules and who cannot afford to pay for legal services. This replaces the civil legal aid scheme. "Legal help" has replaced the terms "advice and assistance" and "certified legal aid" has become "legal representation". Users will have some guarantee of the standards of service of organisations that have been awarded and display the CLS Quality Mark. The Funding Code sets out the help that the CLSF can provide and the requirements that need to be met. In general people will be expected to use conditional fee ("no win no fee") agreements, but it seems unlikely that these will be attractive to lawyers, except in group actions, because the amount of compensation claimed is usually relatively small. The Lord Chancellor has directed that priority should be given to certain cases by the CLSF. These include breaches of human rights by public bodies, and employment rights cases. While this will cover certain discrimination cases, it does not appear to include discrimination in non-employment cases. Since the principle of equal treatment is a fundamental human right, it should be accorded high priority.

Recommendation 46

- The Lord Chancellor should direct the CLSF to give priority to all types of discrimination case in respect of both legal help and representation.

(3) Burden of proof

4.37   Employment tribunal chairmen whom we interviewed indicated that they generally used a model direction based on the judgement in the Court of Appeal decision in *King v. The Great Britain China Centre* [238] Neill LJ in *King* provided the following guidelines:

(1)   It is for the applicant who complains of racial discrimination to make out his or her case. Thus if the applicant does not prove his or her case on the balance of probabilities he or she will fail.

(2)   It is important to bear in mind that it is unusual to find direct evidence of racial discrimination. Few employers will be prepared to admit such discrimination even to themselves. In some cases the discrimination will not be ill intentioned but merely based on an assumption 'he or she would not have fitted in'.

---

[237] Information supplied by the EOC, May 2000.
[238] [1991] IRLR 513, CA.

(3) The outcome will therefore usually depend on what inference it is proper to draw from the primary facts found by the Tribunal. These inference can include, in appropriate cases, any inference that it is just and equitable to draw in accordance with s. 65(2)(b) of the 1976 Act from an evasive or equivocal reply to a questionnaire.

(4) Though there will be some cases where for example the non-selection of the applicant for a post or promotion is clearly not on racial grounds, a finding of discrimination and a finding of different race will often point to the possibility of racial discrimination. In such circumstances the tribunal will look to the employer for an explanation. If no explanation is then put forward or of the tribunal considers the explanation to be inadequate or unsatisfactory, it will be legitimate for the tribunal to infer that the discrimination was on racial grounds. This is not a matter of law, but as May LJ put it in *Noone*, 'almost common sense'.

(5) It is unnecessary and unhelpful to introduce the concept of a shifting evidential burden of proof. At the conclusion of all the evidence the tribunal should make findings as to the primary facts and draw such inferences as they consider proper from those facts. They should then reach a conclusion on the balance of probabilities, bearing in mind both the difficulties which face a person who complains of unlawful discrimination and the fact that it is for the complainant to prove his or her case.

The House of Lords in *Zafar*[239] approved these guidelines, but with the significant clarification that while tribunals may draw an inference where there is a difference of treatment and the employer fails to provide an explanation, or provides an inadequate or unsatisfactory one, there is no requirement to draw such an inference.

4.38 Article 4(1) of the EC Burden of Proof Directive 97/80/EC, provides that:

Member States shall take such measures as are necessary, in accordance with their national judicial systems, to ensure that, when persons who consider themselves wronged because of the principle of equal treatment has not been applied to them establish, before a court or other competent authority, facts from which it may be presumed that there has been direct or indirect discrimination, it shall be for the respondent to prove that there has been no breach of the principle of equal treatment

This provision in effect codifies the ECJ's earlier rulings in this field, whose effect was to shift the legal burden of proof once the applicant has raised a prima facie case of discrimination.[240] The Government, commenting on a draft of the directive in 1997, argued that "the directive would make very little difference to the way in which sex discrimination cases are decided in the UK in practice" and that "there will be no need for legislation in order to formally shift the burden of proof."[241] However, in our view, there is an important difference between the position under the EC Directive and the approach in the *King* and *Zafar* cases. Under the latter, where a respondent fails to provide any adequate or satisfactory reason for a difference in treatment, the tribunal *may* drawn an inference. However under the Directive once the applicant has shown a difference in treatment between himself or herself and the comparator, and the circumstances are such that an inference of discrimination could be drawn, then the burden of proof shifts to the respondent to prove that there has been no unlawful treatment.

4.39 There was a difference of opinion among our respondents as to whether the change resulting from the Burden of Proof directive should be embodied in legislation. One Regional Chairman thought that burden of proof causes few problems and that judicial guidelines are sufficient. However, all the other chairmen interviewed favoured a statutory rule, since this would remove any confusion and would help chairmen when advising lay members who find difficulty in understanding the burden of proof. This is borne out by a recent study of race discrimination

---

[239] *Zafar v Glasgow City Council* [1998] IRLR 36, HL.
[240] See Ellis (1998), pp. 229-230.
[241] House of Lords European Legislation Select Committee, Second Report, (Session 1997-98).

cases in Scotland, which indicates that there would be greater certainty and consistency if there were a reversal of the burden of proof.[242] It would also have important symbolic value in making respondents aware of their responsibility to show a credible non-discriminatory reason for their conduct. Tribunals should always give reasons for drawing or not drawing an inference, and they would be encouraged to do so by a formal reversal of the burden of proof. One Regional Chairman argued for a formulation analogous to the current unfair dismissal provision where the burden is on the employer to establish the reason for the dismissal, but the burden as to reasonableness is neutral. In our view this would not go far enough to satisfy the requirements of the Directive. Although the Directive applies only to sex discrimination, a similar formulation has been used in the draft EC directives under Article 13 of the EC Treaty relating to other grounds of discrimination, and a similar rule should be enacted in the UK.

Recommendation 47

- There should be a statutory reversal of the burden of proof in respect of all unlawful discrimination along the lines set out in Article 4 of the Burden of Proof Directive 97/80/EC

E. Time limits

4.40   The statutory time limit for presenting a complaint to a tribunal in employment discrimination cases is currently three months from the date of occurrence of the discriminatory act. This period may be extended where in all the circumstances of the case the tribunal considers that it is just and equitable to do so, a discretion that is rarely exercised. In county or sheriff court proceedings the period is six months. The CRE in their third review of the RRA noted that "many individuals who experience discrimination in the workplace are not aware of their right to complain to an industrial tribunal and, in particular, are not aware of the three-month time limit to do so." A study into the operation of the DDA found that the three-month time limit was a problem for parties involved in informal attempts to resolve a dispute. Informal dispute settlement processes are time consuming, correspondence between the parties can take several months, and the three month time limit often places the parties under pressure to register an IT1 to safeguard rights.[243] The EOC have also indicated that a longer deadline would help the chances of a negotiated settlement being reached.[244] The Better Regulation Task Force supported an extension.

4.41   There was no agreement among employer respondents as to whether the period should be extended. Some companies feared that parties would lose a sense of perspective on the issue if the time was extended, and also argued that all employment claims should be treated similarly noting that there is a three-month limit for unfair dismissal and other claims. On the other hand, there was general support among organisations supporting complainants that the three-month time limit should be extended. The favoured option was to extend the time limit to six months, as in county court proceedings, and in line with that for claims by ex-employees under the Equal Pay Act. An alternative would be to follow article 46 of the FETO in Northern Ireland, which provides that a complaint must be made to the Fair Employment Tribunal within 3 months from the date when the complainant first knew or might reasonably be expected to have known of the act of discrimination or within 6 months from the date when the act occurred

---

[242] Ross (2000).
[243] Meager et al. (1999), p. 198.
[244] EOC (1998b), p. 14.

whichever is the earlier. In our view it would be best to have a simple clear rule without qualifications depending upon the complainant's knowledge, subject to a discretion to extend in exceptional cases.

Recommendation 48

- The time limit for making a complaint of unlawful discrimination should be six months from the date of the alleged act of discrimination, unless in all the circumstances of the case the court or tribunal considers it just and equitable to hear the complaint out of time

F. Remedies

(1) Compensation

4.42   Compensation for the statutory tort of unlawful discrimination is assessed in the same way as common law damages. Damages are normally concerned to make good, so far as possible, the pecuniary or non-pecuniary loss suffered by the victim by putting him or her into as good a position as if no wrong had occurred. There has been an increase in the average levels of compensation awarded by tribunals in the past decade (see Table 4.3). Between 1991 and 1998 the average compensation awards for all discrimination cases in Britain (excluding interest) increased from £2,020 to £6,944. The average awards for injury to feelings, over the same period increased from £959 to £3,058. While the individual figures for a specific year should be treated with caution, there is a clear overall upward trend in the awards of compensation. The removal of compensation limits, as a result of the ruling of the ECJ in the *Marshall (No.2)* case[245] ensures that "the loss and damage actually sustained as a result of the [discrimination] can be made good in full".[246]

Table 4.3 Average compensation awards £ (excluding interest)[247]

Year	All	Sex (in. MOD)	Sex (ex. MOD)	Race	Disability
1991	2,020	1,896	—	2,289	—
1992	2,683	2,526	—	3,088	—
1993	2,912[248] (4,146)[249]	5,273	2,923	2,900	—
1994	13,142	15,625	4,078	2,685	—
1995	5,617	5,865	3,505	4,962	—
1996	6,799	5,774	5,510	9,641	—
1997	8,222	4,556	—	8,220	3,743
1998	6,944	6,873	—	6,083	11,501

[245] Case C-271/91 [1993] ECR I-4367.

[246] At 4407-4408; but cf. Case C-180/95 *Draehmpaehl* [1997] ECR I-2195, where the ECJ appears to have modified this. Ellis (1998), p. 224 is strongly critical.

[247] The figures are extracts from those given in the Equal Opportunities Review. Figures for compensation for disability discrimination is only given from 1997.

[248] Total excluding MOD sex discrimation cases.

[249] Total including MOD sex discrimination cases.

Table 4.4 Average awards for injury to feeling £

Year	All	All Sex Discrimination	Sex (ex. MOD)	Race	Disability
1991	959	838	—	1,226	—
1992	1,355	1,239	—	1,659	—
1993	1,923	1,398	1,349	2,504	—
1994	1,582	1,576	1,615	1,589	—
1995	2,426	1,924	1,873	3,470	—
1996	2,916	2,565	—	4,170	—
1997	3,019	2,441	—	4,632	1,822
1998	3,058	2,907	—	3,730	2,543

4.43   The most difficult head of damages to assess is that for injury to feelings, which can also include injury to health. Responses to our consultation opposed having fixed guidelines on the levels of damages for injury to feelings. However, the suggestion was welcomed that there should be an up-to-date digest of current awards, going beyond the very useful annual overview in *Equal Opportunities Review*. This would act as an aid to settlement and would introduce more consistency in awards. The Discrimination Law Association have suggested that there should be guidelines indicating the criteria that need to be considered by a tribunal in making an award for injury to feelings. In our view, such guidelines may lead employment tribunals to apply a fixed tariff rather than examine the evidence of individual cases. Tribunals should have evidence presented to them on matters such as medical/psychological conditions; effects of the discrimination on the victim's lifestyle, family, friends and personality; the effects of having to seek a remedy (effects of publicity and having to go to court); the absence of an apology; the effect on trust and confidence.

4.44   In order to comply with the Equal Treatment Directive, the Sex Discrimination and Equal Pay (Miscellaneous Amendments) Regulations 1996 amended the SDA 1975 s.65 so that a tribunal can award compensation for unintentional indirect sex discrimination in employment cases. No such amendment has been made to the RRA, nor are such damages available in non-employment sex discrimination cases. Damages can be awarded for unintentional indirect discrimination on grounds of religion under the FETO. There is no justification for allowing such damages in cases of sex and religion, but not race discrimination, and in employment but not in non-employment cases. Furthermore, allowing compensation to be awarded for unintentional indirect discrimination would assist in tackling institutional racism which the Stephen Lawrence Inquiry Report stated can be unintentional. Such a remedy would provide an incentive for institutions and organisations to take a proactive approach in reviewing their policies and procedures.

Recommendation 49

- There should be an up-to-date digest of current awards for injury to feelings
- Damages should be available as a remedy for unintentional indirect discrimination in respect of all grounds of unlawful discrimination and in all fields to which the law applies

(2) Exemplary (punitive) and aggravated damages

4.45   There was mixed reaction among our respondents to the suggestion that exemplary damages should be available in cases of unlawful discrimination. These are damages which are intended to punish the wrongdoer. In the words of the Law Commission, they "seek to effect retribution, as well as being concerned to deter the defendant from repeating the outrageously wrongful conduct and others from acting similarly, and to convey the disapproval of the jury or court."[250] The Law Commission has suggested that these should properly be called "punitive damages". The award of such damages for racial discrimination has been ruled out by the EAT, departing from earlier decisions, in the case of *Deane v London Borough of Ealing,*[251] because at common law such damages cannot be awarded in respect of a wrong which did not exist before 1964 (the date when the *Rookes v Barnard* decision[252] froze the causes of action for which such an award could be made). The EAT has also held that exemplary damages should not be available in sex discrimination cases for breach of the Equal Treatment Directive.[253] Exemplary damages are not available in Scotland. In our Working Paper No.1, Evelyn Ellis points that although it has not yet ruled specifically on this matter, the ECJ might well regard exemplary damages as a necessary remedy in the armoury potentially available to national courts.[254]

4.46   Exemplary damages are distinguished from aggravated damages which compensate the victim of a wrong for mental distress (injury to feelings) in circumstances in which the injury has been caused or increased by the manner in which the defendant committed the wrong, or by the defendant's conduct subsequent to the wrong. This focuses on the effect on the victim rather than on punishment or deterrence. Aggravated damages are awarded from time to time by employment tribunals in England, Wales and Northern Ireland in discrimination cases, but there seems to be no consistent pattern. There is no remedy of aggravated damages in reparation claims in Scotland. Tribunals in other parts of Britain should make greater use of their power to award aggravated damages. In particular, they should specify the amount of aggravated damages separately from the basic award for injury to feelings, and should follow the Court of Appeal's approach in the case of other torts that, where it is appropriate to award aggravated damages, these are unlikely to be less than £1,000 but would normally not be more than twice the basic compensatory damages unless on the particular facts the basic compensation is modest.[255]

4.47   The Law Commission has recently conducted an extensive review of the law relating to aggravated and exemplary damages,[256] and has recommended that punitive damages should be awarded where in committing a wrong, or in conduct subsequent to the wrong, the defendant deliberately and outrageously disregarded the plaintiff's rights. This would apply not only to any tort or equitable wrong, but also for a civil wrong which arises under an Act, but only if such an award would be consistent with the policy of that Act. The Commission thought that, so far as discrimination outside the employment field is concerned, it would be consistent with the policy of the SDA (and RRA), to award such damages because the Acts allow unlawful

---

[250] Law Commission (1997), para. 1.85.
[251] [1993] IRLR 209, EAT.
[252] [1964] AC 1129.
[253] *Ministry of Defence v Meredith* [1995] IRLR 539, EAT.
[254] Para.6.6
[255] *Thompson v MPC* [1997] 3 WLR 403 at 417.
[256] Law Commission (1997).

discrimination to be the subject of civil proceedings "in the like manner as any other claim in tort". This appears to mean that remedies which are typically available in tort are also available for unlawful discrimination. As regards employment cases, the Acts say that the compensation awarded should be the same as "any damages" which could be awarded for discrimination outside the employment field. The Law Commission concludes that "to refuse to award punitive damages [in an employment case], while awarding them in a [non-employment case], would create an anomalous distinction between English law's protection of individuals from unlawful discrimination within and outside the employment field".[257]

4.48   The Commission proposed that in deciding the amount of punitive damages the court or tribunal would have to consider a variety of matters, including the state of mind of the defendant, the nature of the right infringed, the nature of the harm, and the nature and extent of the benefit the defendant derived from the wrong. Punitive damages would not normally be awarded if the defendant has already been convicted of an offence involving the conduct concerned, and if other sanctions had been imposed. If the Law Commission's proposals were adopted an example[258] of the kind of case in which punitive damages would be available would be where an employee is subjected to a campaign of racial harassment by a group of fellow employees over a long period, ranging from taunting, ostracism, and false accusations of misconduct, to violent physical abuse. Though the victim makes a formal complaint to his or her employer, no proper investigation is conducted and no further action is taken. The harassment continues, and the victim claims compensation. In our view this is exactly the kind of situation in which the tribunal should be able to send a clear signal of outrage and disapproval to the wrongdoers and seek to deter future conduct of this kind by awarding punitive damages.

Recommendation 50

- Tribunals in England , Wales and Northern Ireland should make greater use of their power to award aggravated damages
- Punitive damages should be available for unlawful discrimination as recommended by the Law Commission in respect of England and Wales
- Consideration should be given to the award of aggravated and punitive damages for unlawful discrimination in Scotland

(3) Reinstatement and re-engagement

4.49   It is not open to a tribunal to order the reinstatement or re-engagement of an employee, who has been the subject of a discriminatory dismissal unless the employee presents the case as one of unfair dismissal. As a result the employee with less than one year's qualifying service cannot get back their job. Our respondents regarded this as an anomaly and supported the extension of these powers to the tribunal in discrimination cases, irrespective of the length of service. Such an extension would ensure consistency between the two regimes and may encourage employers to seek proactive ways to accommodate the needs of the employee. Responses to our consultation indicate that, as in unfair dismissal cases, this power would be rarely used either because the victim did not wish to return to the employment of the discriminator, or because the tribunal found that it was not reasonably practicable for the employer to comply with an order. Where an order is not complied with, the tribunal is limited to awarding additional compensation. The order cannot be specifically enforced.

---

[257] Law Commission (1997), paras. 1.63 –1.65.
[258] This example is given by the Commission as a situation in which exemplary damages are not at present available.

4.50   Some of our respondents suggested that consideration should also be given to providing tribunals with the power, in cases of discriminatory recruitment, to order "engagement", on the ground the applicant should as far as possible be put in the same position as he or she would have been in had he or she not been subject to discrimination.[259] A distinction has to be drawn in this respect between being given the job that was applied for and another suitable job. Where the tribunal takes the view that, but for the unlawful discrimination, the applicant would have got the job applied for, then it should be able to order engagement, subject to the rule as to practicability (e.g. where another person has already been given the job on a permanent basis).

Recommendation 51

- An employment tribunal should have power to order engagement, re-engagement or reinstate-ment, unless the employer shows that it would not be practicable to comply with such an order
- If an order is made but not observed, the tribunal should be able to award additional compensa-tion, including aggravated and punitive damages

(4) Power to make recommendations

4.51   The tribunal is able to make a recommendation that an employer take certain action to obviate or reduce the adverse effects of the discrimination on the applicant.[260] The EAT has held that an employment tribunal cannot recommend that an employer promote a successful candidate to the next available vacancy as this would prevent consideration of other candidates.[261] This appears to us to be unsatisfactory for the same reasons as were advanced above in respect of orders of engagement. The tribunal should be able to make a recommendation of engagement or promotion where it is satisfied that but for the discrimination the applicant would have got the job. In non-employment cases there is no power to make recommendations.

4.52   The recommendation must relate to improving the position of the applicant. It is not possible to make recommendations that have a wider effect on the employment practices of the employer. Thus there is no power to make recommendations to change a discriminatory practice where the applicant has left employment.   In Northern Ireland, under the FETO Art. 39(1)(d), a tribunal is able to make a recommendation that the "respondent take within a specified period action appearing to the tribunal to be practicable for the purpose of obviating or reducing the adverse effect on a person other than the complainant of any unlawful discrimination to which the complaint relates". There are two options open for failure to comply with such a recom-mendation without justification. First, the President or Vice President can certify the failure to the High Court which is then able to deal with the respondent as if the recommendation of the tribunal had been an order of the High Court. Alternatively, the President or Vice-President can require the respondent to pay to the Department a pecuniary penalty of an amount not exceeding £40,000.

4.53   The Bar Council's Sex Discrimination Committee voiced concerns that a tribunal's recommen-dation might have consequences for persons who were not parties to the proceedings, and that it would be difficult to identify who has been affected by the discrimination. In our view, the proper way to deal with the wider issues of this kind, is not in an individual case, but through

---

[259] Palmer et al. (1997), p. 533.

[260] SDA s.65 (1)(c); SD(NI)O, art. 65(1)(c); RRA s.56(1)(c); RR(NI)O, art. 53(1)(c); DDA s.8(2)(c).

[261] *British Gas v Sharma* [1991] IRLR 101, EAT. In *Noone v North West Thames Regional Health Authority (No.2)* [1998] IRLR 530, CA, the Court of Appeal similarly refused to uphold a recommendation that the applicant be offered the next available vacancy on the ground that this would subvert the statutory procedures for appointments in the Health Service.

investigations by the commission followed where necessary by an application to the tribunal by the commission (see para.4.26). It must be borne in mind that it is always open to tribunals, in their reasons or oral remarks, to draw attention to general failings in the respondent's organisation which may have contributed to the individual complaint. Our case studies (Appendix 1) indicated that most employers pay very close attention to such remarks. Moreover, if the commission keeps a database relating to particular employers, a series of findings of discrimination should prompt investigations by the commission.

Recommendation 52

- An employment tribunal should have power to recommend that the applicant be engaged in or promoted to a particular job
- The power to make a recommendation that action be taken to obviate or reduce the adverse effect of the discrimination on the applicant should be extended to non-employment cases
- In the event of a recommendation not being complied with in the period specified the tribunal or court should have power to award additional compensation, including aggravated and punitive damages

(5) Interim relief

4.54   We consulted as to whether tribunals should have power to award interim relief, on the grounds that there are circumstances in which a remedy at the end of a hearing cannot adequately compensate an individual for discrimination that has occurred, or where discrimination is ongoing and should be stopped immediately. The CRE thought that interim relief would be a useful mechanism in situations where a public authority respondent institutes disciplinary action very close to complaints of race discrimination. Interim relief could be used effectively to suspend such proceedings pending the outcome of the tribunal proceedings, especially if it is suspected that the disciplinary action may be an act of victimisation. The CRE noted that at present the only way of obtaining any sort interim relief is to seek an injunction in the High Court, which is an expensive and time-consuming process. RADAR and the RNIB argued that tribunals should have the power to order interim relief in disability cases where a person is claiming a reasonable adjustment. The EOC put forward the idea of tribunals having the power to issue interim relief in their 1998 consultative document. They informed us that responses to their proposal were mixed. Some believed that interim compensation orders would be impractical or ineffective, whereas others commented favourably.

4.55   We agree with the Bar Council's Sex Discrimination Committee that a fast-track procedure to enable tribunals to grant interim relief would be likely to be cumbersome, expensive and rarely used, as is the case with the procedure under the ERA 1996, s.129 in respect of unfair dismissals on particular grounds such as union membership or non-membership. There is a particular difficulty in discrimination cases in being able to find, at the early stage, whether the application is likely to succeed, this being a pre-condition for the grant of interim relief. Tribunals already have the ability to fast-track cases for hearing where urgency can be shown. Accordingly, we make no recommendation in this respect.

G. Costs

4.56   Employment tribunals do not normally award costs, although they have the power to do so if the proceedings were brought or conducted "frivolously, vexatiously, or otherwise unreasonably". We sought views as to whether tribunals should have power to award costs to a winning party on wider grounds than at present. Many argued that this would undermine the ethos of the tribunal system of providing an accessible inexpensive route for resolving disputes. The fear of having costs awarded against them would act as a further deterrent to applicants in precarious financial circumstances wanting to bring complaints of discrimination. The Law Society's Employment Law Committee noted that the awarding of applicant's costs against the unsuccessful employer would not usually be a deterrent to firms determined to fight claims, particularly where the complainant is unrepresented.

4.57   There are also powerful arguments against allowing the Commissions to recover their costs from the successful complainant. In view of the relatively low awards, recoupment from any payment made to a complainant whom they supported would result in a hollow victory for complainants. The EOC in their response pointed to their own research which showed that the amount of money which it would have recouped if it were to have taken 10% of all awards over £10,000 in 1996 and 1997 was actually quite small. Furthermore, it would not be just to require respondents to pay costs whenever they lost if they could not collect costs when they won. Thus, if the Commissions were able to recover costs from unsuccessful respondents there would have to be a reciprocal right for successful respondents to be able to recover their costs from either the Commissions or parties and that would be a large deterrent for applicants.

4.58   In relation to disability cases it was suggested tribunals should have the power to award expenses incurred in obtaining medical evidence where the respondent unsuccessfully claims that the applicant does not fall with the definition of "disability" within the terms of the Act. In our view, it would be anomalous to have a special rule of this kind, and tribunals should be able to assess whether the respondent has acted frivolously, vexatiously or otherwise unreasonably in disputing this issue. We make no recommendations for changing the costs rules.

H. Conciliation, mediation and arbitration

4.59   We received a number of submissions suggesting that mediation and arbitration, as well as the present conciliation arrangements, might have an important role to play in discrimination cases. Clarifying the meaning of the terms, conciliation, mediation and arbitration may assist discussion of this.[262] Conciliation may be defined as a strategy whereby a third party assists the parties to a dispute to reach a settlement. This is a voluntary process that can be declined by either party. This is the service currently provided by ACAS in discrimination cases. Mediation is essentially a "facilitative function". The mediator like the conciliator conveys information and clarifies issues but, in addition, gives a view on the strengths and weaknesses of a case and recommends a settlement. The process remains voluntary although any agreement reached can be binding. Arbitration is a process whereby a third party makes an award having heard the cases for both parties. The parties lose their control of the settlement entirely, as the decision is the arbitrator's not that of the parties.

4.60   The present system promotes settlement thought conciliation. Copies of a complaint to an employment tribunal under the SDA, EqPA, RRA or DDA are sent to the Advisory, Conciliation and Arbitration Service (ACAS). In Northern Ireland this function is conducted by the Labour Relations Agency (LRA). Their conciliation officers have a duty to promote a settlement if both parties make a request for settlement or if the officer thinks that there is a

---

[262] The definitions are taken from Corby (1999).

reasonable chance of achieving a settlement. Settlements reached through ACAS conciliation are binding on the parties and prevent the parties from taking the matter to a tribunal.[263] Parties are also able to make binding compromise contracts without ACAS where the agreement is in writing and before signing the agreement the employee has received advice from a relevant independent adviser.

4.61   One of the criticisms of the present system is that ACAS have a duty only to promote conciliation but no duty to promote equal opportunities. They facilitate communication and the exchange of views between the parties but "do not make decisions on the merits of the case nor impose or even recommend a settlement".[264] ACAS conciliation is, "by virtue of its own traditions as well as the legislative framework as interpreted by the courts...meticulously neutral as between the parties. [ACAS] is emphatically not a rights-enforcement agency".[265] ACAS conciliation plays an important role in the settlement process. Tables 4.5-4.7 shows that in the 1990s 36% of SDA cases were settled through ACAS conciliation. For race discrimination claims the figure was 25%, and for equal pay 21%. The figure for DDA cases is 41%.[266] It is to be noted, however, that there is no provision for conciliation in non-employment cases under the SDA and RRA. The DRC has been given the power to make arrangements for the provision of independent conciliation services in respect of non-employment claims.[267] A similar power clearly needs to be given to the EOC and CRE.

4.62   Hunter and Leonard have argued for mediation to be added to the range of dispute resolution options available in the sex discrimination field.[268] This was echoed in responses to our initial consultation paper. Mediation is available in discrimination cases in several countries, including the United States, Australia and New Zealand. A pilot mediation programme was carried out by the US EEOC in 1991. In light of the success of this pilot, the Commission established an ADR task force to examine the possible expanded use of ADR. In 1994 the task force concluded that mediation was a viable mechanism for resolution of employment discrimination claims and recommended the implementation of a programme. Among the advantages of mediation are that it is informal; it reduces delay in settling a claim; it reduces the costs to the parties; it can provide for a wider range of remedies to a situation than is available by taking cases through the tribunals; it offers privacy; and it is particularly valuable to parties who wish to continue their employment relationship. Furthermore, the American experience indicates that mediation can encourage positive employment practices when there are effective internal processes.[269] The privacy offered by mediation can be problematic. In cases of harassment, where the public nature of the employment tribunal process can be harrowing there is an obvious advantage in the privacy offered by mediation. However Hunter and Leonard note that "a privatised dispute resolution process will inhibit both the publicisation and the elaboration of sex discrimination legislation". To overcome this they argue that while privacy and confidentiality should apply to the mediation process there should be a presumption that mediated settlements would become a matter of public record. This presumption would be rebutted if both parties wished to keep the mediated settlement private.

4.63   Other dangers which Hunter and Leonard note in the mediation process for discrimination include the reproduction of financial, informational, skill, status and personal power imbal-

---

[263] SDA, s.77(4)(a), RRA, s.72(4)(a).

[264] ACAS, *Individual Conciliation- a Short Guide* (London, ACAS)

[265] Lewis and Clark (1993), p. 8.

[266] Meager et al. (1999), at p. 114.

[267] DRCA, s.10.

[268] Hunter and Leonard (1997).

[269] Stamato (2000), p. 25.

Table 4.5 Equal Pay Cases 1990–9

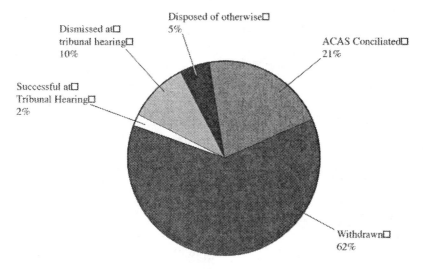

Table 4.6 Sex Discrimination Cases 1990–9

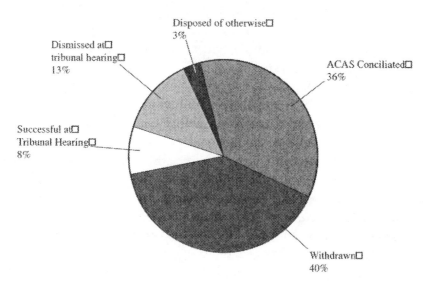

Table 4.7 Race Discrimination Cases 1990–9

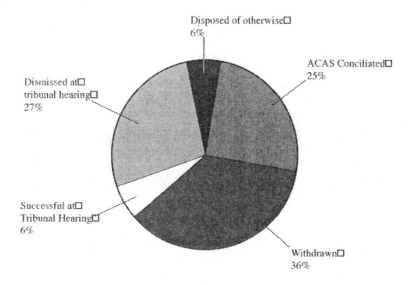

ances between the parties and the undermining of legal rights contained in discrimination legislation. It is important that the mediation process should reflect the aims and ensures compliance with discrimination legislation. Hunter and Leonard favour a "rights based mediation" model for discrimination cases, which "prioritises legal rights and the elimination of discrimination". To be successful, entry into mediation would need to be voluntary rather than mandatory. The option of mediation should be offered as early as possible. The mediator would not be merely a neutral facilitator but rather would have responsibility for ensuring that the objectives of the legislation are furthered through the mediation process and the eventual settlement does not undermine the legal rights of the parties. The mediator would provide information about the legislation in general and the legal implications of the various issues in dispute. The mediator would have a vital role in addressing the power imbalances between the parties.[270]

4.64   So far ACAS has signalled a reluctance to attempt a more proactive approach aimed at reaching settlements which promote equal opportunities. They believe that this would undermine their neutrality. It may be that ACAS will required to take such an approach if they are specified as a public authority in respect of the proposed duty to promote equal opportunities. However, public resources are unlikely to be available for having a separate discrimination mediation service. Accordingly, we would urge support for a privately-funded pilot project, initially perhaps in respect of sexual harassment cases. Consideration should also be given to a requirement for having third party independent mediation in employment cases incorporated into employment grievance procedures.

4.65   Provision now exists for ACAS to establish an arbitration scheme. Parties will be able make a binding agreement to submit a sex, race or disability complaint to binding arbitration under such a scheme instead of going to an employment tribunal.[271] In Northern Ireland the LRA is also empowered to prepare a scheme providing for arbitration for cases that could go to the FET.[272] We understand that initially the arbitration scheme will cover only unfair dismissal. Strong reservations have been voiced about the suitability of arbitration for dealing with the right to equal treatment. Unlike the USA, where the cost and delays of civil litigation have stimulated the use of arbitration in discrimination cases, there is no reason to suppose that arbitration in the UK will be speedier or more cost-effective for the parties than the tribunals, particularly where there are complex disputes of fact or law. Until there has been experience of the operation of the scheme in respect of unfair dismissal, it would be premature to introduce a scheme for including arbitration in discrimination claims. We believe that priority should be given to mediation.

Recommendation 53

- The power of the commission to make arrangements for conciliation in non-employment cases should be extended to all grounds of unlawful discrimination
- A pilot project for mediation in sexual harassment cases, and subsequently in other discrimination cases, should be supported.
- Employers' grievance and harassment procedures should include provision for mediation
- The ERA 1996, s.3 should be amended so as to require an employer to specify in the note about grievance procedures a person or body to whom the employee can apply for mediation of any grievance relating to alleged discrimination or harassment, if other procedures fail

---

[270] Hunter and Leonard (1997), p. 312
[271] SDA, s.77(4D); RRA, s.72(4D); DDA, s.9(6) as inserted by the Employment Rights (Dispute Resolution) Act 1998, ss.7-12.
[272] FETO, s.89.

APPENDICES

APPENDIX 1

Findings from Employer Case Studies

1. Introduction

1.1. Three categories of employers in Great Britain were included in the detailed case studies, carried out between June and November 1999, although in practice, the categories overlap. The aim was to cover a wide range of organisations, sectors and levels of interest. The first category is large employers who are active members of the various equality networks. Requests for interview were made to employers who were members of equality networks such as Organisation Resources Counselors, Inc. (ORC), The Employers' Forum on Disability, Race for Opportunity and Opportunity Now. The second category is employers which have had recent litigation. Approaches were made to organisations which had decisions against them in employment tribunals using lists for 1998. The third category is employers, which are neither active, nor have had recent litigation against them. The Institute of Personnel and Development (IPD) arranged a focus group of 15 of their branch members from England, and the CBI sent a circular letter to members asking for volunteers to participate. Approaches were also made to respondents involved in a survey of flexible working being carried out by the Judge Institute of Management Studies, and interviews on both topics were combined. The latter were chosen because they represented organisations which were not active, nor had they had recent employment tribunal cases against them.

1.2. In September 1999, interviews were held with six large US corporations. Discussions at a two-day meeting of the ORC Workplace Opportunity Network in New York also produced relevant information on experience in the USA.

1.3. In November 1999, interviews were held with six large employers in Northern Ireland from both the private and public sectors.

1.4. Interviews have been classified according to sector, and level of activity. Employers who belong to more than one equality network are categorised as high; those belonging to one or none but with active equal opportunities policies are medium. Employers with neither active programmes, nor membership of an equality network are categorised as low.

Classification of respondents

Sector	Activity Level	Interviewee
Private		
Finance 1	High	HR/EO
Telecommunications	High	HR/EO
Finance 2	High	HR/EO
Food	High	Corporate Affairs
Utilities 1	High	HR/EO
Legal	Medium	HR/EO
Finance3	High	HR
PropertyConstruction/devel.	Low	HR
Catering	Low	HR
Health	Medium	Community Affairs
Utilities 2	High	HR
Housing Association	High	HR

Sector	Activity Level	Interviewee
Focus Group		
Consultancies 2	Low	Partner
Engineering	Low	HR
Police Services	Medium	HR
Higher Education	Medium	HR
Tourism	Low	HR
Hotels	Low	HR
Food	Low	HR
Voluntary	Low	HR
Public		
Postal 1	Medium	Legal
Health	Medium	HR/EO
Transport	Medium	Legal
Civil Service	High	HR
Postal 2	High	HR
Police Service 2	High	HR/Operations
USA		
Motor Manufacturing	High	HR/EO
Utilities	High	HR/EO
IT	High	HR/EO
Pharmaceuticals	High	HR/EO
Telecommunications	High	HR/EO
Finance	High	HR/EO

Three organisations (a local education authority, a multi-national conglomerate, and a multi-national in the food industry) declined to take part in the survey, and several did not reply despite reminders. The latter included two household name retail organisations and a multi-national pharmaceutical company.

1.5. Most of the case studies were of large corporations with established human resources departments, and, in some cases, specialised equality and diversity managers. A few small employers were included in the IPD focus group.

2. Overall effect of the equality laws in employment in Britain

A. How has the law helped secure changes?

2.1. In employment, the anti-discrimination legislation has been the starting point for changes in practices. In most cases, initial action has been triggered by a complaint. A comment from a company solicitor was:

'This company would not have made the progress it has in having an ethnic mix which reflected the area without the law, and we continue to use it to effect change.'

Another said: 'It would not work at all if it was entirely voluntary.'

Only three of the employers interviewed had experience of formal investigations. In two of these, the investigation had caused the company to review completely their recruitment and selection procedures and criteria.

2.2. After dealing with a complaint, a combination of factors determined whether an employer continued to take action and make further changes. As one respondent put it:

'Litigation has a short-lived effect. What is needed is cultural change in an organisation to sustain progress on equal opportunities'.

Another said:

'Timing is very important. If a complaint comes at a time when there is other regulatory activity having a public impact, a complaint can be very powerful.'

2.3.   Many interviewees felt that a key condition for the continuation of high level action was the support and active involvement of a senior, or more important, board level manager. Senior managers are particularly influenced by bad publicity. Often, the senior manager had been sensitised to discrimination and equal opportunities by an earlier experience, sometimes in another company, of managing a department that had had a tribunal case against it. Employers with a high public profile and whose customers were members of the public, for example, retail and financial services, were sensitive about their image, as they believed that adverse publicity from a case could adversely affect their business.

2.4.   Another significant factor in encouraging sustained action is peer or sectoral influence. For example, in the financial sector there are several influential employers who share experience and this spreads good practice among others in the sector. This influence does not exist in most other sectors surveyed. Several experienced respondents said that joining one of the equality campaigns or employer groups also stimulates continued action, and introduces an element of peer competition.

2.5.   For most active employers, monitoring was important as it showed that they were vulnerable and made them continue to review selection decisions. (See paragraph 8.5 below)

One Equal Opportunity Manager said:

'Monitoring is very useful to focus future activities.'

Another said:

'The best way to justify the need for action is to bombard everyone with statistics about the gap in the participation of women and ethnic minorities.'

But the majority of respondents said that they monitored sporadically, and only looked at the data if there was a complaint.

2.6.   Most active employers said that the periodic receipt of complaints enabled them to use the lessons, and any bad publicity, as justification for continuing action to review practices and decisions, and to reinforce the equal opportunities policy through training and guidance for managers.

One Equal Opportunity Manager said:

'Cases demonstrate the gap between policy and its implementation. They are important because they justify the need for my role and for a strong forward looking policy and programme.'

2.7.   The implementation of the DDA had also been used to reinforce equal opportunities messages, and to justify continuing reviews. For retail sector, and service providers, auditing their premises for access by people with disabilities was also a useful reinforcement, especially as it provided a direct link with their core business functions.

2.8.   Only one organisation said that they would have implemented an equal opportunities policy without the influence of discrimination case. But this organisation had had cases against it and had used these to review and improve practices.

2.9.   There was general agreement by all those interviewed that the equality legislation had a significant effect on human resource and other practices, and, gradually, on attitudes. Employers considered that the legislation had also influenced expectations. Most people knew in general terms that they were protected against sex or racial discrimination, although fewer knew that people with disabilities were protected. Not one employer argued that the equality legislation was no longer necessary.

2.10. Most of the more experienced and active interviewees felt that discrimination was now more subtle and covert, and therefore more difficult to tackle. They said that many managers knew what formal language to use, knew how to follow procedures and how to make decisions appear objective. One experienced respondent said:

'There is a difference now in the type of case we are receiving. The complaint now is more usually about the language and lack of sensitivity on the part of managers. It was more a matter of unconscious behaviour'.

Another said:

'Now practices are so much better but attitudes have probably not changed. This is a much more difficult process.'

2.11. Human resource/equal opportunity professionals felt that they needed to find new messages and new techniques to keep their managers up to standard. They thought that those aspects of the legislation with clear tangible rules, such as the requirement to make 'reasonable adjustments' under the DDA, and law on the maternity rights, were much easier to get across to managers (and small businesses). However, concepts such as 'equal opportunities' were not easily explained in practical terms. They felt that a new more effective law would help keep up the momentum, although there were different views on what this might be (see below). Significant numbers (more than half) felt that the best way of getting compliance with the overall aims of the equality laws was to have practical, technical advice from a Commission with specialised expertise.

B. How has the law been unhelpful?

2.8. Several (three or four) less active employers complained in general terms about the demands of regulation on business, especially small businesses. It is worth noting that they were employers who had no experience of litigation and did not have active equality programmes who expressed these views. It is also important to underline the fact that their complaint was not about the protection of individuals against discrimination, which they did not question, but about the additional requirements which they believed were imposed by regulations, to demonstrate that they were complying. Larger numbers of employers in the sample, including some more active respondents, felt that managers saw the equality legislation either as too adversarial or as giving special privileges to those protected. One respondent said:

'There is a problem with racial discrimination cases as managers feel that the underlying assumption is that the individual concerned is racist, and this causes discomfort. Often cases are a result of poor practice, but a case is run on adversarial lines, based on the assumption that they were racist. It is not a genuinely participative process and does not help in getting managers to understand how to behave in a non-discriminatory way.'

Nevertheless all interviewees accepted that laws against discrimination were a necessary price to pay for fairness at work.

3.   Specific experience of complaints procedures

3.1   Individual complaints were the strongest influence on employers. Many examples were given of a strong individual case which came at the right time, raising questions about a selection or other personnel procedure, and produced change in practices. One interviewee commented on a significant case as follows:

'At the time I was able to use the case to demonstrate the need for change. It was a window of opportunity which enabled me to promote change. Since then, there have been so many changes that it is no longer possible to use this argument.'

3.2. Among some of the most active respondents, there was a tendency to be more likely to defend cases to the end. They would settle only if they were vulnerable, either because someone failed to carry out the correct procedure, or the paper trail was poor. These organisations felt that they had developed effective equal opportunities practices, and therefore it was against their interests to settle.

3.3. There was little support for arbitration. Most said that they would not agree to it because they would 'lose control'. One respondent argued for specialist arbitration under the DDA. It would avoid the current system which set one medical specialist against another. It was better to have a panel of three specialists making a decision on whether a condition was a disability and what was a reasonable adjustment.

3.4. Employers were generally content with the tribunal procedures and with the role of ACAS. Some would have liked better weeding out of unmeritorious cases. They said that tribunals were too generous to individuals especially in race discrimination cases. Some of the most active felt that the equality commissions were too unwilling to take a good equality programme into account in deciding whether to support an applicant.

3.5. Several respondents mentioned the difficulties of dealing with sexual harassment cases, which had the potential to attract intrusive publicity, unwelcome to both respondent and complainant.

4. Formal investigations

4.1. Very few respondents had experience of the equality commissions' strategic enforcement powers, although two that had had this experience said that it resulted in wholesale change in practices. Two others had found the threat of a formal investigation had been counterproductive because it had not been carried through. This had undermined the equality manager's credibility and weakened the argument for extensive change. The threat has to be real.

5. Why some employers do not take action

5.1. Respondents who had done little other than issue a policy statement had had no external or internal pressure to take any further action. Either they had had no exposure to complaints, or they had faced only weak cases. They did not feel vulnerable. For example, one company that experienced several complaints each year felt under little pressure because they had only lost one case. In addition, many complainants were not represented. As most cases were about dismissal, they felt that the equality legislation was being used as a substitute for unfair dismissal. Managers in this company were under strong counter-pressure from the parent company to increase profits. As a result, a manager had moved a Black member of staff at the request of a big corporate client, for fear of losing the business.

5.2. Where organisational change was not sustained, it appeared to be because some of the conditions, which have driven progress in the most active organisations, were missing. For example, several respondents had found that when a particular senior manager who had been driving change left the company, equal opportunities initiatives were given lower priority. Structural change such as take-overs and workforce reductions had stifled action because energies were focused on dealing with these upheavals. One respondent said that change had not been sustained because the central equal opportunities unit had been disbanded and no one was looking at the overall picture. It was dealt with on a case by case basis. The central unit had also been making sure that managers received training, but since then it had not been happening.

5.3. Publicity also has a negative effect, especially in organisations without a dedicated equal opportunities unit to absorb some of the pressures and bring out the positive aspects of a case. Some of those interviewed were unwilling to share experience because they feared that they may expose their weaknesses and invite challenges from employees or pressure groups. This also applied to the joining of campaigns such as Race for Opportunity and Opportunity Now.

5.4. Some aspects of the legislation have been less effective. Few respondents were actively reviewing pay structures. Indirect discrimination was not well understood. The lack of complaints about equal pay and indirect discrimination means there is little case law to influence change. Similarly, without legislation, everyone felt that the voluntary code of practice on age discrimination would be ineffective, and no one had taken any initiatives to combat it, even though they conceded that age discrimination was 'widespread.' A typical comment on the voluntary code from one respondent who was not a specialist equal opportunities manager was:

'It is a waste of time.'

5.5. Most interviewees felt that discrimination on grounds of sexual orientation was too sensitive to tackle voluntarily. One respondent with a well-established equal opportunities programme had tried unsuccessfully to introduce sexual orientation into their diversity policy but dropped it because the board 'went ballistic'. However, almost all interviewees accepted that it would become necessary to include age, and sexual orientation in the grounds of discrimination, and a few also accepted that religious discrimination would have to be covered.

5.6. In general, respondents did not find the sex and racial equality codes useful, mainly because they were seen as old. Some commented that the codes were based on an assumed centralised structure which no longer applied, as most organisations had devolved decision making to units. Several mentioned the Disability Code more positively mainly because of its newness and practical recommendations. There was a demand for 'technical' codes with information on current good practice.

6.   Government influence

6.1. Not surprisingly, the public sector was strongly influenced by the lead taken by government. Some of the most active private sector employers also felt that the line taken by government ministers was influential and could help win arguments with senior managers for further action. Government was also seen as a negative influence, and examples were given of lack of support, for example by taxing nursery places, which undermined employers. Many respondents were looking at the government response to the Stephen Lawrence Inquiry report to assess what more they needed to do to change their organisational culture. If the government response were seen as weak, it would be more difficult to justify action within their company. Several felt that the Better Regulation Unit report had been unhelpful because it emphasised the voluntary approach.

7.   Demographic and social change

7.1. Many respondents, especially those in Greater London, were aware that the ethnic mix of the labour market and customer base provided a good business case for an active equal opportunities programme. They were aware that population ageing would affect recruitment, but only a few were considering actively recruiting older people. In retail and financial sectors, customer demands for services to be available for longer hours and weekends, meant that they were considering how to attract and retain women with family responsibilities, and this too provided a business argument for having equal opportunities programmes.

7.2. Some considered that developments in information technology had changed managers' roles. Widespread use of E-mail and Intranet technology resulted in flatter structures, and managers had to become facilitators rather than controllers. Individuals had more responsibility for their output and for decisions. This encouraged the introduction of diversity management. It was believed to be consistent with managers' changing role. Emphasis on maximising individual performance encouraged them to respect and value differences such as sex, age and ethnic background. Other respondents saw diversity policies as consistent with becoming a global organisation. For example one equal opportunities manager said:

'We need a consistent corporate worldview. It is essential to develop values which are appropriate to this, and cultural change and valuing diversity are seen as an essential part of business transformation.'
Diversity policies were not precisely defined. Respondents with these policies emphasised individual treat-

ment, development, and valuing differences. However, the introduction of diversity policies was confined to those employers with long standing equal opportunities programmes. It appeared to be partly motivated by the need to introduce new messages which were not seen as focusing on particular groups, which would appeal to line managers. New initiatives were needed, to help keep up the momentum.

8. Changes to the legislation

A. Positive duty

8.1. There was significant support for the introduction of a positive duty to promote equal opportunities. (The precise terms of this duty were not explored in detail). Some employers saw this as analogous to their duties under the Health and Safety at Work Act. They felt that the focus of regulation by the equality commissions would be on how best to carry out this duty and not on whether there had been a contravention, which was seen as negative, adversarial, and too emotional, especially in the case of racial discrimination. If taking affirmative action was linked to a positive duty to promote equal opportunities or fair participation, it might be more acceptable and more productive than if it were linked with discrimination. This approach was also seen by some to be more consistent with diversity policies, because these are concerned with inclusivity and with accountability to a range of stakeholders.

B. Definition of Discrimination

8.2. Some more experienced employers felt that the definition of discrimination needed to be reviewed, as it was out of date, given recent decisions, such as the acceptance of unconscious discrimination in the Nagarajan case, and the decisions about 'in the course of employment'.

8.3. Several employers referred to workplace bullying, and felt that it was illogical for there to be protection if such behaviour was based on race or sex, but not otherwise.

C. Positive Action

8.4. One employer with considerable experience of using the positive action provisions argued that these were now out of date, in two respects. Positive action has to be for 'particular work'. This was no longer an appropriate concept, because employers' training programmes are linked to giving people specific competencies which may be needed for a variety of positions at a certain level. Secondly the provisions do not allow positive action to be taken for people who receive payment such as New Deal trainees and Work Experience, because they are deemed to be employees. The sections were based on a model of training which has now changed. Very few respondents had used these provisions for increasing ethnic minority representation, mainly because they were considered to be too difficult to justify, and would be seen as 'special privileges'. One respondent said that women's personal development courses had been the single most effective initiative taken in her organisation.

D. Monitoring

8.5. There was also general, but not unanimous, support for a requirement to monitor, so long as this was not accompanied by requirement to report the details to an equality commission. The latter was considered to be counterproductive and also to undermine the very purpose of monitoring, which was to provide a management tool to assess progress. Most employers supported the idea that an overall breakdown should be given in the Annual Report. Several preferred this to be a breakdown of the recruitment rates of different groups, as this was more dynamic, because it would focus on how new entrants reflected the make-up of the catchment area, whereas an overall snapshot of the workforce was a reflection of past recruitment too. Others suggested an overall workforce diversity breakdown would be sufficient. It was felt that a public statement of monitoring results was consistent with their general policy of giving feedback to stakeholders. Several who supported this idea commented that it was not appropriate to include small businesses.

E. Extending the grounds of protection

8.6. Many respondents felt that an inclusive definition was preferable, given the 'fluidity' of identities, the overlap of possible grounds, and also the fact that employers dealt in people, not members of specific groups. A majority of respondents were in favour of extending the law to age discrimination, or if not in favour, they recognised that there was a compelling political case for it. Some felt that it could broaden acceptance of the equality laws because it would include white men. Many felt that they could do little to tackle age discrimination without the support of the law.

8.7. There was some support for including sexual orientation. As with age discrimination, many felt that as other grounds have been added to the original laws, it was difficult to justify excluding sexual orientation, especially in view of recent decisions of the European Court of Human Rights. Several employers felt that sexual orientation was a private matter and they were not convinced that there was a problem of discrimination at work, but nevertheless saw that individuals may need a right to take action if there was discrimination. There was almost no support for extending enforcement beyond giving individual rights of complaint. One respondent suggested that legal protection against discrimination on grounds of sexual orientation could be linked to an individual declaration of their orientation, similar to that related to disability in the DDA.

8.8. One respondent who had recently opened a division in Northern Ireland supported the inclusion of religious discrimination. Others said that they did not feel that religious discrimination was a problem in employment as a person's religion was not visible. One employer with extensive shift working felt that including religion could cause difficulties, as it would increase the numbers who could claim exemption from certain shifts.

F. The Commissions

8.9. Most employers were strongly in favour of a single equality agency, for several reasons. Firstly, employers said that their own equality policies and programmes were unified, especially those with diversity policies. Secondly, they felt that it was inconvenient to have to deal with three commissions. Thirdly, they considered that each commission had a different approach and different priorities, which led to inconsistencies and made it difficult to act on their advice. Fourthly, they felt that it would become impractical to have additional agencies if the grounds of protection were extended. Less active employers in particular did not trust the equality commissions to give advice on problems, because of their law enforcement role, and also because it was felt that the commissions' main interest was in getting high profile test cases rather than in working quietly behind the scenes. Most respondents, including those with experience, said that they did not go to the commissions for technical advice, but used the employer networks or their legal advisors. The active employers 'kept in touch' with the commissions to be aware of their thinking and approach. A few employers who had had contact with local race equality councils perceived their approach as negative and counterproductive.

8.10. Although employers said that they did not use the commissions' advisory services, most accepted that there was a need for a strategic role for the agencies in enforcing the broader aims in the legislation. This aspect was not explored in depth in the interviews, but it appears that employers would prefer the equality agencies to have a more clearly focused enforcement role without the current ambiguities of advisory and promotional roles.

8.11. There was scepticism about the value of a one-stop shop advice agency. Some more experienced employers considered that it would not have the expertise to give detailed advice, and were doubtful about using it.

8.12. It should be noted that views of the case study organisations on the separation of enforcement and strategic roles of the commissions reflect different experiences. As the EOC has pointed out, employers may seek their own legal advice on specific matters, but are keen to do more general promotional work with the commissions such as building awareness, and sharing experience of good practice.

G. Purchasing and contracting

8.12. Some of the most active private sector employers were using their purchasing chain to influence the equal opportunities practices of suppliers, and to widen the pool to encourage more use of ethnic minority businesses. They supported more widespread use of contracting policies, to 'educate' suppliers although they disliked the idea of contracting being for legal compliance. One difficulty of implementing positive purchasing policies is that large companies are reducing the numbers of suppliers used, in order to cut costs, which undermined efforts to bring in small businesses. Two public sector employers had active contracting policies and asked suppliers about their equal opportunities policies. One said:

'The Bernard Manning case requires us to protect customers and staff from racial harassment. We have to extend this to contractors on our premises.'

One specified to agencies that staff supplied under the contract should reflect their (i.e. the purchaser's) workforce diversity. Several other respondents linked equal opportunities with ethical investment, and the need to ensure that their suppliers met their ethical standards.

9. USA

A. How has the legislation helped bring about change?

9.1. All the employers who were interviewed in the US said that contract compliance requirements were the most significant influence on their organisations. The need to have affirmative action programmes which included good faith efforts to reduce under-utilisation, and goals and timetables for achieving this, as part of the process of contacting with federal and state governments, had a big impact. It affected all areas of activity, in contrast to individual litigation, which tended to be seen as a question of the costs of a pay-off, and was delegated to separate units. There were several reasons why this was more significant than even a big expensive case:

- Affirmative action became a mainstream business matter because it was linked with gaining government contracts. In the words of one multi-national EO manager:

'Preparing affirmative action plans was a defining moment.'

- The need for there to be an affirmative action plan for all areas of under-utilisation had a direct impact on operations divisions and senior managers. One EO manager said:

'It provides a mechanism to get EO issues to the top of the house.'

- The affirmative action plan became a strategic business plan used internally to focus where action was needed. It provided an impetus for change.

- The need to define and carry out measures included in the affirmative action plan was pro-active and practical.

- The need to set goals and have timetables gave a benchmark and detailed data to measure progress. It is also used to benchmark with other companies.

All the EO managers said that they would not have been able to sustain the change which had taken place without the OFCCP contracting process. One said:

'The government mandate for this was essential.'

Another said that his company had doubled their representation of women and minorities since adopting affirmative action plans in the 1970s:

'We are now as diverse as we can be.'

9.2. The most effective aspects of affirmative action were considered to be the outreach activities. All those interviewed had detailed programmes to link with local neighbourhoods, churches, and community organisations, minority schools and colleges, and media. More important they all had programmes aimed at 'levelling the playing field', to develop women and ethnic minority executives. Other important measures were the links with community advocacy groups to develop economic ties through dealerships, and supplier development programmes. They measure progress in penetrating minority markets, which gives a clear economic link between, affirmative action and business success.

9.3. Everyone agreed that the OFCCP requirements had a resource cost, especially in setting up systems and dealing with compliance reviews. It was felt that these costs did not outweigh the gains. Some were concerned about the practicality of preparing affirmative action plans and returns in future as businesses changed so rapidly. Even as we spoke, one EO manager said that his corporation had just taken over another, rendering his plans out of date.

9.4. Most of those interviewed had moved to the diversity approach, which stressed individual development and the need to respect and value individual differences. In discussing public and political perceptions of affirmative action, it was argued that the diversity approach could make it more difficult to justify affirmative action because it applied to specific under-represented groups. The social and business purposes of affirmative action needed to be continuously reinforced and explained. Affirmative action was misrepresented and continued to be attacked in the media and in political debate as no longer necessary and divisive.

10.   Northern Ireland

10.1. Employers interviewed in Northern Ireland agreed unanimously that the Fair Employment legislation had made a fundamental difference to equal opportunities. It was described as 'the key driver', and 'absolutely crucial to make things happen'. The requirement to monitor and prepare action plans to reduce under-representation by a deadline was very important. One EO manager said:

'Unless managers are told to do it, they play at it,' and 'everyone was in favour of monitoring but no one did it'

before the Fair Employment legislation required it.

Another said:

'The duty to monitor focused the minds of senior managers. The triennial review put them in the spotlight. It has entirely changed our attitudes, approach and culture. It has proved to be a good thing and we could not do without it. Without legislation, voluntary codes simply do not work. '

The requirement to take affirmative action to reduce under-representation also helped tackle vested local interests.

10.2. Two employers were part of a UK organisation and said that they were struck by the differences in attitudes towards equal opportunities of their colleagues in Great Britain. They were much less ready to take equality into account, and 'were on another planet'. This was because their mainland British colleagues 'knew they would not get caught in the long grass.' Equal opportunities in Great Britain were at the bottom of the line, but in Northern Ireland it was something that had to be done. As competitive pressures increased equal opportunities disappeared.

10.3. Employers in Northern Ireland accepted that many had reservations about the resource implications of complying with the monitoring and review requirements, but all agreed that these had been unfounded in practice. They said that comprehensive monitoring was perfectly feasible, and the main demands on resources came at the outset in setting up the systems. There were some concerns about the additional requirements being added to monitor applications because of practical problems of definition. There were also concerns about the practicalities of monitoring decentralised companies with separate business units, which change regularly because of acquisitions and restructuring. It was felt that there should be stream-lining. One suggested that large corporations should report for the entire group. All however agreed that the gains outweighed the disadvantages.

One commented:

'sadly there must be pain; if you dilute the reporting it won't happen'.

There had been a big selling task and they did not want any dilution.

10.4. The triennial reviews were also thought to be an essential vehicle for a good equal opportunities regime because of the link with under-representation. One employer commented that the requirement to promote a harmonious workplace was important because it enabled them to tackle the informal workplace culture, including sexual harassment.

10.5. All employers interviewed were strongly in favour of a single equality commission, with advice, training and reviews on all protected areas, and harmonisation of codes. Some said that, partly because of the success in bringing sex discrimination cases in Northern Ireland, they had applied the stronger require-ments of the Fair Employment Act to sex equality, although others acknowledged that community background equality had been more actively tackled. They were in favour of a compulsory mediation or arbitration with a neutral third party in complaints resolution, because of the litigious culture in Northern Ireland, and the serious fall-out from publicity for even unfounded cases.

10.6. Although there were some concerns about the resources involved, the public sector employers were in favour of the public duty and the need for impact analysis. It was felt that this would put equality consider-ations further into the mainstream, out of HR into core business operations.

11. Summary of main findings and conclusions

11.1. Looking at the approach to equal opportunities in Great Britain and comparing it with experience in Northern Ireland and the USA, it is possible to identify a fundamental difference. The main impact on employers in the USA and in Northern Ireland is from having to reduce under-representation. This is an inclusionary approach. It requires employers to take practical steps to increase the diversity of their recruit-ment and progression. It is not based on fault-finding and on retrospective analysis of decisions. Reviews of decisions may form part of a review of efforts taken, but the emphasis is on assessing the effectiveness of affirmative action and not on whether there have been specific exclusions. This seems to overcome one of the frequently mentioned perceptions of employers in Great Britain, that the regime is too adversarial, and based on a presumption of fault.

11.2. The second observation is that a requirement to reduce under-representation is a practical and concrete challenge. It can be achieved by using a range of marketing techniques which are already familiar to business. It brings equality considerations into the business arena. Several employers in Northern Ireland and the USA commented that affirmative action planning was in line with other business planning, and could be integrated with it. In contrast, employers in Great Britain were attempting to involve operations managers with more abstract concepts such as equal opportunity and indirect discrimination.

11.3. The third observation is that a requirement to monitor which is tied to reducing under representation appears to be more acceptable than one linked with equal opportunities, because the former is measurable and the latter needs definition. If there were a duty to reduce under-representation or to work for fair partic-ipation, it may not be necessary to make monitoring a separate legal requirement as it would be inherent in the measures to be taken in support of this duty.

11.4. The fourth observation is that HR professionals with experience of a regime which requires monitoring, affirmative action and goals and timetables, are wholly if favour of it and in no doubt that it works. In comparison, reliance on individual litigation seems to work only when there is a combination of several other external and internal conditions, some of which are fortuitous. Formal investigations can also work but the British equality commissions have never had nor are likely to, the resources to have a wide impact. Moreover, employers in Britain are responding to an accusatory process, which provokes a defensive response, and taking action under pressure and not as part of a their own plan. Those who have experienced them do not support the arguments that requirements to reduce under-representation, monitor and take affirmative action are too oppressive. Positive action training has been little used in Great Britain, especially for ethnic minorities. It is seen as too controversial, about 'social engineering', and difficult to justify to white staff. Definitions of work for positive action purposes are based on an assumed more static employment pattern than exists today. However, if part of a plan to reduce under-representation it may become more acceptable as a business matter.

11.5. Employers are almost all in favour of a single equality commission. They see advantages in having an integrated approach to regulation and advice, and it is consistent with the approach adopted by most employers with active programmes. Those who disagree tend to argue that disability is an exception because of the technical questions involved, or alternatively, that there is a political need for separation in the case of disability. Few respondents were confident of having a constructive relationship with the equality commissions because of their role in enforcing the law, and this led some to argue for a separation of the wider advisory, educational and advocacy roles of the commissions. It is worth noting that there was a more constructive relationship with the FEC in Northern Ireland in relation to the triennial reviews, which are seen as less adversarial than the complaints process, and the formal investigation process in Britain. This partly results from the fact that these reviews in Northern Ireland are not investigating unlawful discrimination, but are seeking to assess progress towards fair participation.

11.6. One emerging practical question is the need to distinguish between the legal framework and any consequent reporting requirements. The case study organisations were not against regulation if it is effective, but they were opposed to increased reporting requirements. Moreover, any regulation which includes reporting or monitoring, has to be flexible to meet current business organisation which favours devolution to smaller units defined by core activities and frequent change and restructuring in the face of competitive pressures.

APPENDIX 2

Legislation

UNITED KINGDOM

Armed Forces Act 1996
Courts and Legal Services Act 1990
Disability Discrimination Act 1995
Disability Rights Commission Act 1999
Employment Act 1989
Employment Act 1990
Employment Protection Act 1975
Employment Relations Act 1999
Employment Rights Act 1996
Equal Pay Act 1970
Fair Employment (Northern Ireland) Act 1989
Health and Safety Act 1974
Human Rights Act 1998
Local Government Act 1988
Local Government Act 1992
Local Government and Housing Act 1989

National Minimum Wage Act 1998
Northern Ireland Constitution Act 1973
Northern Ireland Act 1998
Parliamentary Commissioner (Northern Ireland) Act 1969
Pensions Act 1995
Prevention of Incitement to Hatred (Northern Ireland) Act 1970
Protection from Harassment Act 1997
Public Order Act 1986
Race Relations Act 1976
Race Relations (Remedies) Act 1994
Sex Discrimination Act 1975
Sex Discrimination Act 1986
Trade Union Reform and Employment Rights Act 1993
Welsh Language Act 1993

Statutory Instruments

Transfer of Undertakings (Protection of Employment) Regulations 1981, SI 1981/1794
Disability Discrimination (Abolition of District Advisory Committees) Order (Northern Ireland) 1998, SR 1998/230
Disability Discrimination (Meaning of Disability) Regulations 1996, SI 1996/1455
Disability Discrimination (Description of Insurance Services) Regulations 1999, SI 1999/2114
Disability Discrimination (Employment) Regulations 1996, SI 1996/1456
Disability Discrimination (Questions and Replies Order) 1996, SI 1996/2793
Employment Protection (Part-time Employees) Regulations, SI 1995/31
Equal Opportunities (Employment Legislation) (Territorial Limits) Regulations 1999, SI 1999/3163
Equal Opportunities (Employment Legislation) (Territorial Limits) Regulations (Northern Ireland) 2000, SR 2000/8
Equal Pay (Complaints to Employment Tribunals) (Armed Forces) Regulations 1997, SI 1997/2162
Equal Pay (Complaints to Employment Tribunals) (Armed Forces) Regulations 1997, SR 1998/105
Employment Rights (Dispute Resolution) (Northern Ireland) Order 1998, SI 1265 (NI 8)
Employment Tribunals (Constitution and Rules of Procedure) Regulations 1993, SI 1993/2687
Employment Tribunals (Constitution and Rules of Procedure) (Scotland) Regulations 1993, SI 1993/2688
Employment Tribunals (Interest on Awards in Discrimination Cases) Regulations 1996, SI 1996/2803
Fair Employment and Treatment (Northern Ireland) Order 1998, SI 3162 (NI 21)
Maternity Allowance and Statutory Maternity Pay Regulations 1994, SI 1994/1230
Maternity and Parental Leave Regulations 1999, SI 1999 No. 3312
Northern Ireland Act Tribunal (Procedure) Rules 1999, SI 1999/2131
Occupational Pension Schemes (Equal Access to Membership) Regulations 1995, SI 1995/1215
Occupational Pension Schemes (Equal Treatment) Regulations 1995, SI 1995/3183
Race Relations (Complaints to Employment Tribunals) (Armed Forces) Regulations 1997, SI 1997/2161
Race Relations (Complaints to Employment Tribunals) (Armed Forces) Regulations (Northern Ireland) 1998, SR 104
Race Relations (Formal Investigations) Regulations 1977, SI 1977/841
Race Relations (Northern Ireland) Order 1997, SI 869 (NI 6)

Race Relations (Prescribed Public Bodies) Regulations (Northern Ireland) 1998, SR 4

Race Relations (Questions and Replies) Order 1977, SI 1977/842

Sex Discrimination (Northern Ireland) Order 1976, No. 1042 (NI 15)

Sex Discrimination (Amendment) Order 1988 SI 249

Sex Discrimination (Complaints to Industrial Tribunals) (Armed Forces) Regulations 1997 SI 2163

Sex Discrimination (Complaints to Industrial Tribunals) (Armed Forces) Regulations (Northern Ireland) 1998 SR 106

Sex Discrimination (Formal Investigations) Regulations 1975, SI 1975/1993

Sex Discrimination (Gender Reassignment) Regulations 1999, SI 1102

Sex Discrimination (Gender Reassignment) Regulations (Northern Ireland) 1999, SR 1999/311

Sex Discrimination and Equal Pay (Miscellaneous Amendments) Regulations 1996 SI 4380

Sex Discrimination and Equal Pay (Remedies) Regulations 1993

Sex Discrimination (Questions and Replies) Order 1975 SI 1975/2048

Sex Discrimination Act 1975 (Exemption of Special Treatment for Lone Parents) Order 1989, SI 1989/2140

Sex Discrimination Act 1975 (Exemption of Special Treatment for Lone Parents) Order 1991, SI 1991/2813

Statutory Maternity Pay (Compensation of Employers) and Miscellaneous Amendment Regulations 1994, SI 1994/1882

European Community Directives

Council Directive 75/117/EEC on the approximation of the laws of the Member States relating to the application of the principle of equal pay for men and women

Council Directive 76/207/EEC on the implementation of the principle of equal treatment for men and women as regards access to employment, vocational training and promotion and working conditions

Council Directive 77/187/EEC on the approximation of the laws of the Member States relating to the safeguarding of employees' rights in the event of transfer of undertakings or business

Council Directive 79/7/EEC on the progressive implementation of the principle of equal treatment between men and women in matters of social security

Council Directive 86/378/EEC on the implementation of the principle of equal treatment of men and women in occupational social security schemes

Council Recommendation 86/378/EEC on the employment of disabled people in the community

Commission Recommendation 92/131/EEC and Code of Practice on the protection of the dignity of men and women at work

Council Directive 92/85/EEC on the introduction of measures to encourage improvements in the safety and health of pregnant workers and workers who have recently given birth or are breastfeeding

Council Directive 96/34/EC on the framework agreement on parental leave concluded by UNICE, CEEP and the ETUC

Council Directive 97/75/EC amending and extending to the United Kingdom of Great Britain and Northern Ireland, Directive 96/35/EC on the framework agreement on parental leave concluded by UNICE, CEEP and ETUC

Council Directive 97/80/EC on the burden of proof in cases of discrimination based on sex

Council Directive 98/52/EC on the extension of Directive 97/80/EC on the burden of proof in cases of discrimination based on sex to the United Kingdom of Great Britain and Northern Ireland

Statutory Codes of Practice

Commission for Racial Equality code of practice for the elimination of racial discrimination in education

Commission for Racial Equality: code of practice for the elimination of racial discrimination and the promotion of equality of opportunities in employment (1983)

Commission for Racial Equality for Northern Ireland: code of practice for the elimination of discrimination and the promotion of equality of opportunity in employment

Equal Opportunities Commission: code of practice on sex discrimination: equal opportunity policies, procedures and practices in employment (1985)

Equal Opportunities Commission for Northern Ireland: code of practice for removing sex bias from recruitment and selection (1995)

Code of practice for the elimination of discrimination in the field of employment against disabled persons or persons who have had a disability (1996)

Guidance on matters to be taken into account in determining questions relating to the definition of disability
Equal Opportunities Commission: code of practice on equal pay (1997)
Disability Discrimination Act 1995: code of practice rights of access, goods, facilities, services and premises (1999)
The Disability Discrimination Act 1995: A code of practice- duties of trade organisations to their disabled members and applicants (1999)

Non- Statutory Codes of Practice

Code of practice on age diversity in employment (1999)

APPENDIX 3
Comparison of Legislation

Table 1: The Race, Sex, Disability and Fair Employment Legislation

	S D A	SD (NI) O	R R A	RR (NI) O	DDA /DR CA	F E T O	
Definition of Discrimination	1	3	1	3	5 14 20 24	3	The SDA s.1(1)(a) refers to discrimination occurring where a person is treated less favourably on the grounds of "her sex" and on the grounds of "her marital status". In the RRA s.1(1)(a) there is discrimination if a person is treated less favourably "on racial grounds". The FETO is closer to the wording of the RRA. It states that a person discriminates against another person "on the grounds of religious belief or political opinion" if "on either of those grounds he treats that other less favourably than he treats of would treat other persons". The provision of the DDA s.5(1)(a), 20(1)(a) and 24(1)(a) are similar to the SDA in holding that a person discriminates against a disabled person if "for a reason which relates to the disabled person's disability he treats him less favourably than he treats or would treat others".
Indirect Discrimination	1 (1) (b)	3(1) (b)	1 (1) (b)	3 (1) (b)	–	3 (2) (b)	Unlike the other legislation the DDA does not mention indirect discrimination.
Reasonable Accommodation	–	–	–	–	6 15 21	–	Only the DDA creates a duty to make reasonable adjustments
Segregation	26 46	27 47	1 (2)	3(2)	–	–	RRA s.1(2) declares that segregation on "racial grounds" constitutes discrimination. The SDA by contrast allows segregation in certain situations. The DDA or FETO make no comment.
Affirmative Action -	–	–	–	–	–	4 (1)	FETO allows action designed to "secure fair participation in employment by members of the Protestant or Catholic community" there is no equivalent provision in other legislation
Discrimination Against Applicants and Employees	6	8	4	6	4	19	Both the SDA and RRA hold it to be unlawful for an employer to discriminate against a person "in the way he affords him access to opportunities for promotion, transfer or training, or to any other benefits facilities or services". The EAT in *Clymo*[1] held this to refer only to "access" to existing opportunities for promotion. Thus it was not discrimination not to offer job-sharing, as this benefit/service was not available so the applicant could not be refused access to it. To avoid this limitation the DDA refers in s.4(2)(b) to discrimination "in the opportunities which he affords him for promotion" (this covers opportunities etc whether in the form of an existing benefit or not) and in s.4(2)(c) refers to discrimination by "refusing him any such opportunity" this covers an existing benefit. No amendment has been made to the SDA, RRA or FETO. FETO does not explicitly mention promotion. It states that it is unlawful for an employer to discriminate against an employee "in the way he affords him access to benefits or by refusing or deliberately omitting to afford him access to them". This is less explicit than the provision in the RRA that explicitly refers to "opportunities for promotion, transfer or training, or to any other benefits facilities or services". All of these are probably caught within article 19(1)(b)(iii) of FETO that makes it unlawful for an employer to discriminate against an employee "by subjecting him to any other detriment".

[1] Clymo *v*. Wandsworth Borough Council [1989] IRLR 249

Category							Description
Genuine Occupational Qualification	7	10	5	8	5	70	The lists of situations where the exception for genuine occupational qualification apply are different for SDA and RRA. The DDA has no genuine occupational qualification defence but instead allows a defence of justification to a claim of discrimination. The FETO does not have a GOQ exception but contains a list of excepted employments.
Contract Workers	9	12	7	9	12	20	In the SDA and RRA the prohibition on discrimination against contract workers includes discrimination in the "way he affords her access to any benefits, facilities or services". The DDA and the FETO in the parallel sections only cover discrimination in the "way he affords him any benefits". They do not mention "facilities or services". The SDA and DDA do not have an equivalent to the RRA s.7(4) which holds that "nothing in this section shall render unlawful any act done by the principal for the benefit of a contract worker not ordinarily resident in Great Britain in or in connection with allowing him to do work to which this section applies, where the purpose of his being allowed to do that work is to provide him with training skills which he appears to the principal to intend to exercise wholly outside Great Britain".
Partnerships	11	14	10	12	–	26	The RRA and FETO cover only partnerships of six or more partners while the SDA covers all partnerships. The DDA does not cover partnerships.
Vocational Training	14	17	13	15	–	24	There is no parallel provision in the DDA to prohibit discrimination by persons concerned with the provision of vocational training.
Qualifying Bodies	13	16	12	14	–	25	Qualifying bodies are not covered by the DDA. There is no equivalent in the RRA of the provision in SDA s.13(2) which provides that where a body is required to satisfy itself as to the good character of a potential member before awarding a qualification which facilitates entry into a trade or profession, it shall have regard to any evidence that the applicant has practised unlawful discrimination in carrying on any trade or profession.
Employment Agencies	15	18	14	16	19(3)(g)	22	The provisions of the RRA, SDA and FETO are similar. The coverage of employment agencies in the DDA is through section 19 which makes discrimination in the provision in the provision of goods, services and facilities unlawful, and includes amongst the examples "facilities provided by employment agencies or under section 2 of the Employment and Training Act 1973"
Discrimination by Persons with Statutory Powers to Select Employees for Others	–	–	–	7	–	21	This provision is in the FETO and the RR(NI)O There is no equivalent to this provision in the other legislation.
Police	17	19	16	17	–	51	The legislation states that the holding of the office of constable shall be treated as employment. There are exceptions allowed in the SDA for height, uniform and equipment requirements. Police are not covered by the DDA. There is no equivalent provision in FETO but police officers may be covered by virtue of article 51 (Certain Public Authorities to be Treated as Employers).
Other Exceptions	18 19 20	20 21 22	6 9	6(5) 11	–	57 70 71 72 73 74	The SDA also provides exceptions allowing discrimination in relation to prison officers, midwives and ministers of religion. The RRA has an exception for seamen recruited abroad and for employment intended to provide training in skills to be exercised outside Great Britain. The FETO lists exempted employment in article 70 this includes employment as a clergyman. Article 71 provides an exception in relation to employment of schools teachers. Article 72 is an exception for the provision of training in pursuance of affirmative action. Article 73 provides exception allowing an employer to pursue an affirmative action practice in the selection of employees for redundancy as long as the policy is not directly framed by reference to religious belief or political opinion. Article 74 allows for measures aimed at encouraging applications from underrepresented communities. And Article 57 is an exceptions allowing provisions that aim to hire the long term unemployed; such provisions may otherwise constitute indirect discrimination

Education	22-28	24-29	17-19	18-20	29-31	27	Both the SDA and RRA cover discrimination in education. FETO applies only to universities and institutions of further education, it does not apply to schools. The DDA does not create a right to a claim of unlawful discrimination in education but instead creates an obligation on education institutions in their annual reports, to publish information on the ways that they are dealing with the educational needs of disabled persons. This does not apply to independent schools. Section 18 of the DDA specifically excludes educational institutions from the duty on service providers not to discriminate.
							The RRA contains provisions that declare segregation to constitute less favourable treatment (see above RRA s.2(1)). The SDA in s.26 allows segregation in education (single sex schooling). There is also an exception for physical training (SDA s.28).
Planning Authorities	–	–	19 A	–	–	–	The RRA has been amended to cover planning authorities. No amendment for planning authorities in the RR(NI)O, the SDA or FETO.
Goods, Services and Facilities	29	30	20	21	19-21	28 31 (5)	The SDA and DDA includes among its examples of services and facilities covered by this section as including "access to and use of any place which members of the public or a section of the public are permitted to enter". The RRA holds generally that is it is "unlawful for any person concerned with the provision of goods, facilities or services to the public or a section of the public to discriminate". Among the examples of services covered it refers to "any place which members of the public are permitted to enter"; the phrase "or a section of the public" is omitted.
							In the list giving examples of services covered by this section, the DDA omits reference to facilities for education and facilities for transport and travel, these are mentioned in the list for the RRA and SDA. Part V of the DDA makes special provisions on the requirements of public transport. The DDA does however mention access to use and means of communication, which is not mentioned in the other legislation. The DDA, s.20-21, lists the situations in which discrimination is justifiable and also places a duty on service providers to make reasonable adjustments. FETO refers only to "facilities for training" but does not cover education. FETO article 31(5) covers goods, services and facilities provided by schools and colleges.
							The SDA provides a specific exception "where a particular skill is commonly exercised in a different way for men and for women it does not contravene subsection (1) for a person who does not normally exercise it for women to insist on exercising it for a woman only in accordance with his normal practice or, if he reasonably considers it impracticable to do that in her case, to refuse of deliberately omit to exercise it"
Discrimination in the Disposal and Management of Premises	30	32	21	22	22	29	The legislation in the different statutes is essentially the same. The DDA lists the situations in which discrimination is justified. Unlike employment and goods, services and facilities there is no requirement in the relevant DDA provisions for reasonable accommodation.
Associations	–	–	25-26	25	–	–	Section 25 ensures that private clubs are covered by the legislation but provides exceptions for associations whose "main object is to enable the benefits of membership to be enjoyed persons of a particular racial group defined otherwise than by reference to their colour". There is no equivalent provision in the SDA, DDA or FETO.
Exceptions in relation to goods, services, facilities and premises	32-35	33-36	22-23	23-24	32-49	30-31	All the statutes have an exception for small dwellings. The SDA and provides specific exceptions to the prohibition on discrimination in relation to goods, services, facilities and premises for hospitals and for places used for purposes of an organised religion or where facilities are for two people and sharing between men and women is likely to cause embarrassment. Section 33 provides an exception for political parties. Section 34 provides an exception for voluntary bodies.
							The RRA s.23 and FETO article 31(2) provides an exception from the prohibition on discrimination for anything done by "a person as a participant in arrangements under which he (for reward or not) takes into his home, and treats as if they were members of his family, children, elderly persons or persons requiring special degree of care and attention". This covers, for example, foster care and adoption. There is no equivalent to this in the SDA.
							Part V of the DDA makes special provisions on the requirements of public transport.

Barristers	35A	36A	26A	26	–	32	The DDA does not cover discrimination against barristers.
Discriminatory Practices	37	38	28	28	–	–	Both the SDA and RRA prohibit discriminatory practices. There are no equivalent provisions in the DDA of FETO.
Discriminatory Advertisements	38	39	29	29	11	34	The RRA s.29(1) differs slightly from the SDA s.38(1) and FETO. The SDA and FETO require an intention to do an unlawful discriminatory act. The RRA on the other hand require only an intention to discriminate, it is not relevant if the discrimination is lawful or unlawful. The SDA, RRA and FETO prohibit discriminatory advertising in both employment and non-employment areas. The DDA only prohibits discrimination in relation to advertising in employment.
Instructions to Discriminate	39	40	30	30	–	35	The SDA and RRA prohibit instructions to discriminate by a person "who has authority over another person; or in accordance with whose wishes that other person is accustomed to act". FETO does not have mirroring provisions but article 35 holds that any person who "directs, procures or induces to do an act which is unlawful shall be treated as if he had done that act". There is no provision on instructions to discriminate in the DDA.
Pressure to Discriminate	40	41	31	31	–	35	The provisions on pressure to discriminate in the SDA and RRA are slightly different. The RRA makes it unlawful to induce or attempt to induce a person to do an act that contravenes Part II and III of the Act. The SDA elaborates on this by specifying acts "which contravenes Part II or III by ñ (a) provision or offering to provide him with any benefit, or (b) subjecting or threatening to subject him to any detriment". There is no provision on pressure to discriminate in the DDA. FETO article 35 makes it unlawful for a person to direct, procure or induce another to do an act that is unlawful. Article 35(5) mirrors the provision in SDA s.40(2) or RRA s.31(2) in holding that "an inducement consisting of an offer of benefit or a threat of detriment is not prevented from falling within paragraph (1) because the offer or the threat was not made directly to the person in question" but does not include the qualification found in the SDA/RRA that such acts are unlawful "if it is made in such a way that he is likely to hear of it".
Sport	44	45	39	38	–	–	SDA allows discrimination in sport on the basis of sex; the RRA allows discrimination on the basis of nationality, place of birth or length of residence in their selection of sportsmen to represent a country etc.
Insurance	45	46	–	–	–	–	Only the SDA has an exception allowing discrimination in relation to an annuity, life assurance policy, accident assurance policy etc.
Communal Accommodation	46	47	–	–	–	–	Only the SDA has an exception allowing discrimination in relation to residential accommodation that includes dormitories or other shared sleeping accommodation "which for reasons of privacy or decency should be used by men only, or by women only".
Trade Unions etc.	49	50	–	–	–	–	The SDA allows the reservations of seats at a body for one sex. There is no equivalent in the RRA.
Discriminatory Training by Certain Bodies and Other Discriminatory Training	47 48	48 49	37	37	–	76	The SDA, RRA and FETO allow for positive action in training where there is under representation in the work force. Each provides a different definition of under representation. The SDA s.48(1) allows discriminatory training "where at any time within the twelve months immediately preceding the doing of the act there were no persons of the sex in question among those doing that work or the number of persons of that sex doing the work was comparatively small". The RRA by contrast holds under representation to exist if "there are no persons of the racial group in question among those doing that work at that establishment or the proportions of persons of that racial group among those doing that work at that establishment is small in comparison with the proportion of persons of that group (i) among those employed by that employer there; or (ii) among the population of the area from which that employer normally recruits persons for work in his employment at that establishment". The FETO allows religious specific training, and has a definition of under representation similar to that in the RRA. Article 76 allows religious specific training if, within the 12 months immediately proceeding the doing of the act it appears to the Commission that:

							(i) there are no persons of the religious belief in question among those engaged in that employment at the establishment; or (ii) that the proportion of persons of that belief among those engaged in that establishment is small in comparison with the proportion of persons of that belief among all those employed by the employer there or among the population of the area from which the employer might reasonably be expected to recruit persons for employment at that establishment The FETO also contains exemptions for training in pursuance of affirmative action and for measures to encourage applications. The DDA only prohibits discrimination against a disabled person so training or opportunities assisting disabled persons can not be challenged as discrimination by a person who is not disabled.
Acts Safeguarding National Security	52	53	42 69 (2)	42	59	79- 80	The legislation in Northern Ireland relating to race, sex and fair employment all provide an exemption from the prohibition on discrimination where the "act is done for the purposes of safeguarding national security or protecting public safety or public order". This is significantly wider than the equivalent provisions in the GB legislation and the DDA which provides an exception only on the grounds of "safeguarding national security". The CRE (NI) argue that the wider exception in the NI legislation "has the potential to have a serious impact. For example, where a black person is not employed because of a feared hostile reaction to his recruitment by an all white workforce that discriminatory act might be exempt from the effect of the legislation on the basis that it was necessary to protect public order." The RRA s.69 holds that a certificate from a Minister of the Crown "that an act specified in the certificate was done for the purposes of safeguarding national security, shall be conclusive proof of the matter certified". A similar provision is contained in DDA s.52. The Employment Relations Act 1999 removed the power to issue such certificates for employment cases under the RRA and DDA. The provisions of the SDA have been disapplied following amendment by the Sex Discrimination Amendment Order 1988. A similar approach to discrimination on the grounds of religious belief or political opinion in Northern Ireland under section 42 of the Fair Employment Act 1976 was held to breach article 6 of the ECHR. The NIA 1998 now creates a tribunal with power to hear appeals against national security certificates issued by the secretary of state in response to an unlawful discrimination claim against Northern Ireland ministers, government departments or other public authorities. The tribunal has jurisdiction over national security certificates issued in Northern Ireland under the Fair Employment, Race Relations and Sex Discrimination legislation there. The current Race Relations (Amendment) Bill is changing the provisions of the RRA in this area. Clause 6 of the Bill removes the power of the Minister to issue a conclusive certificate in relation to non-employment cases. (as mentioned above the Employment Relations Act 1999 removed the power in relation to employment cases.) It also changes the national security defence so that it is not sufficient that a discriminatory act was done for the purpose of safeguarding national security, it must also be justified by that purpose. The power to issue such conclusive certificates has been found by the European Court of Human Rights, in the case of *Tinnelly and McElduff* 249 EHRR 1999, to be incompatible with article 6(1) of the European Convention on Human Rights. The Bill inserts a new section 67A into the Act which makes provision for courts to adopt certain special procedures when dealing with cases under the Act that raise national security issues. The clause is based on similar provisions for tribunal rules made in Schedule 8 of the Employment Relations Act 1999, which amends the Employment Tribunals Act 1996. However, appropriate rules of court already exist in some cases so provision for new rules of court has not always been necessary.
Codes of Practice	56 A	56 A	47	45	DR CA 9	9	The CRE can issue codes of practice in relation to employment and housing; the EOC can issue codes only in relation to employment. The DRC by contrast can issue codes for employers, service providers and to any other person on any other matter with a view to "(i) promoting the equalisation of opportunities for disabled people and persons who have had a disability, or (ii) encourage good practice regarding the treatment of such persons". FETO can also issue codes in relation to employment and non-employment areas. The CRE (NI) say that this limitation on their power is a "matter which is of practical concernÒdiscrimination in the provision of services and educational facilities ñ particularly with regard to travellers – is still quite common". The DDA also allows the Secretary of State to issue codes of practice.

Formal Investigations	57 58	57 58	48 49	46 47	DR CA 3 Sch3 pt1	11 Sch2	The powers to conduct formal investigation are similar for the CRE, EOC and DRC. In an unnamed investigation the duty of the CRE and EOC is to give general notice of the holding of the investigation. The DRCA provides more specifically that the DRC must give "notice of the holding of the investigation and the terms of reference shall be published in such manner as appears to the commission appropriate to bring it to the attention of persons likely to be affected by it". In addition to investigations at the request of the Secretary of State the CRE and EOC can commence a named investigation where "it believes that a person named may have done" an unlawful act. The DRC can begin a named investigation where it "has reason to believe that the person concerned has committed or is committing any unlawful act". This formulation does not overcome the problems posed by *Prestige*.[2] The FETO allows an investigation "for the purpose of assisting it in considering what if any action for the promotion of equal opportunities ought to be taken by . . . any employer . . ."
Powers to Obtain Information	59	59	50 53	50 48	Sch3	67 Sch2	The powers of the Commissions to obtain information in the course of an investigation are similar for CRE, EOC and DRC. The ECNI has slightly different powers. Article 7(2) gives the ECNI the same powers as the High Court in respect of "the attendance and examination of witnesses, including the administration of oaths and the examination of witnesses abroad and the production of documents". The EOC, DRC and CRE on the other hand have to apply to the County Court for an order requiring a person to comply. The ECNI also has the power under schedule 2 article 8 for the purposes of an investigation to "require an employer or vocational organisation to take such reasonable action as the Commission specifies for communication to his or its employees . . . any written material provided for the purposes by the Commission". The Commissions in Britain have no equivalent powers. Finally the FETO also includes a specific defence for a person who fails to comply with a request for information to show that they had a "reasonable excuse".
Remedies in Employment Cases	65	65	56	53	8	39	Only FETO allows the tribunal to recommend that the "respondent take within a specified period action appearing to the Tribunal to be practicable for the purposes of obviating or reducing the adverse effect on a person other than the complainant of any unlawful discrimination to which the complaint relates". Section 65 of the SDA has been amended to allow for damages for unintentional indirect discrimination in employment cases. Such damages are not available in race discrimination cases. Neither has an amendment has been made to allow for such damages in non-employment sex discrimination cases. The FETO also allows for compensation to be awarded in cases of unintentional indirect discrimination on the grounds of religious belief or political opinion in employment cases but not other cases.
Claims in Non-Employment Cases	66	66	57	54	DRC 10 DDA 25 Sch3	40	The DDA unlike the SDA or RRA contains provisions for the conciliation of disputes arising under Part III of the Act. Section 10 of the DRCA gives the DRC powers to "make arrangements for the provision of conciliation services by any other person for the provision of conciliation services". As mentioned above, the SDA and FETO allow claims for damages for unintentional indirect discrimination cases relating to employment but not in non-employment cases.
Non-Discrimination Notices Actions Plans Binding Undertakings	67	67	58	62	DRC 4	12-17	The EOC, CRE and DRC can all issue non-discrimination notices, but in addition to this the DRC can require the person against whom a non-discrimination notice is served to propose and implement an action plan which aims to prevent further unlawful acts. The DRC can also enter into binding agreements instead of issuing a non-discrimination notice. The FETO allows the ECNI to follow an investigation by securing undertakings from a person to take such actions for the promotion of equality of opportunity as is, in all the circumstances, reasonable and appropriate. If such undertakings are not given or not complied with the Commission can seek directions for the measures to be taken or apply to the tribunal for enforcement of undertakings. A person can agree to voluntary undertakings if the ECNI informs him that it has formed an opinion that he ought to take action for the promoting of equality of opportunity. The ECNI can also seek legally binding undertakings in cases involving race discrimination under the RR(NI)O. This is an improvement on the position of the CRE but the provisions are not identical to those available under the FETO. The FETO allows the ECNI to seek undertakings where it is of the opinion that certain persons ought to "take action for promoting equality of opportunity". The RR(NI)O restricts the ECNI's powers in race cases to seek binding undertakings to prevent discrimination.

[2] Re Prestige Group plc [1984] IRLR 166, HL.

Assistance by the Commissions	75	75	66	64	7	45	The FETO titles article 45 as advice and assistance and in subsection (1) holds that "where a prospective complainant or claimant requests the Commission in writing for advice in relation to prospective proceedings under this part, the Commission shall give him such advice unless it considers that the request is frivolous". This goes further than the more general requirement on the CRE and EOC and under the RR(NI)O to consider the application for assistance and gives them power to grant assistance including advice if they think fit.
Limitation Periods	76	76	68	65	Sch3 3	46	The limitation periods under the RRA, SDA and DDA are essentially the same. The FETO provisions are slightly different. Article 46 holds that "the tribunal shall not consider a compliant under Article 38 unless it is brought before whichever is the earlier of (a) the end of the period of 3 months beginning with the day on which the complainant first had knowledge, or might reasonably be expected to have had knowledge, of the act complained of; or (b) the end of a period of six months beginning with the day on which the act was done". The provisions still allow an application that is out of time where the tribunal considers it just and equitable to do so.
Statutory Duties	–	–	71	67	–	NIA 75	The RRA creates a duty on local authorities to promote equality of opportunity in relation to race. The NIA section 74 creates a duty on all public authorities in Northern Ireland.

Table 2: Sex Discrimination and Equal Pay Act

	EqPA	SDA	
Grounds of Discrimination	–	3(1)	The EqPA only covers discrimination in pay between men and women. If the complaint relates to discrimination against a married person on the grounds of her marital status, only the SDA applies.
The Comparator	1(2)	1(1)	The SDA allows a claim of discrimination where on the grounds of her sex a person treats a woman less favourably than he treats or would treat a man. Thus the SDA allows comparison with the treatment that would be received by a hypothetical man. The EqPA requires comparison with a "man in the same employment"
Questionnaires	–	74	The questionnaire procedure is available in claims under the SDA but not the EqPA.
Time Limits	2(4)	76	The limitation period for bringing a claim under the EqPA is six months. The limitation period for bringing employment cases under the SDA is three months.
Remedies	2(5)	–	Damages, by way of arrears of remuneration, under the EqPA are restricted to a limit of two years prior to the date on which the proceedings were instituted.[2a] There is no equivalent temporal limit on damages under the SDA
Areas covered	1	6(1) 6(6)	Both the SDA and EqPA cover discrimination in aspects of the terms and conditions of employment. It is important to distinguish the areas covered by each. The EqPA covers less favourable treatment in relation to the payment of money regulated by an employment contract. The Equal Pay (Amendment) Regulations 1970 cover less favourable treatment where a matter is regulated by an "equality clause" incorporated into the contract of employment by the Equal Pay Act 1970. These areas are not covered by the SDA. The SDA covers less favourable treatment in a matter which is not included in a contract of employment.

[2a] This is contrary to EC law: Case C-78/98, *Preston v. Wolverhampton Healthcare Trust*, ECJ 16 May 2000.

Table 3: Sex Discrimination Act and European Community Law

	SDA	SD(NI)O	EU Law	
Geographical Scope of the Legislation	6 10(1)	8	ETD1(1)	The SDA is restricted to prohibiting discrimination where it occurs in employment to "any establishment in Great Britain". Section 10(1) then provides that employment is to be regarded as at an establishment in Great Britain unless the employee does the work "wholly or mainly outside Great Britain". The section goes on to state that employment on board ships, aircraft and hovercraft registered in Great Britain is deemed to be inside Great Britain unless the employee's work is performed wholly outside Great Britain. The chief intention behind this scheme would appear to be to protect UK employers where the job is to be performed in a country whose laws do not respect the principle of sex equality. It follows that the Act does not therefore apply to all contracts of employment entered into in this country and that the group of contracts of employment which are excluded from its scope could involve work performed in other Member States of the EU. Article 1(1) of the Equal Treatment Directive[3] opens with the words: "The purpose of this Directive is to put into effect in the Member States the principle of equal treatment for men and women as regards access to employment, including promotion, and to vocational training and as regards working conditions . . .". The European Court of Justice has not had occasion to express its views on the geographical scope of this provision. However, it regards the principle of sex equality as a fundamental human right[4] and is therefore likely to adopt a broad view of this matter. At the very least, it would therefore seem likely that the intention of the Directive will be construed by the ECJ as the prohibition of sex discrimination in employment throughout the area of the EU.
Marital or Family Status	3	5	2(1)	SDA proscribes discrimination against married people on the ground of their marital status; it does not, however, extend to discrimination against unmarried people, or against those who are widowed or divorced. Article 2(1) of the Equal Treatment Directive adopts a somewhat different formulation, providing that "the principle of equal treatment shall mean that there shall be no discrimination whatsoever on grounds of sex either directly or indirectly by reference in particular to marital or family status".
Definition of Direct Discrimination	1(1)(a)	3(1)(a)	Dekker[5]	Direct Discrimination in the SDA requires treatment on the grounds of sex which is less favourable than that received by a member of the opposite sex. Direct discrimination is not the subject of a statutory definition in EC law and the ECJ has on occasion taken a somewhat different view of its constituent elements. This has emerged from its decisions on discrimination against pregnant women. In particular in the Dekker case it held that, where employment is refused for a reason which applies exclusively to one sex, it automatically constitutes direct discrimination; a failure to appoint which is grounded on the applicant's pregnancy is therefore per se unlawful direct sex discrimination. UK case law in interpreting the SDA has effectively reached this position but it may greatly clarify the legal position if the statutory provision could be amended so as to state expressly that, in the case of discrimination on the ground of pregnancy, it is unnecessary to show that a man who was temporarily indisposed (by illness or for some similar reason) would have received preferential treatment.
Definition of Indirect Discrimination	1(1)(b)	3(1)(b)	Directive 97/80 Art.2	Under the SDA indirect discrimination occurs where a "requirement or condition" has an adverse impact on one sex. The EC Directive holds indirect discrimination to occur "where a neutral provision, criterion or practice disadvantages a substantially higher proportion of the numbers of one sex". The case law has suggested that the words "requirement or condition" possess a mandatory connotation: "a must". Thus the EC formulation is wider than the SDA.
Remedies	65	65	ETD 6	The EC Directive emphasises the obligation on Member States to "introduce into their national legal systems such measures as are necessary to enable all persons who consider themselves wronged by failure to apply to them the principle of equal treatment . . . to pursue their claims by judicial process after possible

[3] Directive 76/207, OJ [1976] L39/40.
[4] See eg. Case 179/77 Defrenne v. Sabena [1978] ECR 1365.
[5] Case 177/88 Dekker v. Stichting Vormingscentrum Voor Jonge Volwassen Plus [1990] ECR I-3941

	SDA	SD(NI)O	EU Law	
				to other competent authorities". The remedies available under the SDA may fall short of the standards required by the EC Directive. In particular a section 65(1)(c) recommendation is not, however, effective as a means of specific enforcement because there are very limited sanctions for its non-observance. Furthermore, UK law does not permit the award of exemplary damages in sex discrimination claims.[6] This may fall short of the requirements of EC law in so far as a claim in a comparable area of domestic law (for example, for a common law tort or a breach of contract) could be remediable via an award of exemplary damages.
Burden of Proof	King[7] Zafar[8]	King Zafar	Burden of Proof Directive	The directions on the burden of proof are set out in the case of King and affirmed by the House of Lords in Zafar. These fall short of the requirements of the EC Burden of Proof Directive (see para. 3.49)
Defences and General Exceptions	7(2)(g) and (h)	53(1) 10 (2)(g) and (h)	ETD Art. 2	The exceptions permitted by the SDA are wider and go beyond those that are permitted by the ETD. ETD Article 2(2) allows a Member State "to exclude from its field of application those occupational activities and, where appropriate, the training leading thereto, for which, by reason of their nature or the context in which they are carried out, the sex of the worker constitutes a determining factor". Parts of the SDA which may conflict with the ETD include section 7(2)(h) which provides an exception where "the job is one of two to be held by a married couple". The fact that an employer requires a married couple to perform two jobs is not itself a guarantee that sex is a determining factor for the actual jobs. The exception in the SD(NI)O article 53 for cases concerning national security , public safety or public order is too wide and in breach of the Article 2(2). The employer will only have a defence in EC law where the act done to safeguard national security can be brought within the terms of Article 2(2). Section 7(2)(g) provides an exception where the job "needs to be held by a man because it is likely to involve the performance of duties outside the UK in a country whose laws or customs are such that the duties could not, or could not effectively be performed by a woman". The exception should be restricted to jobs performed outside the EU and should only apply where the law rather than custom would prevent a woman from undertaking the task.
Police	17(3)	19	ETD Art. 2(2)	The exceptions for police officers in SDA s 17(3) are also too wide for EDT article 2(2). The exception allowing discrimination in relation to height require-ments is needed, however the exception for uniform and equipment and allowances in lieu thereof should only be permissible where it is a necessary consequence of the different height requirements for male and female police.
Charities	43	44	ETD Art. 2(2)	The exception for charities in SDA s43 is also too wide for ETD article 2(2). It would permit the recruitment by an employer of persons of one sex only where funds for the payment of the employee were provided wholly or partly by a charity which restricted benefits to that sex. Article 2(2) of the Equal Treatment Directive would clearly not permit such discrimination since neither the nature of the job nor its context would necessarily demand an employee of a particular sex in these circumstances.

[6] See *AB* v. *South West Water Services* [1993] 1 All ER 609, *Deane* v. *London Borough of Ealing* [1993] IRLR 209, EAT; *Ministry of Defence* v. *Cannock* [1994] IRLR 509 and *Ministry of Defence* v. *Meredith* [1995] IRLR 539, EAT.

[7] *King* v. *The Great Britain China Clay Centre* [1992] ICR 516; [1991] IRLR 513, CA.

[8] *Zafar* v. *Glasgow City Council* [1998] IRLR 36, HL.

APPENDIX 4

Consultations and Interviews

Conferences, Seminars and Meetings

Members of the research team participated in a number of meetings and seminars:

Carnegie Foundation on age discrimination

Commission on British Muslims and Islamophobia on religious discrimination

Commission on the future of a Multi-Ethnic Britain on human rights and related subjects

Discrimination Law Association on Equality

Justice on EU and ECHR developments

Liberty on EU and ECHR developments

Institute of Employment Rights on race and disability discrimination

IPPR seminars on the Human Rights Commission

UK round table organised by the European Monitoring Centre on Racism and Xenophobia

ORC Inc. meeting of the Workplace Opportunity Network

Interviews

In the UK we interviewed:

President and a Chairman of Employment Tribunals in Scotland

Four Regional Chairmen of Employment Tribunals in England

The Director of Policy, a Regional Director and inquiry officers, advisers and conciliation officers at ACAS

Directors, policy and legal officers, complaints officers, and case workers at the CRE, EOC and ECNI

A group of employment lawyers in Northern Ireland

The Association of Police Chief Officers

The Fawcett Society

Twelve large employers in Britain in the public and private sectors

IPD focus group of 15 of their members

Meeting to discuss the options paper organised by the TUC with GMB, IPMS, TGWU, UNISON, and FDA

Colin Cramphorn the Deputy Chief Constable of the RUC

A group of six large employers in Northern Ireland from both the private and public sectors

Richard Bennett consultant to the New Zealand Human Rights Commission

In the US we interviewed:

Paul Igasaki, Vice-Chair of the EEOC

Leonard J. Biermann, Director of the National Employment Law Institute (formerly of the Office of Federal Contract Compliance)

Richard T. Seymour of the Lawyers' Committee for Civil Rights Under Law

Bruce McLanahan and other employment discrimination

lawyers under the auspices of Organisation Resource Counselors Inc.

Alfred W. Blumrosen of Rutgers University

Ruth Blumrosen

Sam Estreicher of New York University

Group of six large US corporations

Organisations which submitted a response to the Initial Consultation Paper

Association for Spina Bifida and Hydrocephalus

Bar Council Disability Committee

Barnardos

British Deaf Association

Bristol Lesbian, Gay and Bisexual Forum

Business in the Community

Committee on the Administration of Justice

Communication Workers Union

Commission for Racial Equality for Northern Ireland

Crusaid

Disability Discrimination Act Representation and Advice Project

Early Years Trainers Anti-Racist Network

Employers' Forum on Age

Employers' Organisation for Local Government

Equality Network

Fairplay London

GMB

Graphical, Paper and Media Union
Institute of Personnel and Development
Institution of Professionals, Managers and Specialists
Ipswich and Suffolk Council for Racial Equality
Irish Congress of Trade Unions – Northern Ireland
  Committee
Irish Congress of Trade Unions – Women's Committee
John Grooms – Working with Disabled People
Labour Relations Agency
The Law Society – Employment Law Committee
Lesbian and Gay Employment Rights
Leeds City Council
Lewisham Race Equality Council
LINKS
Men's Movement Northern Ireland
MIND
MSF
National Association of Citizens Advice Bureaux
National Centre for Independent Living
National Disability Council
Northern Ireland Council for Ethnic Minorities
NISPA (Northern Ireland Public Service Alliance)

Public and Commercial Services Union
Plymouth City Council – Personnel and Equal
  Opportunities
RAD- The Royal Association in Aid of Deaf People
RNIB – Royal National Institute for the Blind
RNID – Royal National Institution for Deaf People
The Royal College of Midwives
Save the Children, Scotland
Scottish Association for Mental Health
Society of Black Lawyers
Society of Telecom Executives
Southern Voices
Sue Hastings – Pay and Employment Advice
The 1990 Trust
Third Age
Thompsons Solicitors - Employment Rights Unit
Trades Union Congress
Traveller Law Research Unit, Cardiff University Law
  School
UNIFI
UNISON
The West of Scotland Community Relations Council

Individual submissions to the Initial Consultation Paper

Almeyda G
Bryan R
Budu S
Davis S
Denton
Guest H
Howarth G
Hussain M
Kinrade D
Livie GWG (Employment Tribunal Regional Chairman)
MacMillan J (Employment Tribunal Regional Chairman)
Miller S
Moran E

Morgan A
Nwaokolo S
O'Brian M
Rees A (Employment Tribunal Regional Chairman)
Robinson D
Roe N
Roberts C
Scaife K
Skidmore P (University of Bristol)
Sneath D (Employment Tribunal Regional Chairman)
Taylor A
Tribe C (Employment Tribunal Regional Chairman)
Wellappili T

Those who attended the consultation meetings

Almedyda G
Balouan A
Beirne M (Committee on the Administration of Justice)
Benson B (Disability Scotland)
Balogun A (Society of Black Lawyers)
Bowers J
Bowker G
Brown P (Queens University, Belfast)
Burrows N (Glasgow University)
Carberry K
Carlson M (Bristol City Council)
Casserley C
Chapman F (BECTU)
Cohen B (Commission for Racial Equality)
Cronie D
Cunningham T (Committee on the Administration of

Justice)
Davies S (Citizens Advice Bureau)
Dudgeon J
Dunbar L (Irish Congress of trade Unions)
Eastabrook J (DfEE)
Ellis E. (Birmingham University)
Fothergill S
Garel J. (Avon and Bristol Law Centre)
Gregory J (Middlesex Pay Equality Project)
Haggett E
Hams L (Association for Spina Bifida and
  Hydrocephalus)
Harding C (Trade Union Disability Alliance)
Hill V (Race Equality Unit)
Hope A (ICTU)
Howes M (UNISON)

Hunter P (Scottish Low Pay Unit)
Huyser D (RCM)
Johnson L (Men's Movement Northern Ireland)
Kilpatrick C (Bristol University)
Lafleche M (Runneymeade Trust)
Lane J (Early Year Learning Centre)
Littlejohn D (President Employment Tribunals Scotland)
Livingston S (Queens University, Belfast)
Lustgarten, L (Southampton University)
Magill D (NI Human Rights Commission)
Mason A (Stonewall)
Matchett H (Triangle Housing Association)
May D (BBC)
McBride J (Birmingham University)
McCusker J (Northern Ireland Public Service Alliance)
McInnes I (Labour Relations Agency)
Mill R (Equity)
Modood T (Bristol University)
Moran K (Chartered Society of Physiology)
Morris G (Brunel University)
Nelu AK (Terrance Higgins Trusts)
Neus T (Bristol University)
O'Brien M (Irish Congress of trade Unions)
Orme K (MSF)
Palmer C (Bindman & Partners)

Parsons H (Southwark Council for Community Relations)
Partridge G (AEEU)
Patel D (Malik and Malik, Solicitors)
Poonia K (Bristol City Council)
Rivers J (Bristol University)
Robinson D (Bolton MBC)
Sayer A (Royal Association for Deaf People)
Seery J (UNIFI)
Skidmore P (Bristol University)
Singh K (Sandwell MBC)
Syed M (Derby City Council)
Steele R (Queens University)
Thomas A (RNIB)
Townsend-Smith R (University of Wales)
Tregaskis G (CHE)
Underhill C (Avon and Bristol Law Centre)
Vasista V (1990 Trust)
Vaughan-Willams G (CHE)
Watson J (Lesbian and Gay Employment Rights)
White S (Bristol University)
Willcock A (Society of Black Lawyers)
Woodroffe J (Religious Society of Friends)
Wright M (Organisation for Local Government)
Xavier S (ILMS)
Yu P (Northern Ireland Council for Ethnic Minorities)

Speakers and chairs at the "Options for Reform" consultation conference

Lord Lester of Herne Hill QC (Blackstone Chambers)
Lord Falconer of Thoroton QC (Minister of State, Cabinet Office)
Elmer C. Jackson III (General Director, General Motors, North America)
John Cridland (CBI)
Kay Carberry (TUC)
Sir Herman Ouseley (CRE)
Julie Mellor (EOC)
Bert Massie (Chair, Disability Rights Commission)
Sarah Spencer (IPPR)

Caroline Underhill (Avon and Bristol Law Centre)
Goolam Meeran (Employment Tribunals, Regional Chairman)
Sir Robert Cooper (former Chairman, Fair Employment Commission Northern Ireland)
Joan Harbison (Chair – Equality Commission for Northern Ireland)
Doris Littlejohn (President Employment Tribunals Scotland)
Sir David Williams QC (University of Cambridge)

Delegates to the "Options for Reform" consultation conference

M Allen-Deidrick (Society of Black Lawyers)
Robin Allen QC (Cloisters)
L Anderson (MSF)
C Barnard (Trinity College, Cambridge)
Professor J Beatson QC (Director, Centre for Public Law)
L Benson (NHS Executive)
Professor Bercusson (University of Manchester)
C Bourn (Leicester University)
J Bowers QC (Littleton Chambers)
G Bowker (Equal Opportunities Review)
Professor N Burrows (University of Glasgow)
C Casserley (RNIB)
D Cockburn (Pattinson and Brewer)

E Collins (Equality Commission for Northern Ireland)
C Cork (TGWU)
L Cox QC (Cloisters)
N Cowley (The Equality Authority – Ireland)
N Dandridge (Thompsons Solicitors)
R Dasey (FDA)
S Davies
T Dawson (GPMU)
K Dickson (GMB)
J Eastabrook (DfEE)
Professor E Ellis (University of Birmingham)
M Emmot (IPD)
A Farmer (Cabinet Officer, Regulatory Impact Unit)
Professor S Fredman (Exeter College, Oxford)

J Gardener (BBC)
H Garner (Employers Forum on Age)
R Gidoomal CBE
C Gooding (Employers Forum on Disability)
Professor J Gregory
J Harrington (University of Nottingham)
C Hobby (University of East London)
D Holland (TGWU)
M Howes (UNISON)
P Hunter (Scottish Low Pay Unit)
A Leonard (EOC)
C Low (National Disability Council)
J MacMillian (Regional Chairman Employment
    Tribunals)
M Muir (The Women's Unit)
A McColgan (Kings College, London)
Professor McCrudden (Lincoln College, Oxford)
E Melling (ORC)
J Mellor (Chair, EOC)
C Milne (Chairman Employment Tribunals)
Q Mirza (University of East London)
E Moran (UCL)
Professor G Morris (Brunel University)
R Morris (Traveller Law Research Unit)

J Morris (TUC)
B Nelson (BBC)
G Ong (Royal College of Midwives)
Dr S Palmer (Girton College, Cambridge)
C Palmer (Bindman and Partners)
Stephen Pittam (Joseph Rowntree Trust)
J Prophet (President Employment Tribunals (England
    and Wales))
B Roberts (EOC- Wales)
J Ross (University of Strathclyde)
M Rubenstein (Equal Opportunities Review)
A Sayer (RAD)
Y Strachen (Scottish Executive, Equality Unit)
R Timm (NDC)
R Townsend-Smith (University of Wales)
C Tribe (Employment Tribunals)
P Ward (Northern Foods)
A Watts (HSBC Bank PLC)
Dr C Wilpert (Technische Universitat, Berlin)
Dr R Wintemute (Kings College, London)
 S Witherspoon (Nuffield Foundation)
D Worman (IPD)
J Wren

Submission by organisations in response to the "Options for Reform" paper

Bar Council – Sex Discrimination Committee
Barnardos
Committee on the Administration of Justice
Commission for Racial Equality
Discrimination Law Association
Equality Commission for Northern Ireland
Equality Network
Equal Opportunities Commission
GMB
Justice

Law Society – Employment Law Committee
Leeds City Council
Organisational Resource Counselors – Equal
Employment Opportunity Group
Traveller Law Research Unit
Northern Ireland Human Rights Commission
RADAR
RNIB
Save the Children, Scotland

Submission by individuals in response to the "Options for Reform" paper

Bowers J
Bryan R
Cramphorn C (Deputy Chief Constable, RUC)
Faulkner D (Centre for Criminological Research)
Gill T
Hastings S (Pay and Employment Advice)
Haggett E
Emmott M (Institute of Personnel and Development)
Littlejohn D (President, Employment Tribunals
    (Scotland))

Low C
Morris G (Brunel University)
MacMillan J (Employment Tribunals)
McCrudden C (Lincoln College, Oxford)
Mirza Q (University of East London)
Prophet J. (President of the Employment Tribunals
    (England and Wales))
Spencer S. (IPPR)

APPENDIX 5

Selected Bibliography

Arrowsmith, S. (1995), "Public procurement as an instrument of policy and the impact of market liberalisation" 111 *Law Quarterly Review* 235-284

Arrowsmith, S. (1996), *The Law of Public and Utilities Procurement* (London, Sweet and Maxwell)

Association of Muslim Lawyers (1999), *Religious Discrimination and the Law* (Paper for the Commission on British Muslims Seminar on Religious Discrimination)

Ayres, I. and Braithwaite, J. (1992), *Responsive Regulation: Transcending the Deregulation Debate* (Oxford, Oxford University Press)

Barnard, C. and Hepple, B. A., (1999), "Indirect Discrimination: Interpreting *Seymour-Smith*" 58 *Cambridge Law Journal* 399-412

Bedington, R., Foreman, J., and Coussey, M. (1997) *Decentralisation and Devolution: The impact on equal opportunities* (Ware, Wainwright Trust)

Bercusson, B. and Dickens, L. (1996), *Equal Opportunities and collective bargaining in Europe,* (European Foundation for the Improvement of Living and Working Conditions)

Bercusson, B. (1978), *Fair Wages Resolutions,* (London, Mansell Information Publishing)

Better Regulation Task Force (1999), *Review of Anti-Discrimination Legislation* (Central Office of Information)

Bourn, C. and Whitemore, J. (1996), *Anti- Discrimination Law in Britain* 3rd ed. (London, Sweet and Maxwell)

Cabinet Office (2000), *Winning the Generation Game – improving opportunities for people aged 50-65 in work and community activities*

Carr, J. (1987), *New Roads to Equality – Contract Compliance for the UK?* (London, Fabian Society)

Commonwealth of Australia (1998), *Unfinished Business – Equity for Women in Australian Workplaces: Final Report of the Regulatory Review of the Affirmative Action (Equal Employment Opportunity for Women) Act 1986*

Copus, D. (1999), "A Critique of OFCCP's Comparable Work Theory" (typescript), 20 September 1999.

Corby, S., (1999), *Resolving Employment Rights Disputes Through Mediation: the New Zealand Experience* (London, Institute of Employment Rights)

Coussey (1995), "How Employers used the equal opportunities ten point plan" 103 *Employment Gazette,* pp.317-324.

Coussey (1996), *Developing an Equal Opportunities Guide for small employers: Social Analysis and Research 1,* (London, DfEE)

CRE (1983), *The Race Relations Act 1976 – Time for a Change*

CRE (1985), *Review of the Race Relations Act: Proposals for change- First Review*

CRE (1989), *Local Authority Contracts and Racial Equality: Implications of the Local Government Act 1988*

CRE (1991), *Second Review of the Race Relations Act*

CRE (1995), *Large companies and racial equality*

CRE (1998), *Reform of the Race Relations Act 1976: Proposals from the CRE – Third Review*

Deakin, S. and Morris, G. (1998), *Labour Law,* 2nd ed. (London, Butterworths)

DETR (2000), *Best Value and Procurement – Handling Workforce matters in Contracting: A Consultation Paper on Draft Guidance*

DfEE (2000) *Jobs for all*

Disability Rights Task Force (1999), *From Exclusion to Inclusion – A report of the Disability Task Force on Civil Rights for Disabled People* (London, DfEE)

Ellis, E. (1998), *EC Sex Equality Law,* 2nd ed. (Oxford, Clarendon Press)

EOC (1986), *Legislating for change*

EOC (1988), *Equal Treatment for Men and Women: Strengthening the Acts*

EOC (1990), *Equal Pay for men and Women*

EOC (1998a), *Equality in the 21st Century- A consultation paper*

EOC (1998b), *Equality in the 21st Century – A New Sex Equality Law for Britain*

EOC (1999a), *Facts About Men and Women in Great Britain 1999*

EOC (1999b), *Women and Men in Britain: Pay and Income*

EOC (1999c), *EOC Annual Report 1998: Setting the Agenda for Equality*

EOR (1993), "Defences narrowed" No. 52 *Equal Opportunities Review* 40

EOR (1999a), "Managing diversity an international perspective" No. 86 *Equal Opportunities Review* 33

EOR (1999b), "Equal opportunities policies: an EOR survey of employers" No. 87 *Equal Opportunities Review* 14

EOR (1999c), "Test for victimisation" No. 87 *Equal Opportunities Review* 51

EOR (2000), "Knowledge of Disability is not essential: *H J Heinz Co v Kenrick*" No.90 *Equal Opportunities Review* 49

Equal Opportunities Commission for Northern Ireland (undated), *The Equal Pay Legislation: Recommendations for Change*

Equal Opportunities Commission for Northern Ireland (1996), *Report on Formal Investigation into Competitive Tendering in Health and Education Services in Northern Ireland*

Equal Opportunities Commission for Northern Ireland (1997), *The Sex Discrimination Legislation – Recommendations for change*

Equality Commission Working Group (1999), [Chair: Joan Stringer] *Report of the Equality Commission Working Group*

European Foundation for the Improvement of Living and Working Conditions (1998), *Equal Opportunities and Collective Bargaining*

Fredman, S. (1997), *Women and the Law* (Oxford, Clarendon Press)

Grabosky, P. and Gunningham, N. (1998), "The Agriculture Industry" in Gunningham et al (1998), pp.300-30.

Government of Ontario (1985), *Green Paper on Pay Equity* (Ontario: Government of Ontario)

Gunningham, N. (1998), "Introduction" in Gunningham et al (1998) pp. 3-36

Gunningham, N., Grabosky, P., and Sinclair, D. (1998), *Smart Regulation – Designing Environmental Policy*, (Oxford, Clarendon Press)

Gunningham and Sinclair (1998a), "Parties Roles and Interactions" in Gunningham et al (1998), (Oxford, Clarendon Press), pp.93-134.

Gunningham and Sinclair (1998b), "Designing Environmental Policy" in Gunningham et al (1998), pp.373-454.

Hendy J. and Ford, M. (1995), *Munkman's Employer's Liability at Common Law*, 12th ed. (London, Butterworths)

Hepple, B. A. (1968), *Race, Jobs and the Law in Britain* (London, Allen Lane)

Hepple, B. A. (1970), *Race, Jobs and the law in Britain* (2nd ed., Harmondsworth, Penguin)

Hepple, B. A. (1983), "Judging Equal Rights" 36 *Current Legal Problems* 71-90

Hepple (1994), "Can Direct Discrimination be Justified", No 55 *Equal Opportunities Review* 51

Hepple, B. A. (2000), "Freedom of Expression and the Problem of Harassment" in Beatson, J. and Cripps, Y. (ed.) *Freedom of Speech and Freedom of Information*, (Oxford, Oxford University Press, forthcoming)

Home Office (1974), *Equality for Women* (London, HMSO, Cmnd. 5724)

Home Office (1975), *Racial Discrimination* (London, HMSO, Cmnd. 6234)

Home Office (2000), *Race Equality in Public Services* (London, Home Office Communications Directorate)

Houghton-Jones (1995), *Sexual Harassment* (London, Cavendish Publishing)

House of Commons Northern Ireland Affairs Committee Fourth Report (1999), *The operation of the Fair Employment (Northern Ireland) Act 1989: Ten Years On*, Session 1998-99, HC 98

Human Genetics Advisory Commission (1999), *The Implications of Genetic Testing for Employment* (London, DTI)

Human Genetics Advisory Commission (1997), *The Implications of Genetic Testing for Insurance* (London, DTI)

Hunter, R., and Leonard, A., (1997) "Sex Discrimination and Alternative Dispute Resolution: British Proposals in the Light of International Experience", [Summer 1997] *Public Law* 298-314

Justice (1987), *Industrial Tribunals*

Law Commission (1997), *Aggravated, Exemplary and Restitutionary Damages* (No. 247)

Lester, A. and Bindman, G. (1971), *Race and Law* (Harmondsworth, Penguin)

Lewis, R. and Clark, R. (1993), *Employment Rights, Industrial Tribunals and Arbitration: The Case for Alternative Dispute Resolution* (London, Institute of Employment Rights)

Low Pay Commission (2000), *The National Minimum Wage: the story so far -Second Report* (Cm. 4571)

McColgan, A. (1999), "Regulating Pay Discrimination" (Unpublished, Hart Workshop, Institute of Advanced Legal Studies)

McColgan, A. (1997), *Just Wages for Women* (Oxford, Clarendon Press)

McCrudden (1982), "Institutional Discrimination" 2 *Oxford Journal of Legal Studies* 303-367

McCrudden, C. (1998), *Benchmarks for Change: mainstreaming Fairness in the Governance of Northern Ireland* (Belfast, Committee on the Administration of Justice)

McCrudden, C. (1999a), "Mainstreaming Equality in the Governance of Northern Ireland" Vol. 22 No.4 *Fordham International Law Journal* 1696-1775

McCrudden, C. (1999b), "The Equal Opportunity Duty in the Northern Ireland Act 1998: An Analysis" in *Equal Rights and Human Rights – Their role in peace building: The Equality Provisions of the Good Friday Agreement and the NI Act* (Belfast, Committee on the Administration of Justice) pp.11-23

Meager, N., Doyle, B., Evans, C., Kersley, B., Williams, M., O'Regan, S. and Tackey, N., (1999), *Monitoring the Discrimination Ability Discrimination Act 1995* (London, RR119, DfEE)

Moody, A.(2000) "New Deal and ethnic minority participants," *Labour Market Trends*, 77-82

Morris, P. E. (1990), "Legal Regulation of Contact Compliance: An Anglo-American Comparison", 19 *Anglo-American Law Review* 87-144.

Neumark, D., and Stork W.A. (1997), *Age Discrimination and Labor Market Efficiency- NBER Working Paper 6088* (Cambridge, National Bureau of Economic Research)

Northern Ireland Office (1998), *Partnership for Equality- The Government's proposals for future legislation and policies on Employment Equality in Northern Ireland*, (HMSO, Cm 3890)

Northern Ireland Office (1988), *Fair Employment in Northern Ireland*, (London, HMSO, Cm. 380)

Palmer, C., Moon, G., and Cox, S., (1997), *Discrimination at Work- the Law on Sex, Race and Disability Discrimination* (London, Legal Action Group)

Race Relations Board (1968), Report of the Race Relations Board for 1966-67

Rake, K. (Ed.) (2000), *Women's Incomes over the Lifetime- Explaining the Female Forfeit*, (London, Women's Unit)

Robens, A. (1972), [Chairman] *Report of the Committee on Health and Safety at Work*, (Cmnd. 5034)

Ross, J. (2000), "The Burden of Proving Discrimination", *International Journal of Discrimination and the Law* p.95-118.

Spencer, S. and Bynoe, I. (1998) *A Human Rights Commission: The Options for Great Britain and Northern Ireland* (London, IPPR)

Stamato, L. (2000), "Dispute Resolution and the Glass Ceiling" 55 *Dispute Resolution Journal* 24

Standing Advisory Committee on Human Rights (1997), *Employment Equality: Building for the Future* (HMSO, Cm 3684)

Stephen Lawrence Inquiry (1999), Report of an Inquiry by Sir William MacPherson of Cluny, (London, HMSO, Cm 4262-I)

Street, H., Howe, G., and Bindman, G., (1967), *Street Report on Anti-Discrimination Legislation* (Political and Economic Planning).

TUC (2000), *Straight up! Why the law should protect lesbian and gay workers*

TUC (1998), *Equality in the 21st Century – A TUC Response to the Equal Opportunities Commission*

Varma, A. and Stallworth, L.E. (2000), "Barriers to Mediation", 55 *Dispute Resolution Journal*, 32-43

Whitehouse, S. (1992), "Legislation and Labour Market Gender Inequality: An Analysis of OECD Countries", *Work Employment and Society*, vol. 6, 65

APPENDIX 6

Research Team
Advisory Committee and Panel of Experts

Research Team

Bob Hepple QC is Master of Clare College and Professor of Law in the University of Cambridge, a former CRE Commissioner and Chairman of industrial tribunals.

Mary Coussey is an equal opportunities and diversity consultant and a Senior Research Associate in the Judge Institute of Management Studies, University of Cambridge, a former Director of the employment division in the CRE and head of branch in the Cabinet Office equal opportunities division.

Tufyal Choudhury was Research Associate in the Centre for Public Law, University of Cambridge for this project and (from August 2000) is a lecturer in international human rights law in the University of Durham.

Advisory Committee

Lord Lester of Herne Hill QC (Chair)

Professor Jack Beatson QC – Director, Centre for Public Law

Kay Carberry – Head Equal Rights Department, TUC

Sir Robert Cooper – Chair, FEC, Northern Ireland

John Cridland – Deputy Director-General, CBI

Dr. Shirley Dex – Judge Institute of Management Studies

Doris Littlejohn, CBE – Former President, Employment Tribunals, Scotland

Colin Low – Vice-Chair NDC; member DRC

Julie Mellor – Chair, Equal Opportunities Commission

Sir Herman Ouseley – Former Chair, Commission for Racial Equality

Carolyn Sinclair – Director Constitutional and Community Policy Division, Home Office

Sir David Williams QC – University of Cambridge

and as observers, Bob Niven - Director of Equal Opportunities, DfEE (until December 1999) and then Jenny Eastabrook - Head of Sex and Race Equality, DfEE

Panel of Experts

Catherine Barnard – University of Cambridge

Laura Cox QC – ILO Committee of Experts

Professor Brian Doyle – University of Liverpool

Professor Evelyn Ellis – University of Birmingham

Professor Sandra Fredman – University of Oxford

Tess Gill – Barrister

Professor Christopher McCrudden – University of Oxford

Dr. Stephanie Palmer – University of Cambridge

Michael Rubenstein – Equal Opportunities Review

Rabinder Singh – Barrister

Sarah Spencer – Institute of Public Policy Research

Dr. Robert Wintemute – Kings College, University of London

APPENDIX 7

Working Papers

1. In What Respects Does U.K. Sex Discrimination Legislation Fall Short of the Standards Demanded by EC Law? *Evelyn Ellis*

2. In What Respects Does U.K. Discrimination Law Fall Short of the Standards Demanded by International Human Rights Law? *Tufyal Choudhury*

3. A Critical Review of the Concept of Equality in U.K. Discrimination Law. *Sandra Fredman*

4. Reform of the Disability Discrimination Act. *Brian Doyle*

5. Equal Pay: Lessons from Ontario. *Aileen McColgan*

6. Discrimination on grounds of Religion or Belief. *Tufyal Choudhury*

7. Discrimination on Grounds of Sexual Orientation. *Robert Winemute*

Printed in the United Kingdom
by Lightning Source UK Ltd.
101406UKS00001B/301-368